Practice-based Teaching and Cultural Illumination

# 教学实践与文化传播
## ——以定点帮扶与潮州生活文化为例

戴 凡/主 编

张 佳　符 韵/副主编

·广州·

版权所有　翻印必究

### 图书在版编目（CIP）数据

教学实践与文化传播：以定点帮扶与潮州生活文化为例：汉文、英文/戴凡主编；张佳，符韵副主编. —广州：中山大学出版社，2023.6
ISBN 978 - 7 - 306 - 07783 - 7

Ⅰ.①教… Ⅱ.①戴… ②张… ③符… Ⅲ.①扶贫—概况—凤庆县—汉、英 ②地方文化—概况—潮州—汉、英 Ⅳ.①F127.744 ②G127.744

中国国家版本馆 CIP 数据核字（2023）第 062243 号

| | |
|---|---|
| 出 版 人： | 王天琪 |
| 策划编辑： | 熊锡源 |
| 责任编辑： | 卢思敏 |
| 封面设计： | 曾　婷 |
| 责任校对： | 李昭莹 |
| 责任技编： | 靳晓虹 |
| 出版发行： | 中山大学出版社 |
| 电　　话： | 编辑部 020 - 84113349，84111997，84110779，84110776 |
| | 发行部 020 - 84111998，84111981，84111160 |
| 地　　址： | 广州市新港西路 135 号 |
| 邮　　编： | 510275　　传　真：020 - 84036565 |
| 网　　址： | http://www.zsup.com.cn　E-mail：zdcbs@mail.sysu.edu.cn |
| 印 刷 者： | 广东虎彩云印刷有限公司 |
| 规　　格： | 787mm×1092mm　1/16　15.25 印张　332 千字 |
| 版次印次： | 2023 年 6 月第 1 版　2023 年 6 月第 1 次印刷 |
| 定　　价： | 50.00 元 |

如发现本书因印装质量影响阅读，请与出版社发行部联系调换

# 前　言

## 戴　凡

本书是中山大学2021年秋季学期"创意写作与翻译"课程两个班的学生作品，由两部分组成：一部分是关于云南省凤庆县脱贫攻坚和乡村振兴的故事，另一部分是关于潮州茶文化、食文化、潮绣和潮剧的故事。

选择这两个主题源于我对中山大学为改善凤庆的教育、行政和医疗服务所做的工作的好奇和敬意——这些工作是独具中国特色的扶贫攻坚和乡村振兴的一部分；同时，我一直想找机会体验在中国乃至世界都是很特别的存在的潮州文化。

2021年10月底和11月初，凤庆班和潮州班的师生分别进行了为期一周的实地考察。凤庆班的师生先后乘坐了飞机、火车和汽车，历经14个小时到达凤庆山区，采访了在鲁史中学的中山大学研究生支教团成员、驻村驻县干部以及在凤庆县人民医院工作和对当地医生进行培训的中山大学医疗队。这些派驻人员的服务期从三个月到两年不等。潮州班则在韩山师范学院地理科学与旅游学院·潮菜学院的协助下，在体验潮州茶文化、食文化、潮绣和潮剧的同时，对茶庄茶农、潮菜大师、绣娘、演员和剧作家等进行了采访。

虽然两个班学生的任务性质相同，但课程的运作方式与学生的学习经历和体验却不一样。每个班的12名学生分为三个小组，每个小组负责一个主题。凤庆班的三个小组分别负责支教、驻村驻县和医疗帮扶三个主题；潮州班的三个小组分别负责茶文化、食文化、潮绣和潮剧三个主题。每个小组都有一名中文作者、一名英文作者、一名用中英文写作的学生记者，另有一名学生负责制作相关主题的视频的中英文字幕，视频均由广州新华学院魏东华老师带领的两名学生拍摄并编辑。

本书的创作先由负责相关主题的学生写第一稿，然后由我对作品进行了至少两轮的细致批阅并对学生进行了口头指导。此外，我和张佳、符韵分别进行了编辑。张佳和符韵分别是凤庆班和潮州班的助教，也是本书的共同副主编。张佳负责凤庆部分的编辑和校对，符韵负责潮州部分的编辑和校对。

对学生的指导主要在写作技巧层面上进行，包括作品的结构、叙事视角、叙事声音、对话、细节等；编辑则侧重于语法、句子重组和一些表达方式的改变，以及表达的连贯性和一致性问题。也就是说，我们尽可能保持学生作品的原貌，因为本书不仅要反映"创意写作与翻译"课程的成果，也要反映学生在本课程中的观察、感悟和成长，并通过创意将其表达出来。

如果凤庆班没有中山大学工会，特别是常务副主席许东黎老师的支持，潮州班没有韩山师范学院地理科学与旅游学院·潮菜学院，特别是院长陈菁教授的支持，本课程是不可能为学生带来这本书所描述的体验和感受的。特别感谢涂丽、张哲和张良友老师组织的在凤庆的采访；感谢陈菁教授不仅安排了潮州有关人员的采访，还陪同参加了大部分活动；感谢刘毅教授，他是我在潮州的第一个联系人。我所要感谢的两组相关人员名单很长，本课程制作的两个视频的致谢部分均列出了他们的名字。

我还要感谢本课程的两位教学团队成员：谢桂霞副教授和罗斌副教授。谢老师协助并参加了潮州组的部分调研，她和罗老师一起为本书进行了第一轮编辑和最后一轮校对。感谢我的同事和博士生张思熠，于我在凤庆班和潮州班做田野调查时为我代课。

感谢 Finley MacDonald 的英文编辑工作。感谢张佳和符韵，作为两个班的助教，她们也为两个班的视频字幕和这本集子做了大量的编辑工作。

感谢所有参与课程的学生在课程中的努力和合作以及对课程意义的真诚思考。我希望，这门课程带给我们的共同经历，能成为他们在中山大学学习和生活难忘的亮点。

# Preface

## DAI Fan

This collection features the work of two groups of students attending the Creative Writing and Translation course at Sun Yat-sen University in the fall semester of 2021. It consists of two parts. One concerns poverty alleviation to rural revitalization in Fengqing County, Yunnan Province, in southwestern China; the other regards the tea, cuisine, embroidery, and opera of Teochew culture.

The two themes of the course arose out of my interest and respect for the work that Sun Yat-sen University had been contributing to Fengqing for the improvement of its education, administrative management, and medical service—as part of the nationwide campaign for poverty alleviation and rural revitalization—as well as my admiration for the unique Teochew culture, which bears a distinct presence in China and overseas.

In late October and early November 2021, both groups set out on a one-week field trip: one to Fengqing and the other to Teochew. For over 14 hours, the Fengqing class travelled by plane, train and bus, to the mountainous area to interview postgraduate students teaching at Lushi High School; faculty members serving in the County Administration and Village Committee; and physicians who worked and trained local doctors in the People's Hospital of Fengqing County, serving for periods ranging from three months to two years. While becoming immersed in the material and spiritual life of the Teochew culture through tea sessions, meals and discussions, the Teochew class, coordinated by Hanshan Normal University's School of Geography and Tourism · School of Teochew Cuisine, interviewed individuals on the topics of tea, cuisine, embroidery and opera.

While students in the two classes had similar tasks, the ways the courses were run and the experiences of students were very different. Each class of 12 students was divided into three groups, with each group responsible for one theme. The three groups in the Fengqing class worked on the areas of teaching, county and village administration support, and medical assistance, while the three groups in the Teochew class worked on aspects of tea, cuisine, embroidery and opera. Each group had one Chinese writer, one English writer, one reporter writing in both Chinese and English, and one Chinese and English subtitle writer for the video versions of the two classes, and the videos were shot by the team from Guangzhou Xinhua College, led by Professor Wei Donghua.

This collection is the result of at least two intense sessions of supervision carried out with each student in the course, along with my three rounds of editing and those of Zhang Jia and Fu Yun, who, as associate editors-in-chief, double-checked my three rounds of editing and proofreading, Zhang Jia being responsible for the Fengqing portion, and Fu Yun, for the Teochew portion.

It is essential to note that all supervision of students has been conducted at the level of writing techniques, notably concerning structure, point of view, narrative voice, dialogue, detail, etc., while editing has been limited to grammar, sentence reorganization and certain expressions, along with matters of cohesion and coherence. That is, we have kept the original flavor of the students' writing, as the collection not only aims to reveal what the course has set out to do but also to disclose how students regard their own learning, both at the level of content and creative writing.

The course could not have occurred without the support of the Faculty and Staff Union of Sun Yat-sen University, particularly Ms. Xu Dongli, its deputy chair, and the support of Hanshan Normal University's School of Geography and Tourism · School of Teochew Cuisine, particularly its dean, Professor Chen Jing. Special thanks go out to Tu Li, Zhang Zhe and Zhang Liangyou for organizing local interviews in Fengqing; to Professor Chen Jing for not only organizing interviews with the individuals concerned but also accompanying the class to most of the activities; and to Professor Liu Yi, who was my first contact for the Teochew class. The list of people I am grateful to, in association with both classes, is long. They have been acknowledged in the two videos.

My gratitude goes out to two team members of the course: Professor Xie Guixia, who assisted in the Teochew part of the field trip, and Professor Luo Bin, who, along with Professor Xie Guixia, carried out the first round of editing, and the proofreading for this collection. And I am also thankful for my colleague and PhD student Zhang Siyi who taught my Creative Nonfiction class while I was away with the Fengqing class and Teochew class.

I'm indebted to Finley MacDonald for the editing of the English part of the collection. I'm extremely grateful to Zhang Jia and Fu Yun, who were the teaching assistants for the Fengqing class and Teochew class. They not only helped with the editing of the subtitles for the two videos, but also did enormous work for the current collection.

I thank all participating students for their effort and collaboration throughout the course and their honest reflection on its value. I sincerely hope that the experiences we shared throughout the course remain a highlight of their time at Sun Yat-sen University.

(Translated by Fu Yun)

# 目　　录

## 凤庆报道篇 ························································· 1
 萤火聚星河 ············································· 吕君兰 2
 中大人在路上：从脱贫攻坚到乡村振兴 ············· 屈宁威 13
 以我之力，护你前行 ···································· 王晶晶 20

## 凤庆故事篇 ························································· 27
 弦歌不辍，芳华待灼 ···································· 黄宝欣 28
 "一段扶贫路，一生红塘情"
  ——中山大学脱贫攻坚、乡村振兴纪实 ············· 林冠柔 39
 核桃·医术·朝凤路 ······································· 李心琪 48

## Reports of the Fengqing Field Trip ························· 57
 Starlight ················································ LYU Junlan 58
 We Are on the Way: From Poverty Alleviation to Rural Development
  in Fengqing ······································· QU Ningwei 69
 Sun Yat-sen University's Effort for Fengqing's Development
  ··················································· WANG Jingjing 77

## Stories from Fengqing ·········································· 85
 Into the Mountains ································· MA Weiguo 86
 A Journey of Discovery: The Changes in Poverty-Stricken Areas
  in Yunnan Province ······························ YU Yehui 94
 Two Mountains and Two Hands: Sun Yat-sen University's Medical Support
  for the People's Hospital of Fengqing County ········ TAN Xiaoyan 103

## 中山大学历年派驻凤庆人员名单 ····························· 113
 一线挂职干部名录 ········································· 114
 "组团式"派驻凤庆县医务人员名录 ······················ 115

凤庆历届支教团成员 …………………………………… 117

## 潮州报道篇 ………………………………………………… 119
重品茶香，重识潮州 …………………………… 丁可欣 120
与潮州的相遇和别离
——食文化小组调研日志 ………………… 张　婧 129
潮州纪行 ………………………………………… 谭学铭 140

## 潮州故事篇 ………………………………………………… 151
潮州茶事 ………………………………………… 王　茜 152
潮州随想：食味之极在纯粹 …………………… 林　涵 162
遗憾·不再遗憾 ………………………………… 莫艳池 170

## Reports of the Teochew Field Trip ……………………… 177
Nice to Meet You Again, My Tea and My Hometown …… DING Kexin 178
Meeting and Parting with Teochew: The Research Journal of Teochew
　　Food Culture Group …………………… ZHANG Jing 189
Trip Journals ……………………………………… TAN Xueming 201

## Stories from Teochew ……………………………………… 211
The Story of Tea, the Story of Us ……………… YU Zhigao 212
The Making of Teochew ………………………… HUANG Senyan 218
A Glimpse of Teochew Embroidery and Opera ………… MA Changjun 224

# 凤庆报道篇

　　这部分的三篇报道反映的是凤庆班学生在凤庆期间的调研经历，不仅包括调研内容，而且包括在调研中发生在自己与同学、当地人之间的故事。

# 萤火聚星河

吕君兰

"请吕君兰到 5 诊室 10 诊台就诊!"广州中山大学中山眼科中心的广播响起一阵机械的女声。我走进诊室,递过病历,男医生头也不抬,飞快地翻阅。"2021 年 10 月 15 日,中大五院①初诊……你是从珠海来的?10 月 27 日,凤庆县人民医院?你怎么会去那里?"

"我是中大国际翻译学院的。我们有一门课叫'创意写作与翻译',上周去云南凤庆收集写作素材,反映中大帮扶的成果。"

"还有这种课呀,一个班多少人?"

"将近 20 个吧,一个带队老师,6 个本科生、6 个研究生分成 3 组,每一组负责支教、医疗这些不同的主题。哦,还有助教和摄影团队。"我一边回答,医生一边示意我坐到裂隙灯前。

"病毒性角膜炎。"医生快速翻动着我的眼睑。"这个比较难恢复……拖得有点久了。"他随即转过身去,又看了一遍中大五院的处方,眉头紧锁道:"药不对!病毒性角膜炎怎么开一堆抗生素?"接着,他又从打印机里掏出一张处方单,嘱咐道:"之前开的药都停了,按医嘱用新药。下一位患者!"

我和角膜炎的"搏斗"还要追溯到国庆假期最后一天,当时我因右眼充血到社区医院就诊,拿着"用眼过度"的诊断书和一瓶有助于消除红血丝的药水就离开了。一周后,红血丝还在,于是我就去了中大五院。

"你这是角膜炎。左氧氟沙星,一天滴 4 次;更昔洛韦凝胶也是 4 次,滴了眼药水之后过 5 分钟再用;涂泰利必妥眼膏会看不清楚东西,所以睡觉前用。"医生的手指配合着冰冷的嗓音,飞快地划过长长的处方单。

我倒吸一口凉气:多久才能恢复呢?拜托,一定要在下周去凤庆前康复——身为我们组的记者,如果看不清东西,回来之后怎么写报道呢?

"多休息多喝水,饮食清淡,有的人三五天就好了。三天后复查。"

---

① 中山大学附属第五医院。

三天加三天，我的角膜炎应该会好了吧？出发当日，坐在广州飞往云南大理的飞机上，虽然眼睛仍有点干涩，我自我安慰道：应该是飞机上空气太干燥了。下了飞机，我们直奔高铁站，只在路上匆匆瞥了几眼碧蓝的洱海。从大理到临沧云县的高铁隧道一个接一个，全无风景可言。从云县高铁站到凤庆县城用了一个半小时；从县医院再到凤庆县边陲的鲁史镇，三个半小时的盘山公路，途中风景倒是连绵不绝，只是窗外除了高耸的山坡、葱郁的灌木和干枯的核桃树，再无其他。除了经过澜沧江上的白桥时大家纷纷抓拍，大部分时间大巴车里都一片寂静。

闭上眼睛，持续的耳鸣和突然的拐弯让我难以入睡；睁开眼睛，又感觉恶心犯晕。在闭眼和睁眼的交替中，终于从白天熬到了黑夜，到达鲁史镇时，我的眼皮已经像灌了铅一样沉重。

我们走进四方香饭店，课程老师戴凡教授和我们组四人在同一个圆桌落座，对面坐着四位与我们年纪相仿的年轻人，身着统一的灰色风衣，胸口戴着长方形的"中山大学"胸章。

"支教组今天任务比较重啊，晚上还要采访中大研究生支教团的老师。大家现在感觉怎么样？"戴凡老师问道。

组里的其他两位女生只是苦笑，我不停地揉着眼眶，从泪腺里挤出少得可怜的眼泪稍微润滑一下又肿又干的眼球。

"还好吧，至少刚才我们都没吐。"组里唯一的男生马伟国答道。虽然我们支教组0%的呕吐率远胜医疗组的25%，勉强和驻村驻县组持平，但这两天在鲁史镇的访谈工作全部都由我们组负责——好比同样是伤兵残将，他们有喘息之机，而我们却要直奔战场。

"大家赶紧吃吧，菜已经提前上好了。"支教老师中一位黝黑高大的男生站起来，拿着汤勺在一盆黄色浓汤中打捞。"按照这里的风俗，要把鸡头给最尊贵的客人。"说着就要把捞到的鸡头送到戴老师的碗里，戴老师连连推托。我看着这番和新年饭桌极其相似的情景，和旁边的关慧琳、黄宝欣笑着交换眼神。

"他好老练。"慧琳小声说道。

"谁？"我问。

"许锦涛，支教团的队长，夹菜的那个。"

宝欣拍了拍慧琳的腿，小声说："其实他跟你和伟国一样大，如果不来支教一年，现在也是研一。"

慧琳睁大了眼睛，又点了点头："哎，支教果然让人成长啊！"

许锦涛的老练不仅在饭桌上很突出，饭后的访谈也如此。看着他说话的样子，我仿佛看见了大半个月前采访的首届鲁史支教队队长徐述腾——声音洪亮、逻辑清晰，像演讲一样配合着手势动作。按宝欣的话说，就是"辅导员的感觉"。

支教团的老师依次自我介绍，除了中间最矮的女老师吴雅婷是语文老师，其余三人都是数学老师，尽管只有瘦瘦黑黑的刘超宇是正宗数学专业出身。

"今年老师流失特别严重，很多数学老师都去了县城教书。"来自中山医学院的牛璐璐解释道，接着讲起了她从生物老师变成数学老师的经历。

角落的三个摄影灯围着我们，我感觉眼里的水分在灼烧下蒸发殆尽，每眨一下眼都变得非常痛苦，眼睛和大脑一起出走放空，直到戴凡老师一句"四位同学有什么想问的吗？"，我才回过神来。

我往左看，不只为转移一下尴尬，也为躲避强光。"英文作者伟国，还有中文作者宝欣，有什么细节要问吗？"戴老师追问道。

伟国、宝欣紧盯自己的电脑，一言不发。慧琳打开了大半个月前与上一届支教团的访谈记录。刚才在饭桌上，慧琳问起："我们待会要问什么问题？"我随口一答："好累，没有精力搞提纲了，随机应变吧。"而现在慧琳却直接打开电脑，开始敲打键盘。

"想问一下吴雅婷老师，刚刚说来的时候心理有落差，具体是什么呢？"慧琳问。看着她把页面切到另一个文档，我才发现她已经写了简单的纲要，还列了几个问题。我不安地摆弄着我的电脑，感到身为组长却没有负起责任的羞愧。

"首先是生活上饮水、上厕所等都要慢慢克服吧。比如，有时太阳能热水器储备不够。这几天阴天，我们老师想要洗澡的话也都是没有热水的。但是有些女学生，一方面确实是要洗头，一方面可能是想省钱，就直接去操场上用冷水管子冲一下头。"

"我补充一下，其实学生的宿舍、洗手间、饮水设施都挺原始的。"许锦涛说。我脑海里浮现出半个月前与上一届支教团访谈时他们颇具意味的"知道什么是沟厕吗？"以及那句"沟厕也有合理性，毕竟鲁史缺水，水都是优先供应到食堂的，沟厕一天只冲一次比较节水"。我不禁脱口而出："沟厕？"

"对，就是沟厕。"许锦涛苦笑道，"你们明天可以去看一下。虽然我们已经是第八届支教团了，我住的还是20世纪80年代的老宿舍楼，没有配套的厕所，只能用公共沟厕。之前有点水土不服，得了肠胃炎，每次去厕所都要下四层楼穿过操场。"

"你这一趟肠胃炎下来,短跑速度应该很快!"戴凡老师调侃道。屋内随即充满了快活的空气。

万幸的是,我们在鲁史的第一次访谈就遇到了非常能聊的对象,在我们没有足够话题储备的情况下还是聊了许多我们关心的细节。以至于晚上八点多开始的访谈,一直到十点多才结束(见图1)。摄影灯关闭的那一刻,我合上酸涩的眼睛,眼皮隐隐作痛。慧琳把头靠在我的肩膀上,叹气说:"谁能想到,凌晨三点醒来,到了晚上十点多还要干活呢?困得不行了!"宝欣也倒在慧琳背上,揉着太阳穴,哀嚎着:"下午坐车到现在还晕。"

图1 抵达当晚,课程师生与中山大学凤庆支教小组访谈

"走吧,明天还有一整天访谈呢。"伟国在前面带路,我们一起沿着陡峭的青石板阶梯往上走。夜晚的寒气无声无息地窜进衣服,让人直哆嗦。但没走多久,我就全身冒汗。才走到山腰,我们就已精疲力竭,扶着电线杆大口喘气了。

"你们看!"伟国指了指天空。漫天星斗犹如无数银珠,密密麻麻地镶嵌在深黑色的夜幕上。

"哇……"我们惊呼,"从来没见过这么多星星!"

"这个鲁史古镇还有人住吗?"伟国问。

黄色的路灯照在砖墙上,上面关于茶马古道的壁画述说着往日灿烂的文化,让人不禁遐想这里曾经的热闹风光:数百年前,陡峭的石板路两侧是生意兴旺的商铺,马帮和商人在中间来往穿梭。西行的商人带去丝绸和茶叶,东来的马队捎来边区的药材和盐巴,各个族群在互通有无中相互融合。抗战年代,这条不起眼的小巷肩负起中华民族生命线的重任,军需物资沿着小路翻山越岭、渡河过江,从缅甸等地源源不断地被输送到战争前线。

现在,当年悠扬的马铃声与急驰的马蹄声早已随风远去,曾经马帮来来往往的街道也变得冷冷清清,只留下光滑石板中间的马蹄形凹陷作为历史的证明。瓦房的土墙已经被风磨去了外皮,但是从新刷漆的木板窗框和"临沧市凤庆县历史建筑"的标牌能看得出近年帮扶的痕迹。同样的景观要是放在丽江或大理,到了夜晚游客定会摩肩接踵,但在鲁史——距离大理还有一个半小时高铁和三小时大巴车车程的山区小镇,旅游业只怕是"酒香也怕巷子深"。

"应该有人住,只是睡了吧。我看这里既没什么游客,也没什么夜生活,哪像广东,十点多正是夜宵时间。"我说。

"好想吃夜宵!"慧琳突然喊道,"我晚上都没吃饭,菜都是凉的。"

回想起来我也没吃多少,毕竟齁咸的腌肉、夹杂着辣椒的白菜、浸泡在辣油里的茄子,哪一样都算不上可口,放凉了就更难下咽了。

"刚才老师问我们是不是吃饱了,你还说'晕车吃不下'。"宝欣说。

慧琳沉默了好一会,突然激动起来:"哎,明天晚上是不是就没有任务了?我们可以看看附近哪里有吃的,一边吃夜宵,一边'做数学作业'。"

"做数学作业"是我们组的"黑话"——下午在高铁站吃饭时,我们偷偷买了一副牌,约定有空的时候打。为了不引人注目,就拿"做数学作业"指代。

"想多了,明天朝九晚九全是访谈,晚上九点半才结束。"伟国耸了耸肩,继续往前走。宝欣和慧琳相互搀扶着跟在后面,一声声"好累"听起来像有千钧重。

第二天七点起床,我感觉眼睛像是蒙上了一层雾,还有一丝胀痛感。到牛羊肉米线馆吃早餐时,我小声问组员们:"我的右眼红吗?"

慧琳、宝欣定睛看了一会,点头说:"靠近眼角那里挺红的。"

"怎么了?"伟国问。

"没事,可能是昨天没休息好,水也没喝够,有点疲劳了。"我心虚了,其实应该是病情加重了。但是就算说出实情也无济于事——听首届支教团的徐述腾说,鲁史镇只有一个小小的卫生院,送学生过去也不会治疗,只是让学生躺下来吸氧。何况我们的访谈一个紧接一个,我哪里抽得出时间去看医生呢?

早上第一个采访对象是鲁史中学的校长禹正强,他刚走出校史馆,下一位受访老师就进来了。我们刚靠在椅背上想休息一下,又不得不重新打起精神坐直了腰。同样的情景重复了三四次,上午最后一场访谈结束时,慧琳已经累得趴在了桌上。我从包里摸出眼药水滴上两滴,看到对面的宝欣和伟国也不约而同地往后瘫,眼神空洞。

草草吃过午饭后,我们没怎么休息,很快又重新"开工"。下午的情形仍是鲁史中学的学生们一个接一个地进来访谈。到了下午三四点,连续坐着盯了几个小时电脑的我又感觉眼睛干涩,像是回到了昨晚的状态。

"我们下午的访谈提早结束了,支教组其实已经收集了足够丰富的材料。为了我们将来制作的纪录片更有观赏性,我们要去采集一下鲁史中学的外景,大家可以跟着参观。"戴凡老师和许锦涛走在前面带路,我们一行人穿过操场往宿舍去,先是参观传说中的"沟厕",后又走进新建的教师宿舍。这时,我发现只有伟国还跟在旁边,宝欣和慧琳不见了踪影。我们沿原路折返,刚走到门口,就看到一个熟悉的身影在乒乓球台前笨拙地挪动,宝欣则在旁边抱着手笑嘻嘻地看着。

乒乓球在水泥桌上缓慢地弹跳着,慧琳手忙脚乱地接住,对面的小女生不慌不忙地打回来。看见我们的大部队扛着摄影机凑近,女孩匆匆放下了球拍,害羞地跑掉了。

"这个女孩子真好,刚才她和朋友在打乒乓球,我来之后她的朋友全都跑掉了,只有她一直陪着我。"慧琳看着女孩远去的方向,又追上前去,"不行,我得采访一下她。"

"不错,还会自己给自己加任务了。"伟国点点头,像个老干部。

轻松愉悦的休息时间总是疾驰而行的。晚饭后,医疗组和驻村驻县组都宣称要准备访谈提纲,欢天喜地地回酒店了,空荡荡的校史室里只剩下我们四个学生。强打精神撑完了对最后三个老师的访谈后,却听见戴老师说:"我跟你们大概说一下写作要点。首先是中文和英文的写作者,宝欣和伟国,你们可以先考虑一下用什么视角……"

伟国"嗯"了一下,宝欣却没有反应,手肘放在桌上托着头,像是睁着眼睛在睡觉。我也像她一样用手撑住半边脸,好让疼痛的右眼休息一下。

"慧琳做字幕就要从不同人的访谈里找他们对同一个事件的不同描述,把它们选出来作为纪录片的素材……君兰是记者,需要反映我们支教组在探访中的所见、所闻、所想,写作的形式就比较自由……"戴老师针对每个人的角色都说了一番,最后停了下来:"今天先说这么多吧,看大家好像都要睡着的样子。这个行程确实有点 intense。"

"这个行程确实有点 intense。"从鲁史中学走回酒店的路上,宝欣突然说道,"刚才讲那么多我就记得这个。"

"也可以说:今天安排得非常 overwhelming。"慧琳说。

"你们真是戴老师的得意门生。"伟国也笑了。

我们深一脚浅一脚地走在被挖掘机挖烂的泥路上,抱着沉重的摄影器材,却笑得像过年一样开心——访谈任务终于结束了,可以各搞各的创作了。

没想到的是,任务刚结束,"病号接力"却开始了。我"身先士卒"开始第一棒,又将"接力棒"传到了慧琳的手中。第三天一早等车回县城时,我看见慧琳顶着浓重的黑眼圈,穿着单薄的裙子在十几度的寒风里发抖。

"你怎么那么憔悴?"我走近了看,发现她的眼睛也出现了些红血丝。

"昨天没休息好吧。我看你眼睛也有点红。"慧琳也盯着我看。

"我来之前得了角膜炎,可能复发了。你是怎么了?"我问。

站在旁边的宝欣摸了摸慧琳的头:"她好惨,昨晚熬夜看访谈的视频,在挑要放进纪录片的片段。"

"要什么时候做完?"伟国问,慧琳痴痴地苦笑,好久才憋出来一句"今天。"

"昨天老师12点多给她发微信说'字幕要开始工作了,视频尽量在今天挑完',她就一直做到凌晨。"宝欣摇头。

颠簸的大巴上,我闭上眼睛,却被山路晃得睡不着。看向窗外,只见前排玻璃倒映着笔记本屏幕的影子,慧琳正以二倍速看着之前采访支教老师的视频,时不时把页面切换到文档,把时间代码和说话内容输入进去。我才看了几分钟,晕眩感就席卷而来,不禁暗自佩服慧琳,怎么能在这样晃的路上一直盯着屏幕。

车到达凤庆县城后,我悄悄和戴凡老师说了角膜炎的事情,老师却"喜出望外"："我们下午正好要采访从中大中山眼科中心来援助的刘良平医生，待会找他看看，还能积累视频素材。"于是午饭后，戴凡老师等四人组成的"陪诊团"提着摄影器械和我一起走路前往县医院。大厅空空荡荡的，刘良平医生和他的助手站在二楼夹层等待我们。戴凡老师上前握手问好，又道："这个医院怎么好像没什么人？"

"其实早上还是有不少患者的，现在是午休时间，而且大部分科室已经搬到新建的院区去了，老院区只留下中医和眼科。"刘医生答道。

眼科位于夹层的一端，狭窄的走廊摆了几排座位就成了简单的候诊室。这里没有大城市医院的叫号显示屏，但诊室各个角落摆着眼压计、眼底照相机等视力检查仪器，可谓"麻雀虽小，五脏俱全"。我在熟悉的裂隙灯显微镜前坐下，刘医生一边操作器械，一边讲解："用蓝色光照射，有荧光反应的地方就是有炎症，可以看到角膜浸润快好了。"

刘医生又切换回黄光，把我的眼皮翻起来："比起角膜炎，你的结膜炎更加严重。"什么？还有结膜炎？为什么之前的医生一个都没有诊断出来？

"滤泡增生很明显。"刘医生从打印机里取出两张片子。"你看，如果是正常的眼皮，应该是光滑的，但是现在两个眼睛都有凹凸不平的起伏，这应该是积累了很久的结膜炎，这几天可能没休息好，症状比较明显。"

回到酒店已经接近两点，正是下午该出发的时间。伟国已经和几个同学围在大堂的茶桌边，面前摆着几杯滇红茶。

"这么快看完了？有给你开药吗？"伟国站了起来，特地把位置让给我。

我摊了摊手："医院还没上班，我挂不了号，也没法拿药。医生说现在的药虽然不太对症，但还能维稳，这几天少用眼，回到广州再看医生。"

"那看了有什么用吗？"

"还是有点用的，至少检查了一下，心就放下来了，感觉已经恢复了一半。"

我模模糊糊看到电梯口两个人影互相搀扶着向我们走来——慧琳抱着宝欣的手臂，脸上没有一丝血色。如果说早上的慧琳只是看起来稍显疲惫，那中午的慧琳简直可以说是双眼空洞无神。

"慧琳怎么了？怎么你看起来更像病人？"我问。

"中午没睡。"宝欣打了一个大大的哈欠，说道，"又在看访谈视频。"

"要看几个？还有多少个？"伟国问。

"九个……还有四个……"慧琳拖长了尾音，说话的语气颇有些看破红尘的沧桑感。

"没事吧？其他组负责字幕的人员还没开始干活呢，你晚一点也可以。"我拍了拍慧琳的肩膀，"不然你也和我一样，去享受一下VIP级看病体验。"

一整个下午，医疗组的访谈热火朝天，慧琳则一动不动地坐在桌边，聚精会神地看访谈视频，充分发挥了"心远地自偏"的精神。到了晚餐时间，她下垂的嘴角才稍稍上扬起来。结果听了戴凡老师一句"支教组再加多一个访谈任务，吃饭的时候采访中大附中到凤庆县一中的一位老师"，慧琳的笑容又渐渐收敛，整个人瘫软在宝欣的身上。

晚上回到酒店，慧琳鬼鬼祟祟地溜到前台，接过写着"美团买药"的袋子。我惊讶地问道："怎么了？"

"我感觉快要感冒了，买了点藿香正气水。"慧琳已经快走不动路了，她旁边的宝欣也踉踉跄跄，一直喊道"手痛脚痛""好像得了风湿"。两个人相互挽着胳膊，也不知道是谁搀扶着谁，像是两人三足一样笨拙地勉强往前挪动。伟国叹气："唉，戴老师之前还夸我们组氛围好呢，怎么才两天就这样了。"

我说："是啊，我们组现在就是'老弱病残'组。我是'病'——角膜炎。"

宝欣点头："慧琳是'弱'，我是'残'……那只剩下'老'了，谁是'老'？"

我们一起望向伟国大笑，伟国也尴尬地干笑几声："确实，我1997年的。"

"我1999年。"慧琳说完看着宝欣，宝欣却咯咯笑道："没想到吧，我1998年的！我虽然比你小一级，但是你可要尊称我一声姐姐。"

"那我最小，我2000年，你们还选最小的人当组长，一点都不尊老爱幼。"我摆了摆手。

"唉！我们刚好连成同花顺！"伟国突然激动起来，"对了，我们的'数学作业'一直都没时间做呢！"

我们连连叹气——且不说紧凑的日程能否空出娱乐时间，我们的身体能否消受得起这份"福气"也是一个问题。结果次日早上再见到慧琳的时候，我发现她已经和身边人有说有笑："昨晚把终稿发了过去，现在是'翻身农奴把歌唱'！"

太好了，"病号接力"到此结束吧，我们的任务也越来越少，身体应该也会慢慢恢复的，我想。

不料，当天下午准备下车吃饭时，宝欣猛地从座位上站起来，只听见"咚"的一声闷响，她随即跌回座位，喊道："啊！好痛！"

"你又碰到行李架啦?"伟国小心翼翼地弓着身子站起来。

"好痛!"宝欣一时失了语,不断重复着这两个字。

"我把鞋脱下来帮你按头。"慧琳调侃道,宝欣也笑了。前几天不知是谁也撞到过行李架,当时宝欣说:"小学时候有个同学撞到头,肿起来好大一个包,老师立马把自己的鞋子脱下来,把包按了回去。"听得我们笑成一片,谁知讲故事的人最终变成了故事里的人。

凤庆六天旅程进行到第五天,还是没有人"慷慨解鞋",帮宝欣把头上的包按回去。县医院会议室仍是热火朝天的访谈进行时,隔壁休息室却安静得如同考场:伟国端坐在沙发上,皱起眉头反复修改着英文作品;慧琳盘腿坐在沙发上,时而敲击键盘,时而眯眼小憩;宝欣盯着屏幕没多久,又合上了电脑,皱着眉头,靠在沙发上。

我打了个哈欠,拿出手机准备放松一下,发现微信弹出来宝欣十几分钟前发的消息:"刚才打着打着字,突然眼前模糊了。"

想起之前看过的日剧《非自然死亡》里,一个患者骑摩托车摔到头后当时也只是感觉视力模糊,第二天却因脑溢血暴毙了,我惶恐地赶紧请示老师。

不一会,宝欣也拥有了我体验过的 VIP 就诊体验,只不过不是去昏暗狭窄的旧院区,而是体验了一番中大援建的崭新院区。下午五点,整个外科诊室只剩下宝欣一个病人,诊室前的电子屏还显示着下午最后一个患者的名字。准备下班的骨科医生又套上白大褂,按了按宝欣的头。宝欣痛得嗷嗷大叫,医生却云淡风轻地说:"肿得不是很厉害,视力模糊应该是盯着屏幕太久了,担心的话去照个 CT 看看吧。"

20 分钟后,我们拎着片子回到休息室。伟国马上过来,问检查结果怎么样。

"拍了 CT,照到我的脑袋里有一个瘤。"宝欣一副悲伤的样子,慢吞吞地说,不停叹气。

"啊,那怎么办啊?"伟国整个人僵住了。

"哎,你真是!哪有人撞到脑袋还能撞出肿瘤的。"我抢过宝欣的 CT 袋,拿出那份写着"无明显颅内伤"的检验报告,递给伟国,"你自己看吧!"

伟国接过单子,端详了一会,难以置信地抬起头:"这是什么意思?"

"就是说我的脑子有一个瘤子。"宝欣一本正经地说,没有半点笑场的痕迹。我又气又笑:"别听她瞎说,其实没有大碍,回去毛巾热敷就行了!"

"那刚才你怎么说……"伟国眼含泪水,在白炽灯的照耀下闪着泪花。

"骗你的!"宝欣笑得合不拢嘴,"不会吧……你信了?"

"我才没有！"伟国突然摘下眼镜，双手捂住脸，把头别向一边。

"那你这是在干什么？不会是在哭吧？"我问。

"没有！我就是困了，我要睡觉。"伟国把头埋进沙发缝隙。

看着伟国这番模样，我一边说笑，一边却感觉鼻头一酸。自我们接连生病，自嘲"老弱病残"组以来，"老者"伟国每次上车下车都要提醒一句"小心碰头"，有的时候还用手臂挡住行李架，生怕有人再撞到。

万幸的是"病号接力"没有再继续下去，大家安然无恙地回到了珠海，过了好几天才缓解了"身体被掏空"的疲惫感，回归忙碌的学业生活。六天凤庆之旅看似只是往湖面投入一颗石子，引起一阵波澜又重归平静，但实则却是打了个水漂，余波阵阵。

采访支教团的同学时，他们谈到支教的初心是"用一年不长的时间，做一件终生难忘的事情"。对于我们而言，是"用一周不长的时间，收获了终生难忘的经历"。当一般游客止步于大理时，我们却向群山更深处迈进，亲身体验扶贫攻坚的宏大叙事是如何转化为现实的。支教团所言的"种下一颗走出大山的种子"，变成鲁史学生口中的"想要考上医学类院校"；"考上中山大学"从遥不可及，到如今已有三名鲁史学生走入中大。萤火虽微，但八年来一届届支教团的火种汇聚起来，已能为鲁史的学生点亮满天星辰，照亮前方的路途。而我们作为写作者，感动之余，以我们所见所感讲好他们的故事，同样意义非凡。

好的作者总是从对细节的观察开始。从前我一直是一个粗线条的人，并不在乎身边发生什么事情，以至于回忆时只剩下空洞的情绪，碰到细节性的问题时往往用直觉来填补。诸如牛羊肉米线馆的老板自家不卖油条，却特意从别家买来油条招待我们这类事情，如果不是老师亲口讲述，我只会傻愣愣地吃，绝不会对米线馆为什么卖油条产生一丝一毫的疑问。

这次我有机会以任务的方式强迫自己观察周围的事情，再用访谈的方式刨根问底，其实不仅是为了写作，也为了发掘其中蕴含的生活乐趣。

正如戴凡老师在最后一晚"孔雀宴"上的演讲所说，此时、此地、此刻一定是独一无二的回忆，因为参与课程的同学总要各奔东西，"创意写作与翻译"课程的师生往后也不会再访凤庆。照片和影像能够记录画面，却承载不了最直观的感受与最深刻的情谊，而文字却能做到。纸短情长，愿被我记录下来的人们将来再看到这份不太常规的"报道"时，能够庆幸自己在大学选过"创意写作与翻译"这门课程，这样，我的"挑灯夜战"才变得更加有意义。

# 中大人在路上：从脱贫攻坚到乡村振兴

## 屈宁威

"我们打心眼里希望书记不要走，但是又怕他们在这里吃亏，毕竟我们这里条件不好。"陈大姐笑着说。这句话着实让我心头一颤：她矛盾的说辞透露着一点无奈和心酸。

陈大姐嘴里的"书记"就是郭兴勇书记和蓝澍德书记。从2018年起，中山大学响应教育部扶贫攻坚的号召，向云南省凤庆县红塘村派遣驻村书记，于是书记们与红塘村的缘分就此结下。三年后，我们选修戴凡老师的"创意写作与翻译"课程，来到这里，采访、记录、报道扶贫攻坚中的人和事。从10月24日起到29日，12名学生分为教育、医疗、驻村驻县三个小组，完成各自的采访任务。我和另外三名同学被分到了驻村驻县组，也是在这个主题下，我们得以窥见中大人在扶贫攻坚、乡村振兴中发挥的光和热。写下这些文字的时候，我早已从凤庆回校，但这短短一周的经历却让我弥足珍惜。

时间回到我们到达凤庆的第四天傍晚，在陈大姐家里吃过晚餐后，我们一众20多岁的大孩子瘫坐在客厅的沙发上，盯着电视里正在播放的动画片。片子虽然跟我小时候看的不一样，但也算是一种饭后消遣了。冠柔和烨慧是我们组两个大四的学妹，她俩显然比我更有童心，时不时还讨论一下情节。

"今天，驻村驻县组的同学将享受独有的福利——在陈大姐家的民宿住一晚！当然，我和张佳（博士生助教）也会留下来。"戴老师宣布。这是我们行程中的一个环节，为的就是收集更多创作素材。

外面夜色渐浓，其他组的同学也已离去。组里的同学围坐在沙发上，打开电脑，开始向书记的旧交们打听他们的故事。

"你们印象中的郭书记是怎样的呢？"第一个开口的是露露，我的研究生同学，负责视频的字幕工作。

"郭书记三年前来的时候，大家只当他是一个迷路的外乡人，谁知他主动上来问好，比我们热情多了！"

"对对对！郭书记还给小孩子变魔术，逗他们玩儿！"陈大姐的老公插话道。

"别说小孩子了，也给我变过！骗得我团团转！"一位李姓大哥激动了起来，显然他对这件事印象深刻。

"别说你了，我也被骗过！有一天半夜，郭书记说他回来了，给我发了一个附近的定位，叮嘱我备好茶，叙叙旧。当时我还很开心呢，谁知等我烧好茶，他给我发了句'愚人节快乐！'。我看了看时钟，12点刚过，正好是4月1日。"听了陈大姐老公这番话，场面立马就火热了起来。

"原来郭书记还挺幽默！"烨慧和冠柔都在电脑上记录下郭书记的"玩心"，为她们的中、英文红塘故事提供素材。

"多亏了郭书记，村里有了路灯，晚上回家再也不怕走夜路了。还有我们这门口的水渠年久失修，也是郭书记自己掏钱帮我们疏通的，我们种菜、灌溉都方便了很多。"

我想起，来的路上，有几盏路灯伫立在小路两旁。灯光虽然微弱，但足以照亮四周。可能每次村里人外出务工归家，走在灯光下时都会想起郭书记吧——这个50岁左右，喜欢开玩笑、用真心守护这里的异乡人。

客厅的电视机旁挂着两个精美的相框，隐约看得出，照片里的人不像是本地的。

"啊？这张照片中有我同学。"冠柔凑上前去，说："这个是晓莹，这个是……"

"请问……"冠柔刚开口，陈大姐就接上话："这两张照片里的人是来我们这里住宿的学生，好像……也是你们学校的。"

"这里面还有Stephen老师，还有教韩语的徐老师！"旁边的烨慧也在认真地分辨照片里的外籍老师们：他们围绕一张长桌坐着，透过镜头，看得出他们对乡村生活的好奇。

"说到这个啊，这真是我们村的大事件，我们这辈子都没见过这么多外国人呢！"

"他们来我们这里用餐，那是我第一次做饭给外国人吃，有点让我们家乡菜走向国际的感觉，哈哈哈！而且别的村也都过来看热闹，门口挤满了人。"陈大姐笑得合不拢嘴。

"实际上，当时全凤庆县只要是有微信的人，都知道这件事。"一位村民说。

"别村的人都嫉妒得很呢。"陈大姐的老公满脸自豪。

"他们都问，为什么外国人会来我们这边，我们就说，都是因为蓝书记啊。"

说起蓝澍德书记,我们在到凤庆前就采访过他。当时的蓝书记刚卸任回归中山大学中法核工程与技术学院。从他的口中,我们得知中山大学在红塘村的帮扶情况。从困难人群的定点帮扶到全村的产业发展,蓝书记无不亲力亲为。

到红塘村后,我们一行人也参观了金丝黄菊产业园,那是蓝书记强烈建议的目标地。产业园的门口挂着"中山大学产业帮扶基地"的牌匾。进入园区,仿若置身于一片金黄的世界,连片的菊花地向前铺开,从山脚向上延伸。

"这里真是个'网红打卡'拍照圣地!"医疗组的晶晶一进园就抑制不住自己的拍照欲,拉着露露和其他几个同学跑到中间的一座栈桥上,举起手机,摆好姿势。两边花团锦簇,桥上笑靥盈盈。可没过多久,女生们的热情就因头顶的烈日消退了,她们纷纷逃到了一处遮阳篷下,盯着手机,开始下一步的修图工作。也是在这里,我们和看护菊花园的村民张国凤有了一次交流。

"这个菊花园还是在蓝书记的主持下搞起来的。现在蓝书记已经走了几个月了。"张阿姨感慨道。

"那阿姨您觉得在这里看护菊花园给您的生活带来了什么转变呢?"

"那可太多了!以前,我得去很远的地方采茶,没办法照顾家里。我的丈夫腿脚不便,需要照料。如今,我在家旁边就可以工作,守着这个菊花园,一年有8000块的收入呢。"说起蓝书记,张阿姨的口中时不时就会蹦出一句感谢,草帽下晒得发红的脸向我们昭示着她的敬业和对这份工作的珍惜。

临走时,摄影组的陈建滨和张婧妍将无人机升至半空,掠过我们头顶,拍下这片金丝黄菊园。这也是蓝书记留给红塘村最美好的礼物。

离开菊花园,我们准备前往大摆田完全小学,这所村里唯一的小学也是郭书记和蓝书记特别记挂的地方。

"原来这就是小林老师的画啊!"露露拍了拍我,"早就听说过小林老师,今日终于得以一见他的大作,让我看看这幅漫画上写了什么。"

顺着露露指的方向看去,那些两层建筑物的墙壁上粉刷着巨幅的漫画(见图1)。在这乡间小路上,一股别样趣味油然而生。部分漫画的配文如下:

"你的所有祝福,我会努力实现。"
"如果说书籍是人类进步的阶梯,那手机就是人类近视的电梯。"
落款:小林漫画。

**图1 云南省凤庆县红塘村内的小林漫画**

"小林是谁?"

"小林就是我们中大的老师啊,原本是学医的,后来转型做漫画创作了。"

"哇!那也是一位奇人了。"

"小林老师也是蓝书记请来为红塘村进行艺术创作,配合金丝黄菊园吸引游客的。"旁边的张良友书记解释道。他是接替蓝书记的下一任驻村书记,也是我们此行的领路人。

多亏了这个伟大的时代和在时代中像郭书记和蓝书记一样奋斗的人们,

相对于我小时候,中国的乡村已经发生了天翻地覆的变化。真好。

之后,大摆田完全小学的孩子们纷纷朝着我们一行人敬少先队员礼时,我内心深处最柔软的东西被触碰到了,那份遗失已久的纯真被眼前的他们唤醒了。

"你看他们好有礼貌啊!可能是把我们当老师了吧!"冠柔大概也跟我一样,为此所触动。

在校园逗留的途中,我们还参观了葫芦丝课程。这是一门线上课程,国家一级演奏员陈颖丽老师虽远在广州,孩子们却与之互动得很认真。

"那个小朋友跟不上老师的节奏,好着急啊!"晶晶总是那个发现"亮点"的人。

"还有那个,按错孔了,还吹着呢。"露露附和着。

她们像发现了新大陆,饶有兴趣地观察着课堂上孩子们的一举一动。可能是动静稍大了些,那个跟不上节奏的孩子回头看了一眼,立刻又转了头,散乱的刘海下挂满了害羞。这时,观摩"创意写作与翻译"课程的访问学者俸佳老师凑了过来。

"刚刚有几个孩子跑过来问我认识不认识蓝老师。"

"蓝老师?"

"应该是蓝书记吧,之前采访中他说自己曾在这里教孩子们英语。"

"对哦!然后呢?"

"我就说认识啊,问他们怎么啦。他们想让我告诉蓝老师,说他们想他了。"

后面俸老师又说了什么我不太记得了,只记得当时脑海里闪烁着蓝澍德老师教孩子们 ABCD 的模样,似乎就在眼前这个教室里。

之后在与杨卫林校长的交谈中,我们得知孩子们课上用的葫芦丝是中山大学国际翻译学院捐赠的,他们下课后会把葫芦丝统一放置在阅览室保管。我们也参观了孩子们的阅览室,虽然简单,却也有模有样。

"郭书记为学校添置了很多设备,比如说这里的书柜和学校的音响。"

"这里的书也是捐赠的吗?"烨慧走到一格书柜前,端详着一册儿童绘本。

"是啊,也是捐赠的。"

其实直到从凤庆回来的第二天,我的口译老师 Rita 在微信群里提到要捐书的事情时,我才意识到,原来阅览室的书就来自身边师生的善意。

"郭书记有空就会来学校转转,给学生们变魔术,陪他们玩,也会规范他们的行为。"

"所以,我们进来的时候大家都朝我们敬礼呀!"冠柔的疑惑似乎得到了解答。

"是啊,他们也很想念蓝书记。蓝书记是他们的英语老师,还给他们买了英文的绘本作教材。"

下课以后,有两个小学生接受了我们的采访。他们一个叫赵伟,一个叫王文。他们进来的时候向我们敬了个礼,整了整胸前的红领巾,正襟危坐,略显羞涩。

"你们刚刚上课感觉怎么样?作业多不多呀?"露露放缓了语调。她对孩子的天然亲和力立马给这严肃的场合带来了一丝温馨。

俩人点点头,"嗯"了一声。

赵伟有一个哥哥在鲁史中学上高中,就是我们之前去过的鲁史中学。那里条件虽然艰苦,但来自中大的支教老师们坚持了下来,并成了学生眼里的光。王文有一个姐姐目前在县里读初一,也听过蓝老师的课。虽然两个孩子不善于表达,但我们还是能从只言片语中,知道他们对郭老师和蓝老师的感谢和想念。杨校长告诉我们,他们都接受了郭书记发起的奖助金项目,每年获1000元资助。

临走时,正值学校放学,看着孩子们排着队离校回家,我突然感到,这些小小的个头,承载了太多人的关爱和期待。这时,露露和晶晶开心地跑过来给我看她们手里的巧克力。

"看!这是刚刚那个小女孩给我们的,为了谢谢我们给她拍照!"她们边说边挥手和小女孩道别。

"你还要人家小孩的东西!"我假意指责道。

"才没有,我们拿东西交换的。我们很喜欢她,她也很喜欢我们。"

我佩服她们很快便能和小孩子建立起联系,也感慨孩子们对中大人的信任。很久没有回过小学,早已忘了我的小学生活是什么样的,这些孩子们把我带回了孩童年代。

"你们的孩子有在'大完摆'小学读书吗?"戴老师的一个问题,让大家的脑袋中都出现了一个大大的问号,同时也让我从回忆中回到现实。民宿之夜的访谈随着星星点点的蛙鸣也渐进尾声。"戴老师,您想说的应该是'大摆田完全小学'吧?"露露突然反应过来。

顿时,大家的"笑点"又被"点燃"了起来,烨慧、冠柔还有张佳学姐都笑得东倒西歪，戴老师也尴尬得"扑哧"地笑了。

"哈哈，我们家孩子不在那里上学，在隔壁村的一个学校。"陈大姐笑着回应道。

在这之后，接近一周的云南凤庆之行就临近尾声了。回想起我们驻村驻县组在第一次采访前的那个夜晚，大家拿出所有之前的报道资料，寻找蛛丝马迹，分配话题任务，做足了准备，到真正采访的时候，却被打乱了顺序，只能跟着受访者的思路重新整理问题。经过几天的磨炼，我们慢慢变得游刃有余，尽管也有问不出结果的尴尬，但还是收获了宝贵的一手材料。而最重要的是，在这过程中，中大在凤庆的帮扶足迹和脉络逐渐清晰，这其中的人和事足以被传为一段佳话。

谢谢郭书记和蓝书记，谢谢还在为凤庆努力的人们和即将到来的后继者们，我们会成为你们的传声筒，不辜负你们对这个伟大时代的馈赠。

而凤庆的孩子们因中大师生的帮扶而有了未来的目标。

"我长大要成为一名程序员，为国家科技发展做贡献！"

"我长大要成为一名警察，保卫国家的安全！"

赵伟和王文稚嫩的声音，回应着中大人的努力，承载着乡村振兴的未来。

# 以我之力，护你前行

## 王晶晶

"为了这些人民，我想恳请中大，恳请眼科中心主任继续牵着我们的手，就像母亲保护一个孩子一样，牵着我们的手不断前进，帮助我们迅速提高。"这是凤庆县人民医院眼科副主任李春光在访谈结束时说的话。时至今日，这一字一句仍然回荡在我的耳边……

2019年，中山大学开始以组团的方式派医疗人员到凤庆县进行全面的医疗帮扶，其中眼科就是帮扶项目之一。位于滇西南的凤庆县，自2013年起就是中山大学的定点帮扶县。而本次借戴凡老师开设的"创意写作与翻译"课程，一行人到凤庆县调研，讲述我们眼中的中大扶贫故事。调研团队由戴凡老师、摄影团队、六个本科生、六个研究生、一个博士生助教组成，分别对教育、医疗以及当地产业相关人员进行访谈，李春光医生便是访谈对象之一。我有幸被分配到了医疗组，了解医疗帮扶成果的同时，也收获了许多美好的记忆。

现在仍然能回想起第一天的场景：飞机、动车、大巴，航路、公路、山路，想提笔记录，但由于出发当天凌晨两点半才入睡，身体和脑子似乎都下达了指令——立马睡觉！

睁眼便到了本次行程的第一站——鲁史镇。鲁史镇位于凤庆县东北部，群山环绕，山路崎岖。我只隐隐约约记得，三个小时的山路，头与汽车玻璃窗来回碰撞，醒来后非常疼痛。睡了一天，算是精神了不少，吃完晚饭，我和驻村驻县组的王露露约着出去走走。

一路往前，路旁商铺都已关门。我看了一眼手机，晚上八点。远远望去，看到了一家还开着的小店，我们小跑过去。

"叔叔，麻花还有吗？"吃饭时听支教老师许锦涛提到，这里的麻花很好吃。

"现在没了，明天来吧。"旁边的叔叔对我们说道。

"好的，谢谢叔叔！"

"你们是来旅游的吗？"

"不是，我们是中大的，来做调研。"

"中大的呀！谢谢你们！谢谢你们来到这里！"

谢谢？我不解，为什么要对我们说谢谢？因为我们要买麻花吗？

"你们什么时候走呢？"

"明天。"

"那你们明天再来转转，这附近还有一个戏台。你可以看到，我们这边没什么年轻人，他们都出去打工了，留下的都是老人。我本来也在外面工作，前几天有亲戚生病了，我回来帮她照看店铺。"

"这边的月收入大概多少呢？"

"1800～2000元，商铺的房租一年1000块钱，像卖小吃，一天也就只能卖50元，可能都挣不回本。由于没什么人，很多小店无法开张，年轻人就外出务工了。"

…………

这便是我和露露的第一场"非正式访谈"。虽然似唠家常一般进行，但回去的路上，我和露露都面色凝重。

在医疗组访谈的前一天，我们开始了第一次小组讨论。我一筹莫展，对访谈问题毫无头绪，两个组员谭晓燕和李心琪却已经开始讨论如何写故事了。

"你想好故事的主题了吗？"琪琪问晓燕。

"还没，不是直接写故事吗？"

"这些故事需要一个主题串联起来，你准备用第几人称写？"

"第一人称。"

"我们需要想好主题，明天根据主题有针对性地去问问题。"

…………

"我俩好像局外人！"我对另一个组员黄元亨说道。

听着她俩的争辩，我不由得庆幸自己是组长，不用担心选主题这些问题。只是眼看旁边的元亨一直在打字，争辩也有了结果，我却还没有想出明天要问的问题。最后不知谁提了一句"明天随机应变"，医疗小组的第一次讨论便就此结束。

不一会，元亨便将采访提纲发到了小组微信群里，我大为震撼。关于访谈对象、访谈目的、访谈背景、访谈问题，他都详细列出来了，框架十分清晰。在我看来，整理这些东西应该是组长做的事情，我十分羞愧，同时又佩服元亨。

我开始谴责自己不认真的态度。

出发前,我将此次调研之行看作一次"旅行"。汽车缓缓驶出校园时,我舒了一口长气,心里嘀咕着:我终于可以暂时脱离这个环境了!

研究生生活与我所想的大相径庭,我没想过会这么忙,忙到我开始挤压我的娱乐时间。我开始焦虑,开始逃避,甚至想大哭一场,但我找不到理由停下手中的活。于是,我的心理逐渐"叛逆",我讨厌这样的生活,我讨厌时间被莫名其妙的事情剥夺,讨厌不能做自己喜欢的事情,讨厌这样的环境!本着这样的心态,我来到凤庆,想要借机放松一下,所以对有关学习的事情一律很排斥。但在看到元亨的采访提纲那一刻,我开始反思了:做自己该做的事情并不叫"学习",而是基本要求。

医疗组的采访一个接一个地进行着(见图1):

"李春光医生,您自己对中大的帮扶有什么体会吗?"

"我想代表我自己,也代表我们广大民众向中大、向中山眼科中心说一声'谢谢',然后再向制定这个伟大决策的国家说一声'谢谢'……"

…………

"李海院长,您能谈谈中大的医疗帮扶团队来了之后医院发生的变化吗?"

图1 课程师生对凤庆县人民医院的李海院长进行访谈

"由于中大医疗团队的帮扶,凤庆县医疗水平大幅提升,凤庆县人民医院在云南省县级公立医院综合改革效果评价考核中成绩排名第一。手术台次、出院人次实现'双倍增',基本实现了'大病不出县'。还有一个例子,之前我们有个帮扶医生搭乘本地出租车,当出租车司机了解到这是来自中大的帮扶医生后,要免费送医生到达目的地。"

听到这里,我想起鲁史镇那位叔叔说的"谢谢你们"。我突然懂了,开始感叹这些医生的伟大,感慨自己的渺小。自己无意间成了中大帮扶项目的"受惠者",那一句"谢谢你们"真是受之有愧。我开始思考自己能做什么,记录便显得尤为重要。

驻村驻县组的一个采访地点是在大摆田完全小学。走进校门后,听到的是此起彼伏的问好声:

"老师好!"

"老师好!"

"老师好!"

所有小朋友都在给我们敬少先队礼,好像学校来了什么大人物似的。面对这从未见过的场景,我不禁受宠若惊,开始回应他们的问好:"你好啊,你好啊……"心情也在一片问好声中逐渐变好。

人群中有一个女孩子笑容可掬,落落大方,不似其他孩子的拘谨。我走到她面前。

"老师好!"她笑容灿烂。

"你好呀!你好呀!你几年级了?"

"四年级了!"

叮铃铃铃!上课了,他们回到了教室。我的注意力还在那个女孩身上。不一会儿,下课铃声响起,孩子们又开始向我们问好。我又看到她了,便走过去牵着她的手拍照。

这是我第一次主动去牵一个孩子的手。以前我见到有些孩子没什么礼貌,交谈中还时不时透露出傲气,我不喜欢,也很怕被他们缠上,所以看到孩子我都能躲开就躲开。

这一次不一样,我喜欢这个小女孩,喜欢看她笑,喜欢这些孩子的童真。和他们在一起时,我好像卸下了所有包袱,很放松,也很开心,甚至会开怀大笑。

也许是在他们身上看到了从前的自己,我羡慕他们这般快乐,也希望他们能将这份快乐维持下去,因为这样的快乐我丢失许久了!

以前不懂爸妈为什么一直跟我说，不求我成绩有多好，不求我以后多成功，只要我快快乐乐就好。也不知从何时开始，我的快乐变少了。我拼命想要找回快乐，却无从下手。而和这群孩子在一起，准确地说，和这个女孩在一起，我好像又能感知到快乐这种情绪了。

我不舍地松开她的手，我们要走了，他们要上课了。笑看着她的背影离去，我的视野开始模糊。

看着那个跑去上课的背影，好像看到了10岁的王晶晶，她在向我打招呼，笑着问我："嘿，21岁的王晶晶，你现在好吗？"

我挥手，笑了笑……

我们调研团队在校门口准备上车，恰好学校放学，一群孩子涌过来，向我们打招呼："老师再见！老师再见！……"

"再见！路上注意安全！"

我拿着手机开始记录这一刻。一个小女孩向我跑来，是她，是那个我还不知道名字的女孩！

我向她跑去。

我们抱在了一起。

"姐姐，你们要走了吗？"

"对呀，回家路上注意安全哦！"

随后小女孩跑进了一个屋子。

"露露，你看着她，我到车上拿个东西。"我记得包里还有一块巧克力。我将巧克力递给小女孩的同时，她递给我和露露一人一个巧妙卷。

原来，刚刚那个屋子是小卖部。一股暖流撞击着我的心扉，我忍住眼泪。我是来"帮扶"的，最后却成了"被帮扶"的人。

目送她的背影消失在人海，我拉着露露跑进了那家小卖部。拿着照片询问老板认不认识那个女孩，老板点了点头。我们买了零食，留了纸条，让老板第二天交给她。纸条上写道：要快快乐乐的哦！我希望她能将这份快乐留存下去，希望她的快乐能够温暖到更多的人。

有些地方一生可能只会去一次，所以令人格外珍惜。也许还有机会，但下次不知是何时。正如戴凡老师在最后一晚所说，"大四的同学有的准备找工作了，有的升学深造，我们的博士生助教也要毕业了，'创意写作与翻译'课程的师生以后可能也不会再来凤庆，所以此时此地都是独一无二的。愿同学们以后回忆起大学生活的点点滴滴，会庆幸自己选择了这样一门非常特别的课"。

我有幸通过课程成为中大帮扶项目的一个见证者,见证了中大帮扶给凤庆县人民医院、凤庆人民带来的改变,也见证了凤庆之行对自己的改变。看戏终成戏中人。至此,我才真正理解了鲁史镇的叔叔那句"谢谢你们",读懂了背后真正的含义。尽管我只是帮扶项目的一个小小见证者,但我觉得自己好像在做一件真正有意义的事情。写下所闻所见,愿更多人参与其中,去帮助更多的人。

# 凤庆故事篇

这部分的三篇作品在访谈和田野调查的基础上,分别讲述了中山大学师生在云南凤庆支教、驻村驻县和医疗帮扶的故事。

# 弦歌不辍,芳华待灼

黄宝欣

也许是因为每一天都过得非常充实,时间过得特别地快。

中山大学第十八届研究生支教团来到鲁史中学已经一个月了。一个月前,从凤庆县城到鲁史镇将近三小时的颠簸车程,让徐述腾和队友们对大山的敬畏都上升了一个级别。大家纷纷打趣说,下一次出去就是一年后离开鲁史之时。

徐述腾是这一届支教团凤庆分队的队长。他被分配到的宿舍里,窗户的边框早已生锈发黑,水泥被随意地糊在地板和墙壁上,在昏黄的灯光下,房间显得更加残破。教师宿舍是如此,学生宿舍更不用说。开学之际,校长带他简单参观了一下:八张双层床被拥挤地摆放在小屋内,孩子们的床铺只够一人平躺,上下铺的床边都固定了一条长木板,以免人在夜里翻身时掉下床。

桌子上的高中政治课本已经被翻得有些卷边。短短几周里,徐述腾把课本从头到尾看了很多遍。在开学前的教职工大会上,校长用带有浓浓云南方言口音的普通话向老师们布置教学工作。

"徐述腾老师,负责高一政治课……"

他猛地抬起头,校长的话虽然不好懂,但自己的名字还是听得清的。

大会一结束,他马上找校长:"校长,咱不是都说好了吗?我是来教物理的,我一个物理专业的学生怎么教政治?您是不是弄错了?"

"没弄错,我们不缺物理老师,现在就缺政治老师,学校里好多老师都跑县城去了。"

"那我能不能同时兼任政治和物理老师?我看了孩子们现在的物理成绩,恐怕连会考都过不了。"徐述腾不死心,来云南前,他已经做好了教物理的准备。

"那你让现在的物理老师去教什么呢?他教了一辈子物理,是教得差了点,但他就只会教物理,不像你们大学生,什么都会教。"

徐述腾妥协了,向办公室的老师要了一本高一的政治书。翻开第一章,他只感到很陌生，他已经太久没有接触这些内容了。从现在开始，他既是学生，也是老师。每次课前的晚上，他认真备课，保证给孩子们讲好课。

要讲好课，除了自己掌握好知识，还需要做什么呢？第一节课前，对这个问题，他和队友们想了很久，都担心自己站在讲台上面，下面的孩子们根本不听讲，或者互动时间不搭理他们，这可不是他们想要的。初来鲁史中学时，他注意到教室里的投影设备落满了灰，当地老师一般都只会用粉笔板书，不会也没时间和精力去准备幻灯片，也许这可以吸引孩子们的注意力。

第一节课，徐述腾走进教室时，班内一片沉寂。他做了简单的自我介绍。孩子们都伸长脖子往讲台看。

教室里充斥着微妙的紧张氛围。

"你们有谁愿意当我的课代表？"

意料之中，没人举手。

"那我们玩击鼓传花来决定。"

徐述腾敲着黑板擦，孩子们有节奏地传递着手中的"花"。他随手停下，"花"落在一个腼腆的男孩手中。男孩紧张地站起来，小声地说："老师，我没当过课代表，我不会。"

"你才多大的年纪？年轻人会不会不重要，敢不敢才重要。从今天起你就是我的课代表了，坐下吧。"说完，徐述腾开始操作电脑，放映课件。

第一节课很成功，孩子们的眼睛齐刷刷地盯着大屏幕，精心编排的幻灯片课件似乎有种魔力，牢牢吸引着孩子们。不仅是课件，徐述腾讲课的方式也和以往的老师不同，他用一个个有趣的事例结合知识点，成功地俘获了孩子们的心。

用投影设备效果很好，孩子们都很积极，但这也意味着徐述腾必须牺牲休息时间做课件，一做就是三四个小时。他熬夜在几平方米的水泥地宿舍里一个字一个字地敲打着，一个特效一个特效地编排着，为的是孩子们能在下一节课多学一点。

连着做了一个多月课件，徐述腾开始有点吃不消了。由于没休息够，黑眼圈也慢慢浮现并扎根在他的脸上。月考成绩出来了，学生们的分数和自己的投入并不成正比。他垂头丧气地走上讲台。

"徐老师，您怎么了？"有孩子看出他不对劲。

徐述腾问："你们喜欢老师用课件还是写粉笔板书？"

"课！件！"五十几个孩子异口同声。

徐述腾叹了口气，垂下头不说话。这时，他的课代表站了起来，说：

"老师，您不做课件我们也会认真听课的！"

其他孩子面面相觑，好一会儿才反应过来，也应和着。

他暗下决心，要为孩子们做更多的事。

开学报到的时候，徐述腾和队友们发现很多家长和孩子是背着铺盖走路过来的，有的山路单程就要走两三个小时。孩子们如此每周一次往返，上学是不小的负担。他很快留意到往届支教老师发起的一个项目：在社会上找一些爱心人士给孩子们做一对一资助，每个月给孩子资助200～300块钱作为伙食费。这在很大程度上解决了一个孩子最基本的开销，减轻了家庭负担。徐述腾和队友们决定把项目继续做下去，他负责高中部，另外一名老师陈曦负责初中部。

有了大概的想法，徐述腾在班上鼓励孩子们申请。本以为这个消息会得到很热烈的反响，没想到底下一片寂静。他意识到也许是学生们的自尊心在作祟，便开玩笑道："大家不用不好意思呀，君子报恩，十年不晚。大家觉得自己有需要就申请，写一个申请书给我。"

他没想到的是，当天收到了两个班的80份申请书，每一份申请书上都字字恳切地说明了自己家里的困难条件：

"徐老师您好，我想申请一对一帮扶，我从来没有穿过新衣服，我的衣服都是表哥表姐给我的……"

"老师，我爸爸不能干农活了，他身体不好，我们家没有什么钱了，我怕爸爸不让我读书了，我想读下去……"

…………

孩子们的一字一句令他心如刀割。已经快凌晨三点了，他摇了摇头，把瞌睡虫赶到脑后，将剩余的申请书看完。每一个孩子他都想帮助，但事先联系好的资助人只有不到40个。读完所有申请书的时候天已经蒙蒙亮了，远处也传来了几声鸡鸣。徐述腾决定向孩子们如实说明情况。

"同学们，我先和大家说一声抱歉，老师暂时没有找到那么多资助人，现在需要大家帮助一下老师，推荐一下最需要资助的同学，好吗？"

孩子们纷纷点头，掏出纸和笔默默写了起来。

下课铃响了，徐述腾小心翼翼地拿着孩子们的纸条回到办公室。

"老师，您先资助小慧吧，他们家的房子都快倒了，墙上裂了好大一个口子了，您不信的话我可以和您去她家里看看……"

"老师，我推荐您资助我同桌，我从来没有见他穿过运动鞋，永远都是穿家里做的土布鞋,他真的很困难……"

…………

根据交上来的纸条,徐述腾给孩子们排了序,先帮助最困难的孩子。但他手头上的资助人还远远不够。其实,两三百块钱对一个城市里经济独立的成年人来说,并不是多大的一笔钱,问题是如何取得资助人的信任。他通过微信朋友圈、微博等渠道发送资助说明和请求,希望有更多人能够参与进来。

在做一对一帮扶计划的过程中,大大小小的事都是他一个人做,包括前期与资助人的沟通,让资助人确信自己的钱将被一分不差地打进孩子们的饭卡里;他还负责孩子们和资助人的书信往来,把孩子们写给资助人的信带到镇上的邮局投递出去;资助人会在网上给孩子们留言,他也一一传达。有的资助人中途撤资,徐述腾就自己掏腰包先补上空缺,同时马上寻找下一个资助人。在他的努力下,提交申请的86个孩子在他离开鲁史镇前都得到了一对一的资助,大部分孩子如今还和资助人保持联系。

和孩子们"混"熟以后,徐述腾在课下也和他们打成一片,他更像是他们的大哥哥。这天趁着空闲,徐述腾到篮球场上准备和孩子们"切磋"一番。打得火热之时,他不小心摔了一跤,把眼镜摔坏了。孩子们都围了过来,像做错了事一样。

"没事,咱镇上不是有眼镜店吗?我拿去修修就行了,实在不行就重新配一副。"孩子们这才散开。

鲁史镇说大不大,说小也不小。在这个离县城有三小时车程的深山小镇上,商铺倒是一应俱全,狭小的道路上零零散散分布着一些商住一体的店铺。

晚餐时分,徐述腾拿着眼镜去眼镜店,老板看着"身首异处"的眼镜摇了摇手,说:"你这不行呀,要重新配了。"

验光以后,老板让他挑镜框。这一挑可把他吓坏了,连看了好几副都要1000多块钱。他问老板:"你这里最便宜的要多少钱?"

"最便宜的比较重,800元一副。"

徐述腾摘下验光用的眼镜,说:"太贵了,我不配了。"说着拿起眼镜就准备往店外走。

"唉,你不配了,那我要收你验光费的,50块。"

回到学校，徐述腾和孩子们说起这件事，问大家配眼镜要多少钱。

"老师，我这副要1500块呢！"

原来，镇上的眼镜店一家独大，加上去县城路途遥远，大家要么咬咬牙在镇上配，要么干脆不配。老板把生意都垄断了，价格自然比市价高几倍。徐述腾这才意识到，对班上那些眯着眼睛看黑板的孩子而言，眼镜是奢侈品。

不知道哪里来的豪气，他拍着胸脯和大家说："徐老师保证给你们每一个人都配上眼镜，免费！"

"老师，你可别吹牛呀！"几个坐在后排的男生起哄道："眼镜好多钱一副呢！"

吹牛归吹牛，徐述腾当天晚上就开始想怎么找赞助。几经周折，还是找回那家眼镜店，但老板最低也要收成本价，50块钱一副。徐述腾估算了一下，50块钱一副，全校也要好几百副。那是一笔不小的钱呀！答应了孩子们免费配眼镜的，这可怎么办？

徐述腾想到了润心基金会。基金会答应支持他，但条件是支教结束后，他到基金会工作一年。这样，徐述腾将自己的一年时光"卖"给了基金会，孩子们的眼镜就有了着落。

配眼镜前要验光，这是一项不小的工程，眼镜店老板恐怕是不乐意的。他灵光一闪，想到县医院有熟人，这下事情就好办了。朋友和他说："没问题，这事包在我身上。"

县医院的眼科一共有12人，除了一人必须留下来值班，其余11人在验光当天都来了。徐述腾在学校广而告之，让孩子们只要觉得自己视力有问题的就都测一下，生怕有谁错失了这个机会。验光工程浩浩荡荡地持续了一天，医生们当天晚上住了下来，第二天上午才结束工作。最后，全校385名近视的孩子没花一分钱就配到了眼镜。

很快，第二学期开学了。徐述腾发现班上那个叫李文芝的女生两周没来上课，担心她生病了或是家里出了什么事。放学后，他向校长借了摩托车，骑了一小时山路到了李文芝家里。

"你怎么没来学校报道呢？"

"老师，我不想去上学了。我要和姐姐去宁波打工，我姐打工回来都有新手机了，我也要买。"

原来，在刚刚过去的寒假，孩子们在外打工的哥哥姐姐都回来过年，看到他们衣着光鲜地踏入家门，家里条件一般的孩子就认为辍学打工是一条更好的出路。

回到班上，他对孩子们说："你们现在不要觉得哥哥姐姐风光，等你读完书，一定比他们过得更好。"

几天后，徐述腾发现他好不容易劝回来的李文芝又不上学了。他再一次到她家里问，小女孩扭扭捏捏的，不愿意多说。

徐述腾觉得小女生对他有一些防备，于是叫上队友陈曦和孩子谈。

"老师，我之前和班上的同学都说了，我要去宁波打工。我前两天回去时，他们都笑我，我不好意思再回去了。"李文芝低着头小声说。

这让两人很诧异，孩子原来是这样想的。他向李文芝保证，回到学校后，不会有人笑她，女孩才点头答应。

现在，李文芝在昆明理工大学读大三。今年（2021年）教师节除了祝福，她还向徐述腾表示感谢，感谢他没有放弃年少轻狂的自己。如果没有徐述腾，现在她可能只是一个随处漂泊的打工族。

上课的时候，徐述腾总会有意无意地讲大山外的世界是怎么样的，给孩子们介绍自己在广州的校园生活和正在发生的变化。孩子们都会露出心向往之的表情，这些表情印在了他的心里。他开始萌生一个大胆的想法：带孩子们出去看看外面的世界。

临近支教工作尾声时，中山大学团委让徐述腾线上参与博研慈善基金会的晚会。晚会快结束的时候，主持人问他："徐老师，您太不容易了，离家这么远到深山支教。您有没有什么梦想呢？"

徐述腾知道自己必须抓住这个难得的机会。他清了清嗓子，郑重地说："我的梦想是带我的学生们去一趟广州，看看我的学校——中山大学。"

主持人问在场的各位："大家愿不愿意帮徐老师实现他的梦想？"

马上有人问需要多少钱。

"10万。"

"10万？"

"是的，用作路费、住宿费以及其他开支。我已经有一个很完整的计划书，我给它起了一个名字，叫'青翼计划'。"

拿到了赞助，徐述腾欣喜若狂地和孩子们说这件事，只是这笔钱不可能让所有孩子一起去广州。他宣布："'青翼计划'的资金只允许14名同学参加，我会在各班期末考试成绩前三名的同学里面选，排名靠后的同学也不要气馁，进步最大的同学也会有机会。"

这在班上炸开了锅，对他们来说，到凤庆县已经很了不起了，如果谁去了一趟昆明，那是要吹嘘好一阵子的。而现在，站在讲台上的这个人说，要带他们其中一些人去广州，每一个人的眼睛里都充满了渴望。

"不行，这绝对不行！"
徐述腾怎么也没想到，"青翼计划"最大的阻碍来自校长。
"校长，您没去过广州，您也一起去吧，孩子们都很期待这次活动，我相信他们一定会有很多收获的。"
"徐老师，这道理我都知道，只是，带十几个小孩出去，出了事怎么办？你想过没有？"
徐述腾激动地站起来说："校长，难道我不爱学生们吗？我对他们的爱也不比您少！您看，学校里有的老师还对孩子们体罚，我就算是再生气，也舍不得打骂他们。我只是想带大家去看看外面的世界。"
校长沉默了许久，说："你自己到县城和教育局局长说吧。这么大的事，我也做不了主。"

第二天一大早，徐述腾跑到县教育局。果不其然，局长一听就摇头摆手。
"你一个外来的年轻人，带着我们十几个小孩去这么远的地方，一去就是十天半个月，这怎么行？"
无论徐述腾如何担保孩子们的安全，他都不点头。徐述腾是铁了心要带孩子们出去的。他咬咬牙，主动提出签一份"生死状"——安全责任书，如果出了事，全部责任由他一个人承担。局长见他那副誓不罢休的样子，也不说话了。徐述腾坐在办公桌前写着责任书，局长轻飘飘地冷嘲热讽了一句："小徐，广州这么热，我们这边的学生别说飞机，连车都没坐过几次，那是有可能在路上晕过去的。出了事，你可是要担责任的。"
经过一番周折，徐述腾总算得到了各级领导的许可。转眼期末考试成绩也出来了，"青翼计划"的名单随之尘埃落定。徐述腾坐在办公室处理出发前最后的工作，一个男孩咬着唇走了进来。
"怎么了？"
话音刚落，男孩瘦弱的肩膀抽动了起来。他是班上第4名，但是徐述腾答应了要给班上进步最大的孩子一个名额，于是眼前这个男孩和"青翼计划"失之交臂了。

"你别哭，老师能力有限，这次只能带这么多人去。老师知道你很努力，但我不能对你一个人行特例，这样对别人就不公平了。"

2017年5月27日，徐述腾带着14名同学和4位老师，从鲁史到昆明，再坐飞机到广州。不仅是孩子们，老师们也非常激动。此时，他们都如同未经世事的小孩，对一切都十分好奇：不停地互相发问"这是什么""那是什么"，应接不暇的新鲜事物让他们手忙脚乱。

这时，徐述腾的手机震动了起来。鲁史教师群里在议论道："徐老师真行呀，拿着10万块钱带学生出去玩了。你看这学校连一个正经的操场都没有，划了块泥地就当是操场了。你们说拿这10万块钱建个操场不是更有意义吗？"

徐述腾不明白，在那些老师眼中，什么才是"有意义"的事情。带着孩子们看看外面的世界，去经历一些从未经历过的事情难道不是很有意义的吗？

到了广州，紧凑的行程让他顾不上教师群里那些议论给自己带来的不愉快。他马不停蹄地带着孩子们去参观中山大学南校园。看惯了鲁史中学灰白破败的墙的孩子们，走在红墙绿瓦的校园里显得格外兴高采烈。

第二天，一行人去中山大学的珠海校区参观。校区旁是一望无垠的大海，海面在阳光下波光粼粼，孩子们高兴坏了。赵光炜是高二年级学生的队长，这是他第一次看到大海。他脱下鞋子，挽起裤腿，深一脚浅一脚地走在柔软细腻的沙滩上，朝着海快步走去，直至走到海水能拍打着小腿肚的地方。他弯腰捧起了一口海水喝了下去。

"好咸！"

光炜转过身对着徐述腾露出灿烂的笑容——徐述腾通知他入选的时候，他还害怕自己和大城市格格不入，一度拒绝了这个机会。

刘跃秀比光炜小一届，她看着大海，若有所思。突然有人往她身上泼水，一场水仗就此拉开序幕，孩子们在海水里嬉笑打闹着……

第三天，他们到广州中山大学附属中学听课。第一节是语文课，老师在黑板上写了八个字——"富而无骄，贫而无谄"，让同学们讨论对这句话的理解。和鲁史中学的老师只管在讲台上讲自己的课不同，附中的课堂上，师生间的互动填满了课堂，你问我答，行云流水。

第二节是英语课。英语老师走进教室，说：

"Good morning, class."

"Good morning, teacher."

"OK. Today we're going to…"

英语老师开始讲课，语速逐渐加快，坐在后排的鲁史中学学生开始面露难色，互相交换尴尬的笑容：他们听不懂。接下来的45分钟就有些煎熬了，英语老师的嘴巴在飞快地动，但发出的声音是他们无法理解的。

回到鲁史，学生们在总结大会上分享自己的感受。第一个孩子站起来：
"我们听了中大附中的课，大家都是高中生，别人可以全英上课，我却连一句完整的句子都听不懂，这就是我们的差距。但是，我们和他们是一样的，一样的聪明，只是基础不一样，所以我要更努力地学习……"
"以前，我只在课上听过老师讲广州如何如何，只看到图片，没有什么强烈的感觉。但是这次我自己亲眼看到了，我非常想通过自己的努力改变自己，改变我的家庭，我想报考中山大学……"

学生们一个接着一个发言，到最后都泣不成声。短短一周就像一次洗礼，他们突然长大了，见识到外面广阔的世界，小小的翅膀也在他们身上展开。最终，这14位同学都考上了大学。其中，赵光炜和赵永树相继考上了中山大学，刘跃秀考上了华南农业大学。

在一整年的支教生活中，徐述腾并不是孤军奋战的，来自外国语学院的陈曦一直和他并肩努力。

陈曦教的是高二英语。乡村的英语教育起步晚，师资也不好，孩子们的英语成绩自然不会好到哪里去，平均分都是三四十分。陈曦上了几节课后发现，班上的学生早已对英语失去了兴趣和信心，一副听天由命的模样，调动孩子们的积极性成了她的首要难题。

这个年纪的孩子除了课本，对什么都感兴趣。陈曦到镇上的商铺走了一圈，看到杂货铺货架上放着的小音响，她有了想法。带着音响回到宿舍，打开自己的英文歌单，挑了几首歌词简单的英文歌。第二天的课上，陈曦把歌词拿出来，对班上的同学说："今天我们来学唱英文歌。我们先把歌词读熟了，等会儿课间我们就一起唱，好吗？"

孩子们扯着嗓门，用洪亮的声音跟着陈曦朗读歌词，比以往朗读课文的声音要精神许多。下课铃响了，陈曦拿出音响播放刚播过的歌曲，学生们跟着旋律唱，隔壁班的同学们都闻声过来，争相在教室前后门观看。

光学英文歌是远远不够的，学生们的基础差，教材里的课文和习题不适合他们。陈曦想到自己初学英语时用过的书——《新概念英语》。她找来第二册,在 90 多篇课文中选了 30 篇简单有趣的课文,连同一些配套的语法基础习题,一一整理好后打印给学生作为额外的练习。学英语这么多年,陈曦深知语感的重要性,她抓住各种机会让孩子们放声朗读来培养语感。她还利用周末无偿给留校学习的孩子们开英语补习班,即使不是她教的学生也可以参加。她对英语的热情极大地感染了学生们,英语学习慢慢进入了正轨。

如今,"一对一资助""光明行动"和"青翼计划"已成为中山大学支教团薪火相传的帮扶项目。每一年都有新的研究生支教老师通过层层选拔前往云南凤庆。例如,第 19 届成员是陈佳敏、方仕杰、方媛;第 20 届成员有钟滔、孙雨婷、谢杭、杨文锦;第 21 届成员是刘玲琳、胡玉立、李广涵、叶惠珠;第 22 届的成员有黄晓波、曾小晖、冯思嘉、梁伟诺……

尽管不能在这里一一讲述每一个人的支教故事,但作为一名支教老师,他们做的其实都大同小异。2021 年在鲁史支教的是第 23 届成员吴雅婷、牛璐璐(见图 1)、刘超宇、许锦涛,他们的话恰如其分地表达了各位支教老师的初心:

**图 1 中山大学第 23 届研究生支教团凤庆队成员牛璐璐在鲁史中学讲数学课**

"作为一名支教老师，我想成为走进孩子们心里的老师，想成为帮助孩子们走出大山的老师。"

"作为一名支教老师，我想成为让孩子们喜欢数学的数学老师。我希望通过活泼的数学课堂让同学们不再惧怕数学，让他们热爱数学。"

"作为一名高三支教老师，我会尽我所能帮助他们走出大山，走进大学，走向更广阔的世界。"

"作为一名支教老师，我会努力做一个合格的志愿者，一个合格的人民教师，用一年不长的时间做一件感动自己、感动学生的事。"

……………

中山大学党委书记陈春声曾寄语研究生支教团："一个人的生命周期不算很长，其中有一段时间做一件有意义的工作，这种经历终生难忘，终生受益。中大学生专业水平、智力水平都不错，对职业发展有很好的规划，但更重要的是，中大希望学生德才兼备，有领袖气质、家国情怀，希望他们实实在在地学习和工作，不满足于生活的'小确幸'，要超越这些，要有更高的眼界和胸襟。"

暂别红墙绿瓦的支教团成员在大山深处弦歌不辍，芳华待灼，带着爱与希望砥砺前行。

## "一段扶贫路,一生红塘情"
### ——中山大学脱贫攻坚、乡村振兴纪实

林冠柔

"他……他会给我们变魔术!"大摆田完全小学四年级的王文和五年级的赵伟面对我们这群陌生的"大人",有点不知如何是好,双手不断抬起又放下(见图1)。但是一提到郭兴勇,他们兴奋地说道:"郭书记买了小电驴,逐家逐户去走访,很关心小孩,会给小孩变魔术。"现任红塘村驻村第一书记张良友还带着一点书生气,皮肤也不及之前我们在广州通过视频采访过的蓝澍德书记那般黑。他能经常听到村民们谈论郭书记和蓝书记,以及他们对中山大学的印象,以至于被问起的时候几乎能够将两位书记的故事背出来:"每个村民都会跟你说中大的老师们之前做过什么。"

图1 课程师生在大摆田完全小学采访小学生王文、赵伟

"变魔术!"在民宿里和村民聊天的时候,村民本来拘谨地放在腿上的手也因为谈及书记的亲切而扬了起来。

"不想放他们走啦!"村民们兴奋分享的同时又有点惋惜。"也不能耽误他们的前途,是吧?"他们带有云南口音的普通话不难听懂。

"当时给他做了一本影集。"看到张书记笑意盈盈地站在一旁,一个村民豪放地加了一句:"也会给你做的啦!"

从中山大学2013年起帮扶凤庆县、2018年开始对口帮扶红塘村以来,村里已经经历过三任书记。三任书记给红塘村带来的确实是如同魔术一样的变化。

凤庆隶属于中国西南地区云南省的临沧市,地处云南省西南部,气候宜人。中山大学国际翻译学院"创意写作与翻译"课程的学生在主讲老师戴凡的带领下,踩着10月底霜降时节的尾巴,凌晨从珠海出发,乘坐两三个小时飞机到了空气干燥的云南大理。从大理机场到凤庆县,还要再坐一个半小时的高铁。

凤庆占地14平方千米,从南到北有7000米,县城有八万人左右,总共有13个乡镇。凤庆北端是鲁史,南端是郭大寨。从鲁史中学到凤庆县医院再到红塘村,学生们被分为三个组,分别从教育、医疗和驻村驻县三个方面对中山大学帮扶凤庆的情况进行采访。随行的还有助教和摄影团队,从能做文字转译的"黑科技"到各式各样的摄影设备,设施一应俱全。

在第一次采访开始前,负责摄像的魏东华老师非常亲切地请我们在打好光的现场随便聊天,好让他确认录像的效果。第一次在镜头前难免会有些不自在,这让我有些担心,不知道在正式采访的时候能不能做到让自己和采访者都处于比较放松的状态。

位于大山之中的鲁史只能乘巴士前往。启程前在广州采访过的上一任中大挂职副县长王克这么描述他去凤庆的巴士旅途:"窗外都是黑黢黢的,连路灯都没有,周围是非常多且大的山,从临沧到凤庆就花了三个多小时。"因为他的提醒,我们买了晕车药,车上也备有呕吐袋。充分的应对准备并不能缓解颠簸的山路给我们带来的不适,好几个同学吐得东倒西歪。车上惨淡的光景让人不禁忧心在山里两天的采访条件。所幸,我们这一行得到了县政府的帮助,整段旅程都较为顺利。在从鲁史回来的当天晚上,我们拜访了刚上任的中大挂职副县长张哲。副县长的宿舍干净整洁,一楼接待大厅也布置得很有格调。中式风格的镂空架子上摆满了凤庆出品的坚果、茶叶还有以它们为原料制成的副产品。我们驻村驻县组在凤庆县红塘村的采访之行，就从这里开始了。

到凤庆不过两个月的张哲副县长有一股知性的气质，在茶桌上侃侃而谈。他2008年至2017年都在国外工作，从美国、墨西哥的孔子学院到国内高校，再到凤庆做挂职县长，从高校到地方协管科学、教育、文化、卫生，还要对外招商，工作内容的差异不能说不大，但是张哲副县长告诉我们"人生不可能只有一种工作选择"。他的平易近人使我们卸下了前一晚面对镜头时的不适，采访工作有了一个好的开始。

张哲副县长对凤庆的第一印象是景色很美，还有就是吃住条件和工作环境都不错。但是他待久了就发现，凤庆有许多问题亟待解决。凤庆人民的文化程度不够高，大家能够自觉遵守交通规则，但是未必所有人都能做到不随地吐痰。还有人们习惯用喝酒作为交流的媒介，想要在饭桌上与村民打成一片，就要应对村民们的一轮轮敬酒。因此，伴随着村民亲自酿制的高酒精浓度的酒而来的不仅有热情，还有头疼。

文化程度不够高带来的其他问题也是很明显的，大家对医疗和教育等都不太重视。张哲副县长曾路遇一个村民，脖子上长了一个很大的肿瘤。看到这种情况，大家第一时间肯定会想："为什么不去治病？"张哲副县长对此的分析是：第一，没有钱；第二，不到危及性命的情况就不重视这个病；第三，即使是危及性命，也会觉得反正治不了，也就不治了。每一个可能的原因都是对口帮扶工作希望解决的：没有钱，那就发展产业，招商引资；不重视健康问题，那就发展医疗，争取能让老乡们"大病不出县城"，让"老百姓看到中山大学就是看到希望"。

张哲副县长继续介绍说，在对口帮扶的工作上，医疗方面的目标是把凤庆的县医院建设成云南省前五名的县级医院。对此，中山大学提供了优质医疗资源。经过几年的帮扶，县医院的硬件已经很完善。关于这一点，我们刚到凤庆就有过体验。因为疫情防控的需要，我们要到县医院做核酸检测。虽然核酸采样点设立在医院外部，但我们也稍稍体验了内部的设施：按着地板上标得清清楚楚的指示标识，轻松地找到了厕所的位置。有人开玩笑说："这贴心程度，比得上中大五院了。"

张哲副县长继续介绍说，要带动整个县的发展，年轻人的活力是必不可少的。让年轻人留下来带动整个县，就要发展教育，也要鼓励青壮年劳动力回乡创业。在教育上，中山大学对大摆田完全小学的帮扶是一个好例子。产业上，除了坚果、茶叶，凤庆发展了滇黄精中药材产业，还针对金丝皇菊打造了集旅游景点和菊花茶于一体的产业。

我们直愣愣地听着张哲副县长的分析，间或有学生小口嘬着手里的临沧坚果浆。临沧坚果浆就是凤庆推进产业发展的成果之一。这款饮料确实很好喝，我在采访前转动瓶身看了一圈，临沧坚果下面就明晃晃地写着"Hawaii（夏威夷）"，译名与中文名不匹配这一点让我觉得十分有意思。实际上，临沧坚果就是常见的夏威夷果，而全世界的夏威夷果有约70%是在临沧生产的，给它加上"临沧坚果"的名号也未尝不可。

听说中山大学从凤庆购入产品也是一种消费帮扶，一些产品包装袋上印有中山大学校徽。我们纷纷表示回到学校后一定多多宣传。

"在云南省潜力最大的就是凤庆。"张哲副县长总结道。凤庆的生态好，有超过70%的森林覆盖率；凤庆的气候也是整个云南最好的；在八个县中，文化底蕴最深的是凤庆；城乡差距最小的也是凤庆，它是城乡融合发展示范区；在旅游方面，凤庆有高速公路、高铁和飞机这样的基本交通条件。我们在来的路上也深深体会到了：兜兜转转的山路上，透过车窗看到的不是生机勃勃的绿，就是平静或有些波澜的蓝。在往后几天的采访路途上，我总能看到横跨满山翠绿的水泥桥——因为是拱形，所以我称之为"桥"。是的，凤庆的"桥"不只在水上，还在山中。就像旅程中没有离开过我们的山路一样，沿着将我们带进山中的公路一路往前，沿着将我们带到更高海拔的山路一路向上，横跨峡谷的桥和横跨密林的桥自始至终都在我们的视野里：在凤庆高挂的太阳下，稳稳地伫立在波光粼粼的水面和满山的翠绿中。

我们主要的交通工具一直是那辆核载20多人的巴士。经历过进入鲁史那番"魔鬼训练"，我们已经能够应付乘坐巴士的旅途，但是比起驱车进入山里，我们对进入村落有不同的担忧：村民会不会因"来路不明"、阵仗又大的一行人的突然出现而感到不安？张良友书记告诉我们："这是政府的巴士，村民们只要看到这样的巴士，就知道是来帮扶的人，所以完全不必担心。"

我们第一个目的地是红塘村村委会。村委会就在大摆田完全小学隔壁，偶尔能听见小学生们朗朗的读书声。我们了解了一些基本情况之后，就去参观滇黄精产业基地和金丝皇菊产业基地。又经过一些歪歪扭扭的山路，树叶接连错落地扫过车窗，巴士停下了。下车之后，我们看到一些路障，原本以为只是普通的石墩子，但是据村民介绍，"墩不可貌相"，它们的真身竟是一种中药。我们饶有兴致地围着中药墩子走了几圈，跟着张良友书记离开了路边的树荫，顶着阳光向村子走去。

凤庆已经入秋，但阳光还是很猛烈。也是这样的阳光造就了在它之下辛勤劳动的凤庆人民又红又黝黑的皮肤。张良友书记领着我们去看滇黄精产业基地。

"种植黄精的李茂昌之前在杭州打工。他喜欢中药材，有这方面的优势，我打电话让他回来发展黄精中药材这一块，我们也给他贷了一万块钱。现在他发展得比较好，买了车，一年的营业额有六七十万。"村委会的干部告诉我们。

站在滇黄精基地前面的李茂昌看起来有些腼腆，不爱讲话，在介绍黄精的时候小心翼翼地捧着黄精的幼苗。

张哲副县长曾说："保障健康最重要的就是提高医疗和卫生水平。"此外，他还提及了"厕所革命"。我听了有点不解，直到在滇黄精基地上了一次厕所，才深刻认识到"厕所革命"的重要性。在去鲁史的路上和在鲁史中学参观学生宿舍时，对于露天的抽水马桶、定时冲水的沟厕，在做足心理准备后，都还能够勉强接受。有过使用这两种厕所的经历，我的承受能力有所增强，看到立在滇黄精基地隔壁的一个小木屋的时候，大概也知道会是什么情况了。

挂起用铁丝做的简易锁，我在逼仄的小隔间里小心地转了个身，映入眼帘的是已经堆满废纸的纸篓和同样也是用铁丝挂在墙上的纸巾。这旱厕的主体是不宽不窄的浅坑，挖成了斜坡，排泄物就可以往下流，或许是可以被用作天然肥料吧。上厕所前，我已经观察过周围，没有流动的水源可以洗手。出来之后，我也只能用随身携带的饮用水简单冲了一下手。指路的阿姨或许是因为紧张，一直用小围裙揩着手，笑着说："这是我们这边最好的厕所了，担待一下哈！"我笑着点头说"谢谢"。

凤庆的妇女好似一个模子刻出来的，在家里的男性劳动力向村外流出的情况下，女性成为顶梁柱，扛起一个家庭的重担——在鲁史古道上能看到筛着农作物的阿姨，还能看到坐在家门口娴熟地敲着核桃、买卖只收现金的婆婆。在金丝皇菊产业基地工作的张国凤阿姨也一样。她家里有五口人，丈夫生病，两个孩子在外地打工，过年才回来。在金丝皇菊产业基地招村民来务工之前，张阿姨的生计是采茶，在不是采茶季的时候，只能到五千米外的城里做工。采茶只能带来一般的收入，因为在中大帮扶之前，茶叶的品种和加工方式都比较单一。能在离家较近的基地务工，张阿姨很高兴。

金丝皇菊产业是新兴产业，村民们都没有接触过。起步的第一年，有专门的老师来指导村民如何采菊，之后，技术由已经上手的村民教给后学的村民。第一次务工的时候,张阿姨特地买了新的剪刀。"好像花了八块钱,买了把手柄裹着橡胶的那种新剪刀。"张阿姨比划着,仿佛手里就拿着当时的剪刀。购入一件新物什对张阿姨来说似乎是少有的事,足见张阿姨对到金丝皇菊产业基地务工这件事情的重视。但到了学习采菊的时候,大家才知道菊花是要用手采的,于是剪刀便失去了出场的机会。

对新产业没有概念并不妨碍村民们积极参与,张阿姨说到这里也仍然是一副笑眯眯的样子。她说:"村民们……可以说是一呼百应。"

"去年(2020年)一年来基地务工的村民就有900多个,大家都很积极,因为我们一定会在年底就结清工钱。"张书记补充道。

因为在金丝皇菊基地务工,张阿姨家年收入将近8000元。阿姨一开始似乎是因为有镜头在拍摄她而感到害羞,后来聊开了,我们才知道阿姨还是村里"筑梦舞蹈队"的一名成员。

"还出去比赛过!现在身体不好了,跳不动了。"张阿姨倚着椅子摆摆手。

"比赛?比赛用了什么曲子呀?是民歌、山歌之类的吗?"比赛的事情激起了我们的兴趣。

"跳的是《我的九寨》《茶山情歌》。比赛闯到第三关,就被淘汰啦!"张阿姨看上去对比赛结果并不是十分看重,回忆起来一样满脸笑意,说道:"为了去凤山镇比赛,我们买了新的民族服装,请了一个临沧的老师来教舞蹈……"她还提到郭(兴勇)书记自己掏钱给村里买了三个音箱,其中一个就给了"筑梦舞蹈队"。

"郭书记走的时候我们很舍不得,太舍不得了。我们每个人凑一点钱,给他送了一面锦旗。对蓝书记也是这样,因为他对我们太好了。"仍然是一口浓重的云南口音,讲话的时候,张阿姨眼尾的细纹像是要飞起来。

郭书记掏钱买的另外两个音箱,一个供村里娱乐,还有一个在大摆田完全小学,被好好地放置在新落成的阅览室里。大摆田完全小学是幼儿园和小学合在一起办的学校,每个年级都只有一个班,总共有170多个学生。在阅览室里,大摆田完全小学的校长杨卫林和一位身兼多职的班主任一起介绍了学校的情况,我们就是在这里采访了五年级的赵伟和四年级的王文。

阅览室原本只是铁皮屋,原来的模样被定格在新阅览室墙上的相框里。我们凑近一看才知道铁皮屋里既没有书,也没有相关的学习用具,仅仅放了一些玩具。在蓝书记的联络下,阅览室得到中山大学国际翻译学院第一党支部的捐赠,摆满了书柜的书本也同样由中山大学资助。有了阅览室之后,为了让学生们养成阅读的习惯，课表中增加了每周两节的阅读课，全班学生由老师带着来这里度过专属于阅读的时光。

"喜欢这里吗？来这里一般都看什么书呀？"为了表达亲切，我们探身向前，向两名小学生提问。

原本在静静听着我们和老师们对话的赵伟和王文，听到提问显得有点紧张，但赵伟很快就接上了话头："喜欢。阅读课上老师会带着过来，平常……喜欢看一些关于历史还有兵器的书。"一旁的王文个头比赵伟矮了一截，似乎更怕生一些，但是也说了"喜欢"。

据身兼各科教学任务，偶尔还需要代体育课的班主任所说，老师们基本都是"多面手"，什么都能教，但是"专业性不够强"。所以即使学生需要"德、智、体、美、劳"全面发展，在"美"这一方面，也没有专业老师可以上课。在中大进行教育帮扶之前，大摆田完全小学的孩子并没有接触过才艺方面的课程。

"没办法，我们的老师就算知道几个音符，就算有安排，也因为专业性不够强而教不了。"自从有了多媒体课室，从三年级开始每个班都被安排了远程艺术课程，为学生补充了艺术知识。

"我们这边的学生都是上了初中之后才接触英语的。自从中山大学的学生来给孩子们上英语课，我们学校的学生就比别的学校超前一点啦。"

"那你们之前接触过英语吗？"我们问赵伟和王文。

"有……哥哥教过几句。"赵伟点头，他说的哥哥是在县一中上高二的赵强。

"学了什么样的英语？可以说说看吗？"在我们的鼓励下，赵伟磕磕绊绊地说出了"Good morning." "Good afternoon."和"Good evening."。虽然有浓重的"中国式英语"味道，但我们也热烈地为他鼓掌，赵伟不好意思地笑了笑。

我们又问他："对课上介绍的国家感兴趣吗？以后会不会想出去看看？"虽然赵伟去过离家最远的地方也就是凤山医院，但是面对我们的问题，憨态可掬的他还是表达了肯定："会想看看。"

下午，我们去了五年级的课室，在课室后方观摩了五年级学生的葫芦丝网课。从门口到课室的路上，总有孩子对我们快速地敬礼并喊上一句"老师好！"。教室不大，只坐得下二三十个学生。课前，学生们领到老师分发的葫芦丝。我俯下身问一个小男孩觉得葫芦丝课怎么样，小男孩摇头晃脑地撅着嘴巴，嘟囔了一句："不太感兴趣。"但上课时，他却逐个音符地吹得小脸通红。

  课室后面的黑板上是红彤彤的"迎国庆"黑板报,黑板前的课桌上摞着整齐的生字本。五年级的孩子字迹略显稚嫩,但是一笔一划间展现的认真显而易见,那种认真也体现在五年级的赵伟讲普通话时的一字一顿上。

  "你以后想做什么?"

  "我想当程序员,因为虽然机器是用钢铁做的,但是控制机器还是需要代码。"赵伟脱口而出。

  为了深入了解民情,当天晚上,我们落脚在红塘村属下的红木自然村的民宿。由于山路崎岖,我们的巴士无法在狭窄的单行道上畅行无阻,转弯更是难上加难。天色渐晚,最后十几分钟的路程,我们决定步行前往。沿途可以见到横在路之间的断树,还能看到横跨于电线和路灯之间大片大片的蜘蛛网。

  帮扶之后尚且如此,村干部们描述的在郭书记来之前的那种"满地垃圾""水沟因年久失修而发臭"且"没有路灯"的情况,实在是令人难以想象。太阳的余晖慢慢散去,不安随着夜色而来,但是有着"中山大学捐赠"油漆印子的太阳能路灯,还有修整过的平坦的水泥地,都让走过鲁史山路的我们备感安心。

  到达民宿后,我们在惊讶于村里也有这么干净的住处之余,还在客厅里发现了三幅有中大国际翻译学院外教的照片。

  "哇,这个是教过我们的老师!"

  "是哦,他是不是发过朋友圈?哈哈!我当时看到还觉得很疑惑,不知道是怎么一回事。"

  "这个是西班牙语的外教。"

  "哦!德语的外教也在呢。"

  "好多我们认识的老师啊,他们居然来过这里。"

  我们很兴奋地辨认着照片上的老师,民宿的陈映琴大姐也跟着我们蹲下来,说:"可惜你们这次来没有拍照!如果拍了,我们也把你们的照片裱起来,和这张照片摆在一起。"

  听了这话,抗拒没有滤镜镜头的我们连忙笑着,摆手说拍出来不好看。陈大姐笑嘻嘻地说:"怎么会!把从中山大学来的老师和学生的照片放在家里,我们沾光了。"

  陈大姐谈起这件事的时候,眉眼中还透着欣喜和小小的骄傲:"我人生中最大的荣幸就是接待了来自七个不同国家的人,我做饮食业20年了,没有见过这种大场面。"

"那么除了你们，村里别的人都是什么反应呀？"

"当时听说有外国人要来，大家都走出家门来看呢！"村民们笑说，"整个凤庆基本上有微信的人都知道了，一发朋友圈，很多朋友点赞。"

"当时朋友圈都传遍啦！"

外国人来访，能算上是"红木村大事"，村里出现了万人空巷的盛况。说着，村民们纷纷掏出手机，打开微信，翻找视频给我们看。视频里外教们脑袋上顶着头饰学跳当地舞蹈的片段非常有趣。看到外教们在课堂外随性的样子，我们兴致都很高，又对着照片问陈大姐："你对这里面哪个外国人印象最深刻呀？"

陈大姐回忆了一下，指着戴帽子白胡子的老师说："这个，这个，因为他的中文说得很好。"因为是认识的老师，我们这些学生都笑作一团，继续问陈大姐他说了什么。陈大姐说："他'谢谢'说得很标准！"

据介绍，时任校长罗俊到凤庆做演讲的时候，也住在这里。"这么大的人物，来这么小的村。"陈大姐这么说着，我们也偷着乐，我们也可以说是"打卡"了校长住过的地方。

至于为什么会办民宿，陈大姐说是蓝书记的建议，因为如果没有可以吃和住的地方，游客可能就不会愿意来。由于村里发展了金丝皇菊产业，村民们可以选择做活打工来贴补家用，民宿的农家乐也渐渐有了起色。与周边民宿不同的是，这户人家有室内的抽水马桶。

对于村民们来说，天黑后，精力也有能得以释放之处。红塘村有一个叫作"打歌"的地方传统，简单来说就是唱山歌。结婚，或者是办其他喜事的时候可以从晚上七点到隔天早上七点唱上整一宿。从中大来的驻村书记都住在红木村，走的时候，村民都会自发为他们"打歌"送行。蓝书记走的那个晚上下雨了，村民们也坚持去送。"千里帮扶路，一生感恩情"，影集上短短10个字，是村民们对书记们最真诚的记挂。

"那么，用一句你们想对书记们说的话来结束今晚的畅聊如何？"

村民们先是一起热情地说："欢迎再回来！"顿了顿，似乎觉得这句话不足以表达他们的心意，互相交换了几个憨笑，摆手又说道："不不不，应该是欢迎回家！"

# 核桃·医术·朝凤路

## 李心琪

大巴、飞机、动车、大巴。从凌晨4点到晚上8点,从广东到云南,一行人终于能够解下行囊。

我对着酒店外的山间夜色拍了张照片,连同在大理机场前拍的合照一起发给母亲:我们到鲁史镇了。

"哪里?"母亲很快就回复了,我能想象她两指贴着手机屏幕,一点点放大图片,在14名学生和5位老师的合照中寻找我的身影。

"就是我昨晚跟你说的,我们学院参与'创意写作与翻译'课程的学生到云南省凤庆县调研,鲁史镇是我们的第一站。我们到这里采访当地的老师、学生和从中大来的支教老师。"

"这么高的山,还都是一些土路,晚上出去的时候要小心一点。"母亲发来语音嘱咐,问道:"什么时候回学校?"

"6天后,10月29日。"

"好,注意安全,注意保暖,多拍些照片给我。"

我一一应下。

第二天上午,在鲁史中学的访谈结束后,中山大学研究生支教团凤庆分队队长许锦涛带我们前往最近的饭店。山路陡峭,许锦涛在前头健步如飞,我缀在队尾喘着大气,沿途瞥见几处破败房屋,屋壁土石剥落,房梁横斜刺入蓝天。我一时不察踩到光滑的石子,足底打滑,险些沿着蜿蜒石阶跌入野草堆。好不容易抵达饭店,喘匀气,见小院的餐桌上有一盘核桃,想起母亲爱吃,便随手拍下发给她。

"现在核桃的采摘季刚过,核桃成熟后用竹竿敲下来,接着还要去青皮、晾晒烘烤……"张良友老师是今年(2021年)中山大学派驻云南省凤庆县红塘村的第一书记,到任不过短短几个月,便已对当地情况了然于胸。他坐在院中的竹编小凳上为我们详细介绍凤庆的核桃产业链:"但是核桃的利润不高,而且你们来的时候应该也感受到了这里山路的崎岖,运核桃出去的成本比较高。张哲老师,就是今年中大派来的凤庆县挂职副县长,现在正跟一些企业联系,尝试着去推广凤庆的核桃类产品,比如说你们今天午餐会喝到的核桃浆。"

当地的饮食习惯与广东不太一样,口味更咸,也更辣,桌上的菜经过几轮转动,还剩大半。午饭过后,喝过当地生产的核桃浆,晶晶学姐说想去买点核桃。我们同行的几个学生分为教育、医疗、驻村驻县三个小组,各有不同的行程任务,考察凤庆脱贫攻坚的不同侧面。她与我同属医疗组,访谈任务集中在后几天,因此,教育组忙碌的时候是我们的闲暇时间。她说:"买点特产,才不辜负从凤庆县城到鲁史镇这两三个小时的颠簸山路。"

我们向饭店老板问明了方向,沿着茶马古道往上走。比起广东,云南的天似乎低了许多。午时,阳光照得四处亮堂堂的,令人走在屋檐下都觉得阳光刺眼。路上铺着两掌宽的青石板,两块石板间的缝隙能塞进一个拳头,长满青苔野草。拾级而上,隐约还能见到几个马蹄印留在发黄的石板上。道路两旁是整齐排布的房屋:木制的窗枢门柱、廊上挂着的几盏大红灯笼、斑驳的墙面与黑色的瓦片、飞翘的檐角,像极了一些古厝复原景点。而一旁停靠的一辆摩托车、一辆小轿车,则带着不合时宜的现代人工痕迹。唯一不同的是这里鲜有人至,在小巷里兜兜转转十几分钟也不见他人,只有一只柯基犬撅着屁股闻声而至。

卖核桃的阿嬷坐在一个屋檐下的小板凳上,一条巷子,一个人。她穿着一件印满褶皱的深玫色外套,一顶蓝色的小帽微微挡住额头,露出沟壑遍布的黝黑皮肤。当地人似乎都肤色偏深。返程路上,我们偶遇了一只身材苗条的家猪,它有着野猪一样烟熏般的肤色——似乎连猪也抵挡不住此处的风吹日晒。阿嬷的手也是黝黑黝黑的,指甲很厚,带着点微微衰败的灰。她从面前凳子上的竹簸箕里拣起一颗核桃,双手大拇指捏住核桃,"咔嚓"一声,核桃便碎开,抖下几粒碎屑。印象中的核桃是用核桃钳都难以打开的"铁核桃",如果费劲砸开,就会碎得满手满地都是。我看着阿嬷熟练地掰开核桃,挑出两枚完整的核桃仁,禁不住暗叹——剥核桃也是一门手艺。

一斤剥好的核桃仁15元,不能使用微信支付。远处的便利店难得迎来外地客人,即使不买东西,老板娘也是热情洋溢,皲裂的唇边缀着笑容。待我们换好现金,阿嬷已经装好两袋核桃(见图1)。

核桃被我们带上了前往凤庆县城的大巴车,奶香味萦绕在车厢里,衬着离镇路上化不开的浓雾。倏尔瞥见车窗外一位妇女头顶一掌宽的布带,背负

图1 课程学生在鲁史镇茶马古道与当地人交流

箩筐踽踽上山。

"有些当地人没有交通工具,背核桃、背茶叶都是这么背的。"张良友老师解释道。昨晚与中山大学研究生支教团的几位老师进行访谈时,他们也这么说。有些学生放假前夕没有家长接送,只能拿条布带,头顶一箱书,走几个小时的山路回家,回家后帮忙摘核桃、剥青皮。等到返校的时候,指尖和指甲盖上全是洗不掉的黑色痕迹。

"用头承重,不会勒得头疼吗?"

"那肯定头疼,这么重的东西。"

九曲十八弯的山路晃得人头晕,前排的晓燕学姐吃了晕车药、戴了耳机,做好了万全准备,信誓旦旦这次绝不能像来时那样"一吐到底";而同是医疗组的元亨同学却仍靠在椅背上,悠哉游哉地看着手机里的访谈记录:"之前康复科的郑停停医生也说了,这种负重方式使得很多当地人有些脖颈头部方面的病痛。"

早在出发前的10月10日,我们医疗组四人便前往广州采访了曾赴凤庆医疗帮扶的三名医生代表:中山大学肿瘤防治中心的张玄烨医生、中山大学附属第六医院康复科的郑停停医生和中山大学附属第一医院儿科的张军医生。自2013年起,中大便通过派专家医疗团队赴凤庆带教培训和接受凤庆医生到广州进修等方式，帮助凤庆县人民医院培养专业医疗人才队伍，打造重点科室基地。至今，中山大学已派出36批、400余名专家至凤庆帮扶。郑停停医生便是其中一名。

回到广州已两个月有余，谈及对凤庆的初印象，郑停停医生微眯着眼，徐徐说道："我去了（凤庆）以后，发现康复科有一半以上的颈肩腰腿痛、膝关节痛患者都是女性，（其中）四五十岁的比较多。"

回想郑停停医生的描述，恰与此次见闻相符。来到凤庆短短两日，我便注意到凤庆的劳动力以女性为主：鲁史镇里酒店的前台服务员，早餐店、饭店的老板，甚至连在茶马古道迷路时偶遇的路人，无一例外都是女性。在鲁史中学进行访谈的第一天，随行的摄影老师魏东华应邀为学校的老师拍摄证件照。而在拘谨地排队等待拍照的老师里，女性教师占了绝大多数。也正是基于女性劳动力数量多的情况，郑停停医生多方筹措，创办了凤庆县首个康复医学科女性康复中心，对当地女性常见的颈肩腰腿痛、膝关节痛、产后病痛进行针对性康复治疗。

"康复治疗？不需要借助手术和药物？"电话里，母亲对女性康复中心尤感兴趣，她平时偶尔埋怨父亲的笨拙，说自己当初产后多遭病痛，药物无效，只能硬生生扛过去。

我卸下行囊，趴到酒店的床上，说："医生是这么说的。"

"你说你当初要是学医多好。"母亲正忙着炒菜，电话那头抽油烟机"呼呼"地响。"自己知道病痛，不需要跑来跑去，像你今天说的，鲁史镇里的人出来看一趟病要走两个多小时的山路，多遭罪。"

以前闲聊时，母亲曾说我幼时多病，镇上医院治不了，县里医院看不好，每次只能奔波到市医院去。"那时家里没有车，公交车也少，只能走半个小时到公交站，再坐两三个小时的车去泉州。小孩子病起来反反复复的，三天两头就要跑一趟。都不用说花了多少钱，这一路下来得花费不少功夫。"母亲笑着说："现在知道你有多难养了吧。"

看一趟病真不容易。娇气的孩子才有此等待遇，若是平时康健的大人，非得遇上大病方才如此兴师动众。年幼多病的我或许给母亲留下了某些阴影，她一度企图说服我读理科，当个医生。我不知道如何回复，低头默默吃核桃。

母亲又道："那你们中大的医生回来之后，当地人看病怎么办？"

"医疗帮扶就包括帮忙培训当地的医疗人员，况且现在网络通信这么发达,还可以借助一些线上渠道。"我想起之前访谈时医生们谈到的线上多学科会诊,"不同的科室可能还有不同的方法,像医学影像科之类的应该还可以借助设备远程操作,下午去县医院访谈的时候我再问问。"

到达凤庆县人民医院的时候已近三点。新建的院区背靠青山,白墙一尘不染,空气中只有淡淡的青草味,会议室里则溢满冲开的茶香。

摄像摄影组首先忙碌起来,在狭小的会议室前后各摆上两个补光灯,照得我眼前反光,只怪眼镜累赘。抬眼看见凤庆县人民医院的院长李海在门外徘徊,随后挑起悬挂的几根电线,侧过身子,避开补光灯,大步走入会议室,坐在我身旁。

"通过此次课程我们主要想了解中大在凤庆的帮扶情况。"课程主讲老师戴凡教授向李海院长微笑致意,双手交叠,腕间玉镯轻叩桌面。她介绍道:"坐在我们旁边的是医疗组的四个同学,晶晶负责记录小组的整个访谈情况,元亨负责视频片段选取和字幕翻译,晓燕和心琪分别写英文故事和中文故事。等一下他们也将根据您的介绍向您提一些问题。"

李海院长将手中的黑皮笔记本打开摊在桌面,右手执笔,开口时却不需看笔记一眼。"我们凤庆县医疗需求很大,2017年中大七院①开始对凤庆县人民医院进行医疗帮扶……中山大学对我们是真帮扶,真派专家,专家落地后,真的提高了我们的医疗水平,使百姓享受真正的三甲医院的(医疗)水平。"

院长讲得流利,我的手指在键盘上飞舞,偶然抬头瞥见其他三位组员以及戴凡老师皆是指尖忙碌不停。我抽空往医疗组的微信群里发了一句:"院长说得好全面,都不需要问别的了。"

"是。"元亨回道。说是这么说,院长一停下,他立马开问:"您刚才提到中大医生医德医风特别好,以至于患者都称赞他们,请问有具体的事例吗?"院长收拾得一丝不苟的头发掉下一缕,竖在额间。"像我们ICU的周俊老师,有一次我们一起做一个活动,都快要吃饭了,突然说有个病人有点状况,他接到电话立马就赶去了。我记得那天晚上抢救到九点多钟才结束。还有儿科的张军老师,对新生儿的救治都是亲力亲为,为患者考虑,在用药这一方面是很细致的,用最有效而又便宜的方案。"院长举了几个例子,思考时眉眼仿佛都在用力,挤出几条抬头纹。

---

① 中山大学附属第七医院。

两天后，我们在对儿科纪元红医生进行访谈时也听说了张军老师这件事。经病人家人同意，戴凡老师将纪元红医生发来的照片转发给我们。那是一个皱皱巴巴的婴儿，被包裹在褓褓里，小小的拳头紧攥着，泛着红，又带着点紫。25周时，他的母亲先兆流产，孩子出生时体重只有800克，两个小时之后呼吸困难。恰逢张军医生在凤庆帮扶，他立马开展手术，成功挽救了宝宝的生命。

其他几张照片是宝宝康复出院回家后拍的：直到满月时，他仍然有些瘦弱，穿着一件大红色的连体衣，露出的手脚细如竹竿。这令我想起自己满月时候的照片，同样穿着大红色连体衣，却是又大又圆的一团，隔着屏幕都能清晰看见包子一样的拳头。

"不过宝宝现在恢复了健康，孩子的父母给张军老师送了一面锦旗。在张军老师回去的时候，他们跟我一起去送她。"纪元红医生的声音温柔却有力，说道："张军老师回到广东后，也继续通过微信跟进这个孩子的情况。"

在微信群跟进患者后续情况是中大医疗帮扶团队的工作常态。医生们从凤庆回到广州后，除每周一次的线上多学科会诊外，还时常在微信上针对一些疑难情况进行探讨。凤庆县人民医院肿瘤科的杨春龙医生就向我们展示了他们与中山大学肿瘤防治中心的张玄烨医生的微信交流记录。截图里，肿瘤科医生群里的某位医生说道：

"拟今天给予FLOT方案①化疗……奥沙利铂按$85mg/m^2$算得143.56mg d1，实际使用143mg d1；亚叶酸钙按$0.2g/m^2$算得0.338g d1，实际使用0.33g d1……"

我不明其意，心中猜测是关于药的剂量。

张玄烨医生很快就回复："能耐受吗？术后可以换两药方案。"

"我们搞不定的事情，就问张玄烨老师，我们科室的医护群，还有我们医生群，她都在。我就感觉她虽然回去了，但还是我们的靠山。"眉间的沟壑为杨春龙医生平添几分严肃感，讲到这里时，他却突然笑了，胸前蓝色的工作牌晃动，磕在桌沿，发出轻响。

"咔嚓"，李海院长盖上笔帽，将黑笔夹在笔记本中，起身结束了这场访谈。

"总结得很好哦。"院长离开后，戴凡老师点着头与我们交谈，让我们做

---

① FLOT是化疗药物组合的名字缩写，包括氟尿嘧啶、亚叶酸钙、奥沙利铂、多西紫杉醇。

笔记时可以将重点内容进行标记，方便之后整理材料。魏东华老师仍在摆弄机器，摄像组的建滨和婧妍还在调整补光灯的位置，检查收音麦克风的电池。

课程助教张佳学姐走进会议室，说下一个访谈对象眼科刘良平医生的患者恰好也来医院了，准备向刘医生送一面锦旗。实在是意外收获，戴凡老师的眼睛都亮了。我往左挪了一个位置，摆好张佳学姐递来的一杯茶水。

刘良平医生穿着白衬衫蓝西装，面对着我们一行人"长枪短炮"的架势，似乎有些拘谨，胸背挺得僵直，双手置于桌前交叠，黑框眼镜微微反着白光。患者是一位女性，40来岁的模样，穿着一条绿色的碎花裙，长眉细眼，化着淡妆，身上香水味浓郁。走近的时候，我注意到阿姨手中拿了一面锦旗，有些欲盖弥彰地往身后藏。

阿姨向我们讲起自己的求医历程：自己年纪不大，却得了白内障，去了几趟医院，都没有接受治疗。知病不医的情况在凤庆并非个例，常有患者因各种误解放弃治疗。之前采访张玄烨医生的时候，她说起曾经有一位患了晚期肺鳞状细胞癌的患者，得知自己得了晚期癌症之后就直接回家，放弃治疗了，直到后来疼痛难忍，在医生们的反复劝说下才接受化疗。

于是，我向阿姨询问凤庆当地关于就医方面的传统观念。阿姨立马打开了话匣子，坐直身子，细眉飞舞，热情控诉着她的"受骗"经历："我之前就听人说，白内障要熟透了才能摘除，大家都这么说，谁知道……"

"不对不对。"一旁的刘医生听到阿姨的话叹了口气，忍不住插话："白内障要尽早就医……"一时间会议室里两道声音交织，传统民间观念与现代医学知识交汇碰撞，"撞"得后排的摄像机不知该往何处转。传统误解无疑影响着凤庆人民的身体健康，白内障患者等待"熟透"才来就诊，而肿瘤患者更是自视"无救"而放弃寻医，一步步拖延，最终导致疾病治愈难上加难。难怪现阶段中大医疗团队高度重视乡镇医疗科普、凤庆胃癌早筛等预防性工作。通过前往乡镇开展讲座，发布文章、视频以进行科普宣传等途径，中大专家医疗团队逐渐扎根凤庆本土，打响了知名度。

"我听前面访谈的医生说，之前有个医生打车，说是中大来的，司机直接就不收钱了。"

阿姨接过戴凡老师的话，说道："大家都知道县人民医院来了一批中大的专家，我朋友也跟我说了，要我赶快来给专家看看。"她的语气中带着几分庆幸。"现在我裸眼的视力比我之前戴眼镜的视力都更好，我开车都不需要戴眼镜。所以我一直对刘主任说，我非常感谢，如果没有中山大学对我们凤庆县的对口扶贫，我现在肯定还是看不见。"

访谈的最后，阿姨拿出锦旗，笑着将它打开，上面用金粉写着"感谢：中山大学中山眼科中心白内障科主治医师刘良平"，中间是"医术精湛，仁心仁术"八个大字。身后，会议室黑色的皮质座椅上留下了一片金粉。

当天访谈结束后，车还没来，一行人往医院门口走去，元亨、晓燕、晶晶和我，我们医疗组四人凑在一起聊着下午的访谈。

"你说如果剥核桃也算是一门手艺，那医生的技术是否是一门更了不得的手艺？"走到医院门口，我仍在苦苦思考中文故事的切入角度，问身旁的晓燕学姐。见她仍旧戴着耳机，我便开玩笑道："别听BBC[①]了，想想我们的故事要怎么写。"

"没有听BBC。"晓燕学姐哭笑不得。"医生的技术肯定算是一种手艺啊。"

"可是手艺感觉更偏向于手工技艺？医生做手术能算是做手工吗？"

她捏着下巴，微微抬头，下午为了拍摄特地打上的一片腮红，此时被路边隐隐约约的灯光映得失了色。"那是更高级的手艺。"

回酒店的路上，我一直在琢磨这个问题。我想说医术是手艺，因为医术需要日复一日的反复练习，需要精细到每一刻度，每一位医学生完成从学生到医生的蜕变都需要很长时间的积累沉淀；同时，医术也是更高级的"手艺"，因为医生医病，医身，更医心，不仅拯救患者的生命，更为他们带去情感的关怀。

我将自己的观点发给母亲。她向来不喜这些文绉绉的话，嫌看得眼累，发来语音问我要依据。

"比如说凤庆县人民医院的李春光医生，他从学生变为医生，首先得经过很多年的理论学习、临床训练，可是这还不够。他要从一名普通医生向一名医术精湛的医生转变，需要接触无数名患者，进行无数台手术，解决无数个病例，也需要接受更专业、更先进的培训，所以他离开凤庆到广州的中山大学中山眼科中心进修。这一过程需要很多时间、金钱、精力等成本，和练就一门手艺活不是类似的吗？"

母亲没有立马回复。

---

[①] 指英国广播公司的电台节目。

"吃核桃吗?"我正拧眉思考,被突然的声音吓了一跳。

晶晶学姐与我共住一个房间,递来另外一袋未剥开的核桃。我拿起一颗,循着记忆中卖核桃的阿嬷的手法,用力一掰——核桃碎了一地。她笑着给我做示范,说:"对着中间掰,像这样。"

我想起了以往见到的手艺传承——戏班里的大师傅给小徒弟传授唱功技巧,工匠教会徒弟沉心静气、精雕细琢。于是,我脱口而出:"好的,师姐。"

晶晶学姐没注意,转身继续收拾桌上化妆品的瓶瓶罐罐。我将核桃壳投进垃圾桶,又挑挑拣拣,拿出一粒看上去最好掰的核桃。这次,我很容易便掰出规整的两瓣——原来剥核桃手艺的传承只需要一瞧、一掰。

我吃着核桃,翻着白天的访谈记录,看到自己着重加粗的一句话:"为了这些人民,我想恳请中山大学中山眼科中心继续牵着我们的手,就像是一个母亲保护孩子一样,牵着我们的手不断地前进,帮助我们迅速提高。"李春光医生的这句话令在场许多人湿了眼眶,我心中百感交集,宛如之前看到电影《百鸟朝凤》中,焦三爷与徒弟游天鸣坐在门槛前一教一学吹唢呐时的感慨万端。以往的手艺传承,如吹唢呐的技艺,大多是一代传一代;如今医术"手艺"的传承,却是横跨千里、从一个地区到另一个地区的"传承"。李春光医生从凤庆到中山大学中山眼科中心进修,刘良平医生从广东到凤庆进行医疗帮扶,两人"一来一往",恰是医术传承的双向途径。

那么,医术之外呢?对口帮扶又算不算是"传承"?一所高校对一个地方的帮扶,是否也算是更广泛意义上的"手艺传承"?

手机震动了一下,是来自母亲的最新消息,她只回复了一个字:"是。"我盯着它看了好几分钟,直到这个字的笔画在我面前旋转重组,才托着脑袋转向窗外。

窗外,夜色掩去青山踪影,道路正在施工,楼房错落有致,天空中闪过几丛光球。远远望去,凤庆县人民医院的灯牌依旧明亮。

# Reports of the Fengqing Field Trip

**The three reports in this section constitute narratives from a field trip in Fengqing County, Yunnan Province, and the included stories recount the work and experiences of the writers, relating what transpired between them, their classmates, and the local people.**

# Starlight

## LYU Junlan

*Next patient: LYU Junlan*, read the screen at the entrance to the doctor's office at Zhongshan Ophthalmic Center, Sun Yat-sen University (hereafter SYSU) in Guangzhou. I went in and handed over my medical records.

"First diagnosis at the Fifth Affiliated Hospital of SYSU on October 15th... Are you from Zhuhai?" The doctor turned the pages rapidly. "October 27th, the People's Hospital of Fengqing County. Why were you in Yunnan?"

In the Covid era, travelling to border regions is considered risky.

"I'm from the School of International Studies at SYSU. I have a course called 'Creative Writing and Translation', and I went there last week to collect writing material on poverty alleviation."

"That's meaningful! How many people were there with you?"

"About 20, one teacher leading the team, six undergraduates and six graduate students, divided into three groups. Each group dealt with different topics, like voluntary teaching, medical aid and the 'First Party Secretary' of the village. We also have two teaching assistants and a three-person camera crew." While I was answering, the doctor motioned me to sit before the slit-lamp microscope.

The doctor quickly checked my eyelids. "Viral keratitis. It'll take a month or two to recover. But you are using the wrong medicine!"

No wonder I was sick for so long. Since my eyes suddenly turned red on the last day of the National Day Holiday, October 7th, I had seen three doctors in the Fifth Affiliated Hospital of SYSU. All said it would take less than a week to recover.

On the day of departure, my eyes felt a little dry on the plane from Guangzhou to Dali, a tourist attraction in Yunnan Province, but I convinced myself that was because of the dry air on the plane.

Disembarking, we hurried to the high-speed railway station, from which we took an hour-and-a-half ride to Yun County, the only county in Lincang City connected to the high-speed rail network. We were stunned by the vast blue Erhai Lake in Dali, but on the train to Lincang, there was nothing but one dark tunnel after another.

From Yun County to Fengqing County, and then from its center to a marginal area, where Lushi Town, our first destination, was seated, the landscape was profuse but monotonous. For three and a half hours on the zigzagging mountain road, the view gave nothing but towering hillsides, lush shrubs, and withered walnut trees. It was almost impossible to sleep with the constant ringing drone in my ears and sudden turns that plagued me with dizziness. At 8:00 p.m., when we finally reached Lushi, my eyelids were so heavy that it was a struggle to keep my eyes open.

"The group for interviewing the volunteer teachers has a heavy task today," said Prof. Dai Fan, the lecturer of the course. "We are going to interview the teachers from the Postgraduate Voluntary Teaching Group of SYSU. How do you feel right now?"

"Fine," replied Ma Weiguo, the only gentleman in our group. After all, none of us threw up on the bus like a few fellow students.

"Let's get started. The dishes have been ready for a while." One of the volunteer teachers, a tanned boy, stood up at the table, having fished in a bowl of thick yellow soup. "According to the custom here, the chicken head should be given to the most distinguished guest." Prof. Dai repeatedly waved him off, but the volunteer teacher insisted, after the manner of toasting at the Spring Festival feast, which features customary insistence and refusal.

"He's so sophisticated," whispered Guan Huilin, a member of our group.

"Who?" I asked.

"The 'toaster', leader of the SYSU voluntary teaching team. His name is Xu Jintao."

Huang Baoxin patted Huilin's leg and whispered, "He's the same age as you and Weiguo. He'd be also in his first year of graduate studies, but he joined the one-year voluntary teaching program before his graduate program."

Huilin nodded, wide-eyed. "Ah, voluntary teaching makes people grow up."

Xu Jintao's sophistication was not only obvious at the table, but also in the interview. His way of speaking reminded me of Xu Shuteng, the leader of the 18th Voluntary Teaching Group at Lushi High School. When we interviewed him half a month ago, he struck us as a sophisticated cadre, speaking in a compelling voice and gesturing with both hands.

Volunteer teachers introduced themselves in turn. The shortest female in the middle, called Wu Yating, taught Chinese. The other three were all math teachers, although the skinny Liu Chaoyu was the only undergraduate who majored in mathematics.

Niu Lulu, from Zhongshan School of Medicine, SYSU, told us why she had switched from biology to math. "Many math teachers left for high schools in Fengqing for better pay."

Three camera lights in the corner surrounded us, and I felt the water in my eyes evaporating under the heat. Every blink had grown raw and agonizing.

Prof. Dai looked at me. "Any questions?"

I looked at my team members, not just to escape embarrassment, but also to avoid the glaring lights.

"English writer Weiguo, and Chinese writer Baoxin, take the opportunity to ask for some details!" said Prof. Dai. Weiguo and Baoxin fixed their eyes on their laptops.

The subtitle maker, Huilin, spoke up, "I have a question for Wu Yating. You mentioned that you were depressed by the conditions at first. What made you feel so?"

Glancing at her laptop, I caught sight of notes and a few questions. I fiddled with my laptop uneasily.

"I was struck by the living conditions. For example, the solar water heaters don't work on cloudy days." Wu brushed the greasy hair behind her ears. "Some girls wash their hair in cold water in order to save money from paying for hot water. They wash their hair with cold water from a hose in the playground, even in such cold weather."

Xu Jintao jumped in. "The dormitories, toilets and drinking water facilities here are all very primitive."

Half a month ago, when we interviewed the previous volunteer teachers, they smiled almost mischievously. "Do you know what a trench latrine is?" And then they added, "Anyway, a trench latrine works well. Lushi is short of water, and trench latrine only needs to be flushed once a day."

I couldn't help whispering, "Trench latrine."

Xu Jintao nodded with a bitter smile. "That's it. Although it is already the eighth year since the first Voluntary Teaching Group came to Lushi, I still have to live in an old no-toilet dormitory built in the 1980s. Last month, I had gastroenteritis. Every time I went to the latrine, I had to walk down four flights of stairs and jogged across the playground."

"You would be a much faster runner after you recover!" Prof. Dai joked. The air inside the room was filled with instant cheerfulness.

Fortunately, though we didn't prepare enough questions, the group was able to gather quite a few details. The interview, which started at 8:30 p.m., did not end until 10:00 p.m. The moment when the camera lights switched off, I let my fiery eyes close. Huilin put her head on my shoulder and sighed, "I cannot hold on any longer. I've never been up at 3:00 a.m. in the morning and still working at 10:00 p.m." Baoxin also fell against Huilin's back and wailed, "I am still dizzy from the bus ride."

"Let's go back to the hotel. We'll have a whole day of interviews tomorrow." Weiguo led the way, and together we climbed steep, mossy stone steps on the slope. The night chill had crept into our clothes, but soon we were bathed in sweat. Halfway up, we clung to a telegraph pole, panting.

"Look!" Weiguo pointed to the sky. Stars like countless silver beads were embedded in the night.

"Wow!" We exclaimed, "I've never seen so many stars!"

"Why are there no lights?" asked Weiguo. "Are there residents in Lushi Ancient Town?"

Yellow streetlamps shone on the brick wall, on which the mural depicted the Ancient Tea Horse Road, all the glory of the good old days. The sound of horse bells and hooves was gone with the wind and the streets where horse gangs came and went were deserted, leaving only horse footprints on the slabs as tokens from history. The mud walls of tile-roofed houses had been stripped of their skin, while the freshly painted wooden window frames and signs read, "Historic Buildings in Fengqing County, Lincang City". At night, a similar site in Lijiang or Dali would be packed with tourists. However, in Lushi, a mountain town requiring an hour and a half by high-speed train and a four-hour bus ride from Dali, there was not even one tourist.

"Residents here must be sleeping by now," I replied. "They don't have much nightlife. Unlike Guangdong, 10:00 p.m. is just time for midnight snack!"

"I'm desperate for midnight snack!" cried Huilin. "I didn't eat dinner at all. All the food was cold!"

I didn't eat much at dinner either, the preserved meat was too salty to swallow, the eggplant had soaked up the chilli oil, and even the cabbage was stir-fried with chillies.

"Ah!" Huilin shouted. "We will be free by tomorrow night! We can 'do our math homework' while having midnight snack."

"Do math homework" is our code for playing card games. After lunch at the high-speed railway station earlier that day, we bought a pack of poker cards and planned to play during our spare time.

"Stop daydreaming! Interviews will start at 9:00 a.m. and continue until 9:00 p.m. tomorrow." Weiguo shrugged his shoulders and walked on.

When I got up at 7:00 a.m., I felt my eyes on fire, and in front of my eyes was a kind of mist. At the breakfast place, I whispered, "Is my right eye red?"

Huilin and Baoxin checked and nodded. "It's red near the corner of the eye."

"What's the matter?" asked Weiguo.

"Nothing. Maybe I didn't rest well yesterday." I knew it must be the keratitis getting worse, but telling the truth was of no help. According to Xu Shuteng, who came to Lushi for voluntary teaching eight years ago, there was only a small health center in Lushi Town, where "Doctors there do nothing but let patients inhale oxygen". Besides, our task in Lushi was a whirl of interviews, leaving no time for medical treatment.

The first interviewee that morning was the headmaster of Lushi High School. As soon as he walked out of the school history museum where the interview was held, the next interviewee came in. No sooner had we settled back in our chairs than we pulled ourselves up again. At the end of the last interview in the morning, Huilin was already lying on the desk, while Baoxin and Weiguo also fell back with hollow eyes. By afternoon, it was the students' turn to come in one by one for interviews. After looking at the computer for hours, my eyes felt dry again, as they were last night.

After dinner, both the medical aid group and the village support group went back to the hotel, purportedly to prepare for interviews of the following days. We were the only four students left in the school history museum. After finishing the last three interviews with local teachers, Prof. Dai said, "I would like to give you a general outline of the writing. First of all, Chinese writer Baoxin and English writer Weiguo, you can think about whether to write your story in the first-person or the third-person perspective..."

Weiguo nodded, Baoxin did not respond, as if she were sleeping with her eyes open. Inspired by her posture, I supported one side of my face with my hand so that my sore right eye could close unnoticed.

"And the subtitle maker, Huilin, you should find different descriptions of the same event from the interview recordings, and select them as material for our documentary. Reporter Junlan needs to reflect on what we saw and heard during our visit to Fengqing, and you can compose it in a relatively free form." Prof. Dai finally stopped, "Let's call it a day. You all look like you're falling asleep!"

As soon as we were out of the gate of Lushi High School, the cold fresh air of the night woke us up. We were walking on the dirt road, holding the heavy camera equipment, but we were all cackling with delight, as the interviews were finally over. Over the next few days, other groups would interview, and we would have time to write our stories.

Unexpectedly, interviews were replaced by sick relay. On the morning of the third day, while waiting for the bus to the county seat, I noticed Huilin shivering in the cold wind, with dark circles around her eyes.

"You're looking haggard." As I looked closer, I saw that her eyes were red, too.

"I didn't rest well," Huilin said. "Why are your eyes still red?"

"I had keratitis before I came here. But don't worry. I'll see a doctor as soon as we get to Fengqing."

Baoxin touched Huilin's head and said, "Poor girl! She spent nearly the whole night watching video clips of our interviews."

"When's the deadline?" Weiguo asked. Huilin smiled bitterly. "Today."

Baoxin said, "The teacher sent a message at midnight: 'Try to finish the video selection for the documentary by the end of today.' That's why she worked so hard."

On the bus to the county seat, I closed my eyes, but the mountain road kept me awake. I saw a laptop screen reflected in the front glass. Huilin was watching the videos at double speed. From time to time, she typed in the time code and the content of the speech in a file. After peeking for just a few minutes, dizziness overpowered me. I couldn't help admiring Huilin. How could she keep staring at that screen on such a bumpy and zigzagging road!

As soon as we arrived at the county seat, I told Prof. Dai my eye trouble.

"What a coincidence!" said Prof. Dai. "We are going to interview a doctor from Zhongshan Ophthalmic Center, SYSU in the afternoon. He should be able to help."

So, after lunch, Prof. Dai, Mr. Wei, the camera man, Mr. Zhang (a local village secretary) and Wang Lulu (reporter from the medical aid group) accompanied me to the county hospital. The hall was empty, and Dr. Liu Liangping and his assistant were waiting for us on the mezzanine floor. Prof. Dai shook hands with him and said, "The hospital seems not so busy."

Dr. Liu replied, "It's lunch break. Besides, most departments have been moved to the new site. Only the departments of Chinese Medicine and Ophthalmology are left in this old site."

After the usual eye exam, I sat down in front of the slit-lamp microscope. While operating the instrument, Dr. Liu explained, "Under the blue light, where there is fluorescence reaction, there is inflammation. You can see that the corneal infiltration has nearly recovered."

Dr. Liu switched back to the yellow light and turned my eyelids up, said, "But your conjunctivitis is more serious than keratitis."

What? Conjunctivitis? Why didn't any of the previous doctors tell me?

Dr. Liu pulled two slides from the printer and said, "You see, the normal inner eyelid should be smooth, but now they are abraded. This must have accumulated for a long period, and these days without enough rest, your symptoms have become more severe."

It was nearly 2:00 p.m. by the time we got back to the hotel. Weiguo and several classmates had gathered around the tea table in the lobby. Before them were cups of black tea, a specialty of Fengqing County. Weiguo stood up and offered his seat to me.

"So soon? Have you been prescribed any medicine?"

"No. I didn't register, and the pharmacy is not open during noontime."

"So, what's the use of seeing a doctor?"

"It's still useful. At least now I know I'm far from recovery and should see a doctor as soon as I get back to Guangzhou."

I saw two vague figures walking toward us. Huilin was supporting Baoxin, whose face was utterly bloodless.

"What's wrong, Huilin?" I asked.

Baoxin gave a big yawn. "She's been watching that endless interview videos during noontime break."

Weiguo shook his head. "You've been watching it all day. Haven't you finished yet?"

"I'm only halfway!" cried out Huilin. "Five finished but four to go."

In the afternoon, the group responsible for investigating SYSU's medical assistance did their interviews heatedly, while Huilin sat motionless at the desk in the adjacent room, frowning. She reminded me of Tao Yuanming, an ancient hermit who said that even if he were in a noisy place, he would have lived a life of a hermit, because "A secluded heart makes the place also secluded."

As dinner was served, a faint smile finally flickered across Huilin's lips, but it soon vanished as Prof. Dai announced that our group would interview a volunteer teacher from the Affiliated High School of SYSU over dinner. Huilin rolled her eyes and then collapsed on Baoxin's shoulder crying, "Help! All I want is a relaxing dinner."

Finally, back at the hotel in the evening, I saw Huilin sneak by with a bag labelled "Meituan Medicine Delivery".

"What's that?"

"It's ageratum-liquid. I feel like I'm about to catch a cold." Huilin could barely walk, and Baoxin, next to her, stumbled and kept moaning, "My hands and feet hurt" and "I feel like I have rheumatism". They were holding on to each other, staggering along like a clumsy couple in a three-legged race.

To my surprise, the next morning, I found Huilin dancing and laughing, "Task's done and Dobby is free!"

I thought, "Great, let the sick relay end here."

However, when we were getting off the bus for dinner, Baoxin got up from her seat and bumped her head. After a muffled thud, she fell back crying, "Ouch! It hurts!"

Weiguo stood up. "You hit the luggage rack again?"

"It hurts!" Baoxin repeated again and again.

"Let me press your head with my shoe." Huilin teased, while Baoxin cried and then laughed. A few days ago, when someone hit the luggage rack, Baoxin told us a story from her primary school days: when a pupil bumped his head, the teacher took off her shoe to press the bump down. Unfortunately, the storyteller now became the miserable pupil of her story.

On the fifth day of the six-day trip to Fengqing, while Prof. Dai and the group responsible for medical assistance investigation were interviewing local doctors and patients, we remained in the quiet lounge room next door. Weiguo was frowning as he revised his English work; Huilin was tapping on her keyboard, and squinting from time to time; Baoxin would stare at the screen and then lean back with a look of pain.

I checked my phone and saw a message from Baoxin ten minutes ago. "While I was typing, my vision suddenly blurred."

Was it the result of concussion from hitting her head? In a TV series called *Unnatural Death*, a man fell off a motorcycle and his vision blurred. In the end, he died of a cerebral haemorrhage.

Soon Baoxin recieved the same "royal" treatment that I had a few days ago, in the brand new hospital built with the assistance of our university. At 5:00 p.m., the entire surgical office was empty. The orthopaedic surgeon, ready to leave, put his white coat back on and checked Baoxin's skull. Although Baoxin was screaming in pain, the doctor said with a casual air, "The swelling is not very severe, and the blurred vision may be due to looking at the laptop for too long. You can do a CT scan if you are worried."

Twenty minutes later, we returned to the lounge. Weiguo immediately stopped us, asking about the test result.

"The CT scan shows a tumor in my head." Baoxin took on a sorrowful demeanour, spoke slowly, and sighed incessantly.

Weiguo froze. "What? You…"

I grabbed Baoxin's CT bag, pulled out the test report that said *No obvious intracranial injury*, and handed it to Weiguo. "Read it yourself!"

Weiguo examined the report for a moment, and looked up incredulously, "What does this mean?"

"It means there's a tumor in my brain," Baoxin replied solemnly.

I grinned, "That's nonsense. As for the swelling, the doctor said a hot towel would help."

"Then why did you just say—" Weiguo's eyes were shining in the incandescent light.

"Just kidding!" Baoxin doubled up with laughter. "No way! Did you believe me?"

"Of course not!" Weiguo removed his glasses. He covered his face with both hands and turned his head away.

"Now, what are you doing?" I asked. "Come on, are you crying?"

"No! I'm just sleepy." Weiguo buried his head into the gap on the sofa.

Fortunately, the sick relay ended at Baoxin. We returned to Zhuhai "intact", but it took days to recover. The six-day trip to Fengqing, started like a stone tossed into a lake, initiating a ripple and returning to calm, proved to be a skipping stone, evoking new reflections again and again.

While we interviewed volunteer teachers at Lushi High School, they spoke of their initial intention in voluntary teaching: *To do something unforgettable in the space of a year*. For us in the creative writing course, this motto could be adapted into, *To harvest unforgettable memories in the space of a week*.

While regular tourists stop at Dali, we headed into the remote mountains and witnessed how the great dream of poverty alleviation was becoming a reality. "We're planting a seed in students' hearts," the volunteer teachers said, "a seed that encourages them to get out of the mountains and explore the wonderful outside world." They were managing to do so, as students we interviewed told us of dreams of entering medical schools beyond the mountains.

"Before the volunteer teachers came, it was something of a mission impossible to send our students to key universities," said the headmaster. His words were echoed by local teachers. However, it's not that way anymore, as three graduates were admitted to Sun Yat-sen University through the special enrollment plan for rural students these years. "The moment when our students got the news," exclaimed the headmaster, "the volunteer teacher jumped up. I've never seen him so beyond himself!"

"Our influence is limited," said a volunteer teacher. Every one of these volunteers shines like a firefly. But over the past eight years, the light of every volunteer group became like stars in the sky, illuminating the road ahead for students in Lushi.

One day in late autumn, we passers-by looked up at the same starlight, and we marveled at its brilliance.

# We Are on the Way: From Poverty Alleviation to Rural Development in Fengqing

## QU Ningwei

"We sincerely hope that the Party secretaries would never leave, but we are also afraid that they would have a tough time here. After all, the material conditions here are poor," said Chen Yingqin, a villager, with an awkward smile. These words hit me hard. Her contradictory thoughts conveyed a sense of sadness.

The Party secretaries Chen was referring to are Guo Xingyong and Lan Shude. In 2018, Sun Yat-Sen University (hereafter SYSU) responded to the call of the Ministry of Education for poverty alleviation and began to send officials to Fengqing, a small county of Yunnan Province in Southwest China, to serve as the acting Party secretaries of Hongtang Village Committee. Since then, the bond between the secretaries and Hongtang Village was formed. Three years later, through the Creative Writing and Translation course, offered by Prof. Dai Fan, we came here to interview, record, and report on the people and events in this poverty alleviation campaign. From October 24th to 29th, a group of 18 people were divided into three groups bearing respective report duties: education, medical care, and the development of village and county. Three other students and I were assigned to the group responsible for village and county. It was also in this group that we were able to get a glimpse of the effort of the SYSU poverty alleviation team. As I write these words, I have already come back to school from Fengqing, but the experience of this trip is utterly unforgettable and precious.

On the evening of the fourth day of the field trip, following dinner at the guesthouse run by Ms. Chen Yingqin, we sat on the sofa in the living room, staring at the cartoons on the TV. Though it was a little bit different from what I watched as a child, they were still kind of entertaining. Guanrou and Yehui, two undergraduates in our group, were more child-like than me and lost themselves in discussing the plot.

"Today," Prof. Dai announced, "the students in the village and county group will enjoy an exclusive benefit! One night in Ms. Chen's guesthouse! And of course, Zhang Jia (Prof. Dai's assistant) and I will be with you." This was a planned part of our trip, aimed at gathering additional writing material.

As it grew dark, students of other groups caught the bus back to the hotel, while the rest of us sat around on the sofa, turned on our computers, and began to ask the villagers about the secretaries.

The first to speak up was Lulu, my graduate classmate and the one in charge of video-subtitling in our group. "What do you remember about Secretary Guo?"

"When Secretary Guo first came here three years ago, everyone just thought he was someone who lost his way. He came up to say hello."

"Yes, yes, yes! Secretary Guo even did magic tricks for the children!"

A villager surnamed Li spoke up, "Never mind the kids, he got me too! I've gotten fooled myself!"

"Never mind you," said Chen's husband. "I have also been fooled! I remember once, Secretary Guo said he had come back here, and sent me a location on WeChat, urging me to prepare tea so that we could catch up on old times. I was very happy. But when the tea was ready, he texted me a 'Happy April Fool's Day!' I looked at the clock. It just ticked midnight. The first day of April arrived."

"So, Secretary Guo is quite humorous!" Yehui and Guanrou both noted down Guo's "playfulness" on their laptops.

"Thanks to Secretary Guo, the village has street lights, so we don't have to walk home in total darkness anymore. And that ditch in front of our door had been in disrepair for a long time. It was also dredged with the help of Secretary Guo, using his own money. Now it's a lot easier for us to grow vegetables and irrigate."

I remembered that when I was walking down the road, there were indeed a few streetlamps on both sides of the path. Although the light was dim, it was enough to light up the way. Perhaps, each time the villagers return home from work, they will think of Secretary Guo, a fifty-year-old man who likes to joke around, but also loves and cares for this place with all his heart.

I noticed two beautiful photos hung next to the TV in the living room, and the people in the photos did not look like locals.

Guanrou noticed this too. "My classmates are in it. Yeah, this is Xiaoying and this is…"

"I just realize that these were students who came to our accommodation at that time, just like you guys, also from your school," said a villager.

Yehui was also trying to identify the foreign teachers in the photo, who sat around a long table. "There's Teacher Stephen here, and Teacher Seo who teaches Korean!"

"It was a big event in our village! We'd never seen so many foreigners in our lives!"

Ms. Chen couldn't stop smiling. "When they came to dine with us, it was the first time I ever cooked for foreigners! It felt like making our hometown food international! People from other villages came over to see what was going on. The place was packed."

According to them, at that time, this big news was spread through WeChat moments to the whole Fengqing County.

"People from other villages were envious."

"They wanted to know why foreigners came to our village, and we said, it's all because of Secretary Lan!"

Speaking of the Party Secretary Lan Shude, we had interviewed him before we came to Fengqing. Back then, Secretary Lan had just completed his job as the Secretary. We first learned from him about the poverty alleviation work in Hongtang Village. From the targeted family assistance to the industrial development of the whole village, Secretary Lan involved himself in almost everything.

That morning, we also visited the Imperial Chrysanthemum Garden, highly recommended by Secretary Lan. At the entrance, a plaque read "Industrial Support Base of Sun Yat-Sen University". Entering the park, we were immersed in a golden world, a chrysanthemum field spreading upward to the foot of the mountain. Pulling Lulu and several other students to the middle of a wooden bridge, Jingjing, a member of the medical group, held her phone high. Flowers blossomed on both sides, and on the bridge, the girls were smiling. But it didn't take long for them to be driven away by the scorching sun. They ran to an awning, where they started photoshopping the pictures on their phones. That was where we had an exchange with Zhang Guofeng, a villager who looks after the chrysanthemum garden.

"This chrysanthemum garden was initiated by Secretary Lan. Now he has gone back to SYSU for a few months."

"So, what changes have been brought to your life after getting the job in the chrysanthemum garden?"

"There's a lot to say! In the past, I had to travel to pick tea-leaves, and each time I came home late, I was unable to care for my family. Plus, my husband needs my care because he has trouble with his legs. Now, I can work right next to my home. As the caretaker of the chrysanthemum garden, I have an extra income of 8000 yuan a year."

Speaking of Secretary Lan, Zhang's words were filled with gratitude. Before leaving, Jianbin and Jingyan, two students responsible for photographing, swept a camera drone over our heads to capture the image of us in the Imperial Chrysanthemum Garden. The garden is the most beautiful gift that Secretary Lan left to Hongtang Village.

Having left the Imperial Chrysanthemum Garden, we headed to Dabaitian Elementary School, the elementary school in the village, and a place that Secretary Guo and Secretary Lan were especially concerned about.

Lulu patted me. "So, this is Xiao Lin's painting! I've heard a great deal of him."

Looking in the direction Lulu was pointing, I glanced at the walls of several two-storey buildings, painted with huge comics, adding special interest to this country road. Some of the comics read as follows:

"All your wishes, I will try to fulfil."

"If books are the ladder to human progress, then cell phones are the ladder down to ignorance."

"By Xiao Lin"

"Who is Xiao Lin?" I asked Lulu.

"Xiao Lin is a teacher at SYSU. He was trained as a medical student, but later became a comic book creator."

"Wow! What a story."

"Xiao Lin was invited by Secretary Lan to make these cartoons so that the Garden would attract more tourists," explained Mr. Zhang Liangyou, our guide on the trip, who had taken over Secretary Lan's job.

Soon we got to a display house which was filled with tea products such as black tea, green tea, and chrysanthemum tea.

"The tea here, of all varieties, is grown and processed in Hongtang village. This is Yunnan Special Black Tea; This is Classic Black Tea, and this is Yunnan Gushu (ancient tree) Black Tea..." The excitement and pride on Liangyou's face conveyed his heartfelt love for this place.

Guanrou called us over for a look. "Look! There are also tripods here and stands for the spotlight, the same as Mr. Wei's." Mr. Wei was the teacher responsible for photographing in our company, a "good old boy" with an unmatched sense of humor.

Lulu immediately recognized it. "This is meant for live streaming to sell products online!"

Yehui jumped in. "Yes—Mr. Wang Ke had helped Fengqing to do a live streaming broadcast." I recalled that in a previous interview, Wang Ke, the deputy County Magistrate of Fengqing County dispatched by Sun Yat-sen University, had mentioned that more than 500000 yuan were made in just two hours during a live-streaming broadcast. Wang Ke has just finished his two-year duty in Fengqing and returned to SYSU. The day before, we had an interview with his successor, Mr. Zhang Zhe, who gave us an introduction to Fengqing's educational, medical and industrial development. One of the things that struck me was how well Mr. Zhang Zhe knew the area within just several months.

He had an extremely good grasp of data. "Fengqing County has an agreeable climate. It is home to 380000 people. It occupies 14 square kilometers and administrates 13 townships. It is 1500 meters above sea level, and 26 ethnic minorities dwell here..."

After a cup of hot chrysanthemum tea and a rest, we set off to Dabaitian Elementary School. The country road was lined with small houses, showing the changes that have taken place here. I must say that the countryside in China is much different from what it was when I was a kid.

When we entered Dabaitian Elementary School, the children all saluted us. They were not even of my waist-high. I was very touched. It seemed that Guanrou was touched too. "Look how polite they are! Maybe they see us as teachers!" During the stay in school, we went to visit the cucurbit flute course, an online course, where the children interacted with a teacher thousands of miles away in Guangzhou.

"That little pudgy boy can't keep up with the teacher, and they are getting so anxious!" Jingjing is always the one to notice the fun thing.

Lulu cut in, "And that one is pressing on the wrong hole but still blowing."

As if discovering a new world, the children watched every move we made. The little pudgy boy glanced back and immediately turned away, cheeks blushing under scattered bangs. At this time, Feng Jia, a visiting scholar associated with Prof. Dai, came over.

"A few kids just ran up to me and asked if I knew their teacher, Mr. Lan."

"Mr. Lan?"

"I think it's Secretary Lan. Didn't he say in the interview before that he used to teach English to the kids here?"

"Right! So?"

"I said I knew him, and asked them what I could do for them. They said they wanted me to tell Mr. Lan that they missed him."

I didn't remember much of what Jia said, but I felt as if I were seeing flashes of Mr. Lan Shude in my mind, teaching children the English alphabet in the classroom right in front of me.

Afterwards, we had a conversation with Headmaster Yang Weilin and learned that the cucurbit flutes used by the children were donated by the teachers from Guangzhou. After class, students would leave the instruments in the reading room for the next class. We then visited the simple but neat reading room.

"Secretary Guo bought a lot of equipment for the school, such as the bookcases here and the school's stereo."

Yehui stepped to a bookcase and examined a children's picture book. "Are the books here also donated?"

"Yes, they are."

It wasn't until the day after I returned from Fengqing, when Rita, my teacher for the Interpreting course, invited the students and teachers in the WeChat group to donate books, that I realized the books in the reading room came from teachers and students around us.

"Secretary Guo would come around the school whenever he could, doing magic for the students, playing with them, and teaching them good manners as well."

Guanrou exclaimed, "He did a great job! Everyone was saluting us when we came in!"

"Yes, they also miss Secretary Lan. He taught them English and bought them English picture books."

After class, two of the children joined us for an interview. One was named Zhao Wei and the other Wang Wen. They saluted as they came in, straightened their red scarves, and sat upright, slightly shy.

"How did you guys feel in class? Is homework too much?" Lulu slowed her way of speaking, showing her affinity with children, relaxing both kids.

The two of them nodded.

In the follow-up chat, Zhao Wei mentioned his older brother, currently attending high school at Lushi High School, which we had previously visited. The conditions there were tough, but the volunteer teachers from SYSU overcame the difficulty and became the source of inspiration for the students. Wang Wen has an older sister who is currently a junior high school student in the county and was also a student of Mr. Lan. Although the two children were too shy to say much, we gathered how much they appreciated and missed Mr. Guo and Mr. Lan. Headmaster Yang told us that they had both benefited from the scholarship program initiated by Secretary Guo and Secretary Lan, which came to 1000 yuan a year.

As we were leaving, the school day ended, with children lining up to leave school and go home, carrying the love and expectations of so many. Just then, Lulu and Jingjing dashed over to show us some chocolate.

"Look! The little girl just gave it to us to thank us for taking photos for her!"

I faked an accusation, "How could you take something from a child?"

"No, we made an exchange. We like her a lot, and she likes us a lot."

I was impressed by how quickly these two were able to bond with kids, and by how much the kids trusted people from SYSU. It had been a long time since I had left elementary school. These children helped me recollect a bit.

"Do any of your children go to Dawanbai Elementary School?" A question from Prof. Dai brought me back from reveries.

Lulu spoke up, "Professor, I think you mean Dabaitian Elementary School."

At once, Yehui, Guanrou and Zhang Jia burst into a peal of laughter. Prof. Dai also laughed.

Ms. Chen clarified, "Oh, Dabaitian. My daughter doesn't go to school there. She attended the other school in the neighboring village."

Right then, I recalled what Zhao Wei and Wang Wen said about their hopes.

"I want to be a computer programmer, to contribute to the national technological development."

"I want to be a policeman, to safeguard the nation."

I wish their dreams are fulfilled.

The night at the guesthouse brought us close to the end of our week-long trip to Fengqing, Yunnan. Looking back to the night before our first interview, the entire group felt nervous, and we pulled out all previous reports, looking for clues to help us assign everyone's tasks. However, when we interviewed, our prepared sequence of questions was disrupted, and we had to adjust to the interviewee's style. After a few days of practice, we grew increasingly proficient. Despite a few awkward moments of fumbling for questions, we managed to gather valuable first-hand material. Most importantly, during this whole process, SYSU's work in Fengqing and the footprints of SYSU's poverty alleviation team grew increasingly clear. Their stories are worth spreading.

Thank you, Secretary Guo and Secretary Lan and those who are still working hard for Fengqing, along with those who will succeed them. We will be your storytellers, striving to keep alive the contribution you made to this era.

# Sun Yat-sen University's Effort for Fengqing's Development

## WANG Jingjing

"I would like to end my speech by expressing my gratitude for the assistance from the affiliated hospitals of Sun Yat-sen University. In the future, please continue holding our hands, and together, we make our way forward," said Li Chunguang, Deputy Director of the Department of Ophthalmology of the People's Hospital of Fengqing County, at the end of the interview.

To this day, these words still echo in my mind. In 2019, Sun Yat-sen University began to send medical staff to Fengqing, providing comprehensive medical support, including ophthalmology.

Fengqing County, located in the southwest of Yunnan Province, has been a designated county for Sun Yat-sen University's support since 2013. We are students of the Creative Writing and Translation course offered by Prof. Dai Fan from Sun Yat-sen University. We were in Fengqing for a field trip to gather material for writing. Our team consisted of Prof. Dai, a photography team, six undergraduate students, six graduate students, and a PhD teaching assistant. We would interview local people concerned in education, medical care, and local industries. Deputy Director Li Chunguang is one of the interviewees. I am fortunate enough to be a member of the group responsible for investigating the medical assistance, and I gained a lot during the trip.

I can still recall the day we left for Fengqing: airplane, train, bus through airways, highways and mountain roads. I was asleep most of the time, as I got up around 3:00 a.m. to catch the plane. When I opened my eyes, we had arrived at the first stop of this visit, the town of Lushi. Lushi is located at the northeast of Fengqing, accessible only through rugged mountain roads. All I can recall was the three-hour drive on the mountain roads, during which my head rocked back and forth against the window, adding to my headache. After dinner, I felt much better. So I went for a stroll with Wang Lulu, a member of the group responsible for investigating local industries.

Along the way forward, most of the roadside stores had closed. It was eight o'clock in the evening. Looking into the distance, we saw a small store open and went over there.

"Excuse me sir, are there any more fried dough twists?" I had just overheard the volunteer teacher Xu Jintao mentioning that the fried dough twists here were delicious.

"They are sold out! Come tomorrow."

"Okay, thank you!"

"Are you tourists?"

"No, we're from Sun Yat-sen University. We came here to learn about Fengqing."

"From Sun Yat-sen University! Thank you! You are so kind!"

Thank you? I didn't understand. Why did he say that? Just because we wanted to buy fried dough twists?

"When are you leaving?"

"Tomorrow."

"Come back here if you have time before departure. There's an opera stage near here. As you can see, there are few young people. They've all gone away to make a living elsewhere, and the ones left behind are old people. I've been working out of town. A few days ago, my relative got sick, and I came back to help her look after the store."

"So how much is the salary here?"

"The profit is about 1800~2000 yuan per month, and the rent is 1000 yuan a year. If you sell snacks here, you may only earn 50 yuan in a day and cannot make ends meet. So having few shoppers leads to stores' closing down, which leads to the departure of more young people."

…

This was our first "informal interview". It gave us a heavy heart on the way back.

The day before the medical group interviewed, our group discussion began. I felt at a loss and had no clue how to ask interview questions. Xiaoyan (Tan Xiaoyan, a member of our group) and Xinqi (Li Xinqi, a member of our group) got into a heated discussion about how to write the story.

"Have you thought of a theme for the story yet?" Xinqi asked Xiaoyan.

"Not yet, don't we just write the story directly?"

"You need a theme to bind these stories together. Which point of view are you going to write in?"

"First-person."

"We would need to ask questions based on the theme tomorrow, so it is necessary to choose a theme."

...

"We both seem like outsiders!" I said to Yuanheng (Huang Yuanheng, a member of our group).

I was very glad that I was the group leader and didn't have to worry about finding a theme, while Yuanheng next to me kept typing at his laptop. By the time Xiaoyuan and Xinqi's conversation came to an end, I still couldn't come up with any questions for tomorrow's interview. Soon after, Yuanheng posted the outline of the interview in our WeChat group. The names of the interviewees and the purpose and background of the interview as well as related questions were all listed in detail.

I realized that outlining is something the group leader should do. At that time, I was highly ashamed and appreciated his work. I began to feel really bad for not involving myself enough for the work.

Before leaving the campus, I saw this visit as trip. As the bus slowly drove off campus, I took a long breath and muttered, "I've finally escaped this environment."

Postgraduate life was different from what I had expected. I was so busy that I had started to squeeze down my recreation time, and I was extremely anxious. I wanted to escape, to cry, but I couldn't find a reason to stop studying. Therefore, a kind of rebellious mentality arose in me. I hated it. I hated the deprivation of my time. I hated that I could not do what I like. I hated this environment. With this mindset, I hoped that this trip could help me relax.

But as soon as I saw the outline, I began to reflect on myself. Doing what you should do is not called "studying", but meeting the requirement for a student.

The medical team started to interview.

"Deputy Director Li Chunguang, what is your opinion regarding this kind of support?"

"On behalf of our vast number of residents and myself, I would like to say thank you to Sun Yat-sen University, to Zhongshan Ophthalmic Center of Sun Yat-sen University, and then to this great policy. For the benefit of residents in Fengqing, I would like to ask Sun Yat-sen University and the Director of Zhongshan Ophthalmic Center of Sun Yat-sen University to hold our hands, like a mother protecting her child, and move forward, and finally, to help us improve skills."

…

"Director Li Hai, what are the changes that have taken place in the hospital since the arrival of the volunteer doctors?"

"With the help of doctors from Sun Yat-sen University, the level of medical treatment in Fengqing has been greatly improved, and in terms of the comprehensive assessment for public hospitals at the county level in Yunnan Province, the People's Hospital of Fengqing County ranked number one. The number of surgical units and discharges achieved a double increase, basically achieving the goal that 'major diseases can be cured in local regions'. People could feel the changes so well that when a doctor told a taxi driver that he was from Sun Yat-sen University, the driver gave him a free ride."

After hearing this, I couldn't help thinking of the shop keeper in Lushi Town saying "Thank you!" and it dawned on me how wonderful these doctors are and how insignificant my contribution was. I had unintentionally become a "beneficiary" of the gratitude for Sun Yat-sen University's support. So, it was especially important to write about my experience.

As we approached Dabaitian Elementary School, a place where we are going to do some interviews, the greetings were lavished upon us.

"Hello, teacher! Hello, teacher! Hello, teacher!" cried out the children, as if we were celebrities. I was flattered and began to respond to their greetings, "Hello, hello." The experience was so overwhelming that my spirits gradually rose.

In the crowd, I saw a girl smiling. Unlike the other children's formality, she stood relaxed. I walked up to her.

"Hello! Teacher!" She greeted me with a smile.

"Hello! What grade are you in?"

"I'm in the fourth grade."

*Ding, ding, ding, ding*! The bell was ringing. The children hurried back to the classroom. My eyes were still fixed on that girl, feeling sorry that I would not see her again.

When the class was over, the children poured out of the classroom, and the greetings started again. Once more, I saw the girl! I walked over to her to take pictures with her. This was the first time I held a child's hand. I have been afraid to play with children, either boys or girls, because some children I have met struck me as impolite and ignorant. Most of the time, I wished to get as far away as possible.

It was different this time! I liked this little girl, loved to watch her laughing, and I began to appreciate the innocence of children. Before them, I started to unguard myself. I felt so relaxed and carefree that I joined them in laughter.

Maybe I saw my old self in them. I envied them for being so happy, and I hoped they could maintain this happiness. I had lost my happiness long before. In the past, I didn't understand why my parents kept telling me that what they wanted was just my happiness, instead of great achievements in studying or enviable longevity. I didn't know when I had become so unhappy. I desperately longed to regain my happiness but to no avail.

Unexpectedly, with those children, with this very girl, I could feel a touch of happiness.

I reluctantly let go of her hand. We had to leave, and they had to go back to class. I smiled as I watched her disappear into the classroom.

My vision began to blur.

I looked at the back of the girl. Her sprinting to class felt like that of the 10-year-old Wang Jingjing. She smiled and asked me, "Hey, 21-year-old Wang Jingjing, how are you doing now?"

I responded to her with a big smile.

When the children poured out of school, our whole research team was standing close to the gate of the school.

Children rushed towards us, saying, "Bye teacher! Bye teacher! ..."

"Bye! Take care!"

I took out my phone and snapped pictures.

A girl ran towards me. Having recognized her, I ran to her and hugged her. It was her. It was the girl, whose name I didn't know yet.

"Miss, are you going away?"

"Yes, be careful on your way home!"

Then the little girl ran into a house.

"Lulu, watch her! I need to go back to the bus and get something." I ran to the bus.

I remembered there was a bar of chocolate in my bag.

After grabbing the chocolate, I immediately got off the bus. The little girl stood next to Lulu. I gave her the chocolate, and at the same time, she gave each of us a chocolate roll. It turned out that the "house" was a grocery store.

A stream of warmth struck my heart, and I struggled to hold back my tears. Why? Why had I come to help, only to be helped?

As she disappeared into the crowd, I dragged Lulu into the store. With the photo of the girl in my phone, I asked the store owner if he knew her. He nodded. We bought her snacks and left a note. Then we asked the owner to give these snacks to her the next day.

On the note, I wrote, "Be happy!" I hope she can always be happy. And I hope her happiness can warm more people in the future.

I may come to Fengqing only once in a lifetime. So, I cherished every moment here. There might be another chance to visit here in the future, but I don't know when that will be. Just as Prof. Dai said at the night of our departure, "Some of our senior students are preparing to find jobs. Some are going on for further studies. Our Ph.D. teaching assistant will graduate sooner or later. We may not come back to Fengqing in the future, so this place and this moment are unique to all of us. I hope that when you think of your college life or postgraduate life later, you will be glad for having chosen such a very special course."

I was fortunate to be a witness to Sun Yat-sen University's poverty alleviation project, seeing all the changes brought by Sun Yat-sen University's effort to the People's Hospital of Fengqing County and the residents in Fengqing. I am grateful as well for my growth during this visit. Just as the saying goes, "People watching the play become the characters in the play." At this moment, I understand the "thank you" from the man in Lushi Town, and the meaning behind it. Although I am only a witness to Sun Yat-sen University's poverty alleviation project, I feel as if I have touched something meaningful, and I am proud to be a witness.

Having written down what I have heard and seen, I hope more and more people can participate in this effort and more people may benefit from it.

# Stories from Fengqing

In this section, the three reports constitute narratives concerning a field trip to Fengqing County, Yunnan Province, covering the students' visits to a range of locations and their reflections on their experiences.

# Into the Mountains

## MA Weiguo

On Oct. 24th, 2021, with 12 classmates from the Creative Writing and Translation course, I participated in the investigation of poverty alleviation through education in Fengqing, a county that was formerly one of the poorest in Yunnan Province. After three hours on a bus ride from a train station in Yun County that didn't exist until one year ago, I finally set foot, dizzy and tired, yet filled with curiosity, on this wooded land.

I had frequently heard about the graduate volunteer teachers who taught in the mountainous areas, but I never got a clear picture of what their life was like. That's why I was so excited when I got the chance to investigate their stories as part of the Creative Writing and Translation course at Sun Yat-sen University. Our mission was to investigate poverty alleviation in the education sector, and gather both the results and stories in the process. Sun Yat-sen University had been providing material and personnel in support of Fengqing County, and now it was time for us to interview people and see what changes have been brought about.

One teacher spoke to us is a graduate of Lushi High School called Liu Yuexiu, currently a student at South China Agricultural University, who had held Xu Shuteng as her idol. She would often say, "I want to grow up like Xu Shuteng." I was surprised because Xu Shuteng was not a pop star. He was someone I had interviewed two weeks earlier, a smiling man in black-rimmed glasses, a former volunteer teacher.

At 23, before he started his master's program, Xu Shuteng taught for one year in this remote Lushi Town, where he taught Liu Yuexiu back in 2016. Currently, there are poverty alleviation programs in China encouraging graduates to fill teaching positions in remote areas before they pursue their master's degrees. These programs aim to generate a balance between impoverished and developed regions; sending teachers to Fengqing amounted to an example of one of these programs.

It took Xu Shuteng more than 15 hours to make the trip from Sun Yat-sen University, his alma mater, to Lushi High School. He had to travel by shuttle bus first, then an airplane, train, and finally bus again, and finally made it to the mountains, where he saw nature at its most untouched. Beautiful as the shades of green might be, they presented a formidable barrier, bumpy and rough roads being the only connections to the world outside.

Building connections proved to be one of the achievements of Xu Shuteng. Not only did he deliver knowledge as a teacher, but he also formed connections between this small village and the world beyond the mountains.

He initiated a program called One-to-One Sponsorship, in which a sponsor from the outside world provides a monthly contribution, ranging from 120 yuan to 200 yuan, to a student in need. This would cover half of a student's monthly expenses. Many sponsors provided both emotional and financial support for the students, even after they graduated from school. Zhao Guangwei, a former Lushi High School student, currently studying at South China Agricultural University, still occasionally visits his sponsor in Guangzhou, besides having regular conversations on WeChat, a popular APP for instant messaging in China. "I talk to my sponsor about the problems I was having in my life. For example, I sought advice from my sponsor when I was not sure about my future."

The program didn't run without any obstacles. Xu Shuteng told us, "Sometimes sponsors had to halt financing due to issues on their part, but I wouldn't cut off the support. Instead, I would immediately look for another sponsor, assuring the students that all things will be taken care of."

The first night when Xu Shuteng received students' applications for the one-to-one sponsorship program, he was sleepless. After going over all of the applications, he was deeply troubled by the tough lives these families were leading. In the end, he selected over 80 applications in total. He was not sure whether he could find that many sponsors, so he asked the kids to write him notes describing which families were having the greatest difficulty. Some kids were very straightforward in their recommendations.

"Mr. Xu, please help Hong. His house is about to collapse. I saw a big crack in it a few days ago. I'll show you the crack if you need evidence."

Another child wrote, "Hey Mr. Xu, help Ming. I've never seen him wear sneakers. All he has are the shoes that his family made from cloth."

Xu Shuteng sought sponsors through every possible channel: his friends, the Weibo (similar to Twitter) account for Sun Yat-sen Graduate Students for Educational Aid, and also the WeChat account. It proved highly time-consuming for him to verify sponsors and assure sponsors that the money would be given to the students. "I had raised 970000 yuan for the students by the time I left Lushi High School," said Xu Shuteng.

"I also started the 'Glasses Project'." Xu Shuteng told us, "I broke my glasses in a basketball game and had to fix them. I learned that the average glasses cost about 1000 yuan, a price that most students couldn't afford, leaving them squinting instead."

He worked with several contacts for the provision of free glasses for students, thus many students got glasses for the first time in their lives.

Reaching out to these contacts and connections proved to be hard work. Thankfully, Xu Shuteng was not alone. Every year, around four graduates of Sun Yat-sen University arrive here. As volunteer teachers, they would interact with more than 300 students. When two terms are over, another four graduates will come to take the baton.

This year, the jobs are passed down to Xu Jintao, Niu Lulu, Wu Yating, and Liu Chaoyu, all of whom had only been here for two months when we interviewed them.

Most of the interviews were conducted at Lushi High School. As it was under reconstruction, the road in front of the school gate was a mire. The school was cleaner, with the school gate as a dividing line between the orderly campus and the dusty exterior.

As I walked past the teaching building, some of the students noticed us and straightened up, sneaking a peek and then turning away. They were too curious to stay focused. Trying to disturb the class as little as possible, I strode quickly past.

In the School History Museum, where accounts and images of distinguished students like Liu Yuexiu were hung upon the wall, we conducted a few interviews, and I saw some familiar faces up there, such as Li Rong and Zhao Yongshu, students I had interviewed two weeks earlier.

Pointing at the picture of Zhao Yongshu, the headmaster of Lushi High School told us, "It was so clear that Zhao Yongshu returned from the Youth Wing Program with more confidence, ambition and perseverance."

Zhao Yongshu was at first unwilling to take part in the Youth Wing Program. The headmaster decided to intervene. He and the teachers talked to his parents, letting them know that this was a great opportunity to broaden Zhao Yongshu's horizons, to help him go beyond the mountains. At last, Yongshu was convinced. As a result, he was motivated to adapt, think, and make public speeches replete with personal insights. When he came back, he was no longer the shy student who didn't believe in himself, but someone who knew he had potential.

Yongshu wasn't the only student who benefited from the volunteer teachers. A student called Liu Yang, after her grandfather passed away, was having a very hard time, with nightmares each night. Her teacher Xu Jintao discerned her weariness and asked her if she would like to talk about what was troubling her. Liu Yang's parents were seldom home because they worked in another county, just like many other parents of rural kids. Liu Yang was at her most distraught point when they broke their promise of coming home for her birthday. But thankfully, Xu Jintao was there to wish her a happy birthday.

This reminded me of another story about special occasions. On Sep. 10th, Chinese Teachers' Day, graduate teacher Liu Chaoyu was anticipating some postcards that teachers would usually receive from students on that day. However, as the day wore on, he didn't get any. Then came time for his class. "I went to the class in low spirits, but I was greeted with a 'Hi! Teacher (Liu)' that was louder than usual. Throughout the class, students were more active and smiling. I couldn't tell for sure, but I had a feeling that this was their gift for Teachers' Day. No postcards, yet there were heart-warming smiles," said Chaoyu.

There were many other examples showing the rapport between the volunteer teachers and students. Many local teachers said, "Maybe it's because they are younger and can understand kids better, or maybe the graduates feature a more flexible teaching style." Either way, many students told us they were able to bond with the volunteer teachers with remarkable rapidity. Luo Shunyi, a student at the school said, "I found my eye contact with my biology teacher Niu Lulu especially soothing. I want to be as gentle as Lulu." When Niu Lulu had to switch to another class, many of her students broke down in tears.

The same thing happened to Xu Jintao when he was teaching Chinese. After one month of teaching in 10th grade, he was reassigned to teach math in the 11th grade. During his last Chinese class, students read out loud an article called "Autumn Nostalgia". As the story progressed to where the mother passed away, "I was touched to see tears streaming down the faces of some students as they shared the feeling that they didn't want to lose someone—in their case, me."

Wu Yating considered that, besides smiles and tears, words also provided a powerful tool for students to express their feelings. So, she decided to improve their language ability by assigning them a weekly diary. Student Chen Yanyan reported, "Students are now more expressive in classes than before. I think the weekly diary made us more engaged in discussion. Now, when teachers ask questions, we raise our hands more often."

Yu Zhengqiang, the headmaster of Lushi High School commented, "Graduate teachers took so many steps to bring out the vitality and ambition of students." The Youth Wing Program was one of the most influential activities. Every year, students who achieve good performances or make the greatest progress will receive a trip to Guangzhou, where they will get a glimpse of modern higher education and lifestyles. They will visit Sun Yat-sen University, one of the top universities in Guangzhou, one of the four first-tier cities in the country.

A Lushi High School graduate He Yingzhe said, "Even though we had known something about urban life on TV, it was never a reality for me until I saw it with my own eyes, as I thought, that kind of thing could only be seen on TV. I met many students from other regions in the program and learned about the ways they learned. They seemed very knowledgeable, while our classmates at Lushi High School know little. I immediately realized that if I were to become as knowledgeable as they were, I would have to do well in the College Entrance Exam and get out of this small town."

During the sharing sessions, when the 2017 Youth Wing Program ended, Xu Shuteng said, "Everyone cried." All 14 students, including Zhao Guangwei, who is now a student studying at South China Agricultural University, were overwhelmed by feelings that they couldn't articulate.

Guangwei said during our interview, "The most significant impact the journey had on me is that I'm able to have this Zoom interview with you in Guangzhou. It made me determined to get out of the mountains and to study in Guangzhou." When they got back to Lushi High School, changes could be noticed in their attitudes, ambitions and actions. They set their sights on top universities, such as Sun Yat-sen University and grew more eager to learn in classes.

In addition to the students who were inspired by the program were the local teachers who accompanied the students. Xu Shuteng told us, "One teacher used to be resented by students for some reason. After the program, he changed his approach, both in teaching and in daily interaction. Now he has become popular among the kids."

This serves as a great example illustrating that educational aid extends beyond local students to teachers and the school.

The headmaster was especially proud of their progress. "The graduate teaching group fills a gap in our faculty. They are quick about getting into their teaching role and exploring new teaching practices. The past few years have witnessed evident breakthroughs after the arrival of the graduates. The number of students entering prestigious universities increases year by year."

Some students acknowledged the differences between volunteer teachers and local teachers. "They are younger," said student Chen Quan. "They know better about how we learn. We like their classes more because the atmosphere is more vibrant." While the local teachers have a master-to-apprentice relationship with the students, the graduate teachers are like brothers and sisters.

"We have regular sharing sessions for teaching methods," a local teacher Ji Yuansu said. "They bring new ideas and methods into our teaching." Many teachers agreed, lauding the graduate teachers' classes. The teaching method that the local teachers applied was to directly inform students of knowledge and information, while the graduate teachers tried to engage students in the process of discovery. Niu Lulu said, "When teaching negative numbers, I don't just tell them that there are numbers like $-1$, $-2$ and that $-30$ are smaller than 3. Instead, I'll draw a number axis first, showing them the sequence of numbers, so that they'll have a graphic understanding of the relationship between numbers."

In 2019, nine students from the school got admitted into first-tier universities, a record high in their history of 45 years. In 2020, a student attained a score of 636 in the College Entrance Exam, the first ever in the school to pass 600. This year, one of the students earned the highest score ever among liberal arts students in Fengqing County.

There's no way of telling precisely to what degree volunteer teachers contribute to the progress, but the headmaster, teachers and students would all agree that it is a change that they need.

The voluntary job brings no less benefit to the volunteers themselves from Sun Yat-sen University. Xu Jintao said, "While the job is only for a brief year, the impact it has on us is everlasting. I knew the conditions were not so good here, but I didn't know it was this bad. I was shocked to discover how well the students handle their life circumstances." He once met an orphan girl who lived with her grandfather because her father had passed away and her mother had abandoned her. "Her personality was outgoing and positive as if nothing bad had ever happened to her." Saying these words, Xu Jintao raised his eyebrows in admiration.

Wu Yating and Liu Chaoyu are also inspired by the students, so much so that they made a vow: "We'll do anything in our power to help them enter the bigger world." Wu Yating told us about one particularly hard-working student. After the National Holiday, Wu Yating noticed how dark the student's hands had become and knew he must've been collecting and peeling walnuts all holiday long since many families grew walnuts. "This student had told me that he wanted to get out of the mountains. I thought to myself, I must make sure that his hard work will pay off, for he's such a diligent kid, shouldering the responsibility of his family like that."

Niu Lulu decided that she would take part in more projects like this. "The affiliated hospitals of Sun Yat-sen University have some other similar programs to help people in remote provinces like Tibet and Xinjiang. Previously, I never paid attention to them. However, this volunteer experience has made me want to do more to help the disadvantaged. If I have the opportunity, I would like to use my medical skills to help more people," she said.

Hearing Niu Lulu's long-term plan, I came to have a much better understanding of poverty alleviation through education. The volunteer teachers came here and became inspiration for people, especially children in the mountains. One year later, the inspiration will give birth to bigger dreams that would spread beyond the mountains, as some students would set foot in other cities after their graduation. Years later, some of them may come back to the mountains with new dreams, making contributions to the community in various ways.

The chain reaction of dreams is a product of poverty alleviation through education, forming a link between volunteer teachers and students. These two groups would never have met otherwise. One life helps another, and then the circle of life passes it on. As I rode in the bus back to Sun Yat-sen University, I brought with me two suitcases, four tired limbs, and a brand-new appreciation for life. I used to think of life as an endless straight line going forward, but now I have realized that it is a circle, a spiralling one carrying all that we have received and all that we will give.

# A Journey of Discovery: The Changes in Poverty-Stricken Areas in Yunnan Province

## YU Yehui

I was touched, watching children in Hongtang Village practice playing cucurbit flute (or *hulusi* "葫芦丝" in Chinese) with their music teacher, who was providing instruction via an online meeting platform. As China's economy took off, Sun Yat-sen University (hereafter SYSU) has provided instruments, teachers, and technology to this mountainous area, contributing to an improvement in the quality of the villagers' lives and profound changes in their mindset. The sound of the cucurbit flute stirred my memories of learning to play this musical instrument. The song was familiar to me. But I was lucky to be taught in a classroom with a teacher standing right in front of us, face-to-face.

Watching the cucurbit flute class on the screen was just the prelude to our discovery of how the lives of people living in poverty-stricken areas have been improved since China made a lot of effort to alleviate poverty throughout the country.

Two weeks later, as students in the Creative Writing and Translation course, we set off with our teachers to Fengqing to generate a report on SYSU's work.

"The ride to Fengqing would be quite bumpy," said Wang Ke, the Deputy County Magistrate whom we interviewed three weeks earlier. Nevertheless, I was still looking forward to the trip, anticipating stories from the local people, the medical team, and the officials dispatched from SYSU.

Fengqing is a county tucked away in the mountainous area of Yunnan, a southwest province in China. Restricted by the lack of roads and a lack of human and technological resources, it had been identified as a poverty-stricken county. Since the 18th National Congress of the Communist Party of China in 2012, to realize a moderately prosperous society, China has placed priority on poverty elimination. As a result, SYSU has paired up with this beautiful county since 2016, dispatching its administrative staff and Party secretaries as on-post first Party Secretary in Hongtang Village and Deputy County Magistrate of Fengqing. Support from SYSU is in almost all aspects of life, from substantial assistance both in terms of the equipment used in education, industries, and medical services as well as personnel assistance, such as volunteer teachers who are the future postgraduates, professors, researchers, to doctors from the affiliated hospitals of SYSU. As a result, Hongtang Village has seen the poverty headcount ratio drop from 36% in 2014 to 1.18% in 2019, accomplishing the task of eliminating absolute poverty in December 2019.

Yunnan is a province in a mountainous area, so on the winding road to Fengqing, we experienced rugged scenery as well as the jolting of our bus, as if we were on a roller coaster. For us, the road was beautiful yet uncomfortable, but for locals, the extreme distance hinders communication as well as development.

Zhao Wei, an 11-year-old boy studying at the primary school in Hongtang Village, told us that it took him half an hour to reach the bank of a river to wait for the bus to his school. The school is called Dabaitian Nursery and Elementary School, or *Wanxiao* for short, a school that covers preschool to primary school education. Adjacent to *Wanxiao* stands the building where the Party Secretary and resident working team members work.

"The reason why Hongtang Village is struggling does not lie only in that it is situated in a remote area but also people's lack of insight and vision for development," said Secretary Lan Shude, the second Party Secretary dispatched from SYSU.

Since 2016, SYSU has dispatched three secretaries to Fengqing, the first being Guo Xingyong, followed by Lan Shude, and followed by Zhang Liangyou who is currently serving in Hongtang Village. Since the revenue in Hongtang mainly derives from tea leaves and walnuts, the dispatched secretaries, together with local officials, have been aiming to boost the local economy by creating new industries and businesses, so that villagers would be able to earn more through their effort.

As Guo's successors, Secretary Lan and Secretary Zhang are tasked with revitalizing the rural industries. According to Zhang, "Realizing rural vitalization begins with the local industries." While focusing on the main crops, walnut and tea leaves, which account for 60%~70% of people's income, they also explored new industries, such as raising the imperial chrysanthemum, to generate opportunities for locals to earn more.

Though Fengqing had been planting walnuts for decades, it was not until SYSU came to assist did this industry form a chain and begin to generate greater revenues. "Fengqing is a must-visit place if you want to investigate and survey the walnut production in Yunnan," said the current Deputy County Magistrate Zhang Zhe, a dispatched official from SYSU to Fengqing County. The rise of the walnut industry in Fengqing was made possible through the effort of a series of Party secretaries and the local government as well.

Wang Ke served as Deputy County Magistrate between 2019 and 2021. He managed to boost the sales of walnut products by introducing live streaming as a way of marketing. "Hearing that this is promoted by our Deputy County Magistrate, Dr. Wang Ke, people were eager to buy our products," said the Deputy Director of Rural Revitalization Administration, Yang Wei. "Wang was very happy on that day. He wore a traditional national costume and the sales were great," smiled Yang.

"The two Deputy Magistrates who served in our county are highly educated, and we benefited a great deal from their knowledge and understanding. I learned many great things from them." Talents prove to be the most critical help that SYSU has provided for Fengqing. Zhang Zhe believes that SYSU should exert its effort in medical care, technology, and education, which are the real strengths of the university.

Medical services, in particular, had been a big problem for Fengqing people.

When asked about the farthest place he had been to, elementary student Zhao Wei replied, "The farthest place I've been to is the People's Hospital of Fengqing County. Grandma was hospitalized, so father took me on his motorbike to visit her in Fengqing, and then we rode back home."

SYSU has shown its medical muscles, providing financial and personnel support to the People's Hospital of Fengqing County and to this county, which lacks advanced medical resources and experienced doctors. As Zhang Zhe pointed out, if SYSU could jointly run a hospital that bore the university's name in Fengqing, people would invest their time and money in the local hospital instead of turning to hospitals in Kunming, the provincial capital of Yunnan. Of course, with continuous help from SYSU, the People's Hospital of Fengqing County has seen a rapid improvement in its facilities and doctors' professional skills, since doctors were also getting opportunities to obtain further education at the university in Guangzhou, in addition to hand-on training in Fengqing when the SYSU doctors were there.

A local official in the village said, "Few of us have worked beyond the village, so we are unable to think in a far-sighted way. I am grateful that in these two years, with Lan as our Secretary, a plan was put in place for developing Hongtang. Lan created a long-term plan for industries and tourism, based on his investigation of the village and his consultations with experts back at SYSU. " It took Lan a week to investigate and finish this plan, which was included in a 10000-word report after discussions on WeChat.

But other than serving as Secretary, Lan also took a job teaching in *Wanxiao*, as the school was really in need of teachers, especially English teachers. He taught English in *Wanxiao*, which made the primary school the first to have English classes in Fengqing—a rare educational opportunity for children living in poor mountainous areas.

With the aid of equipment and financing from SYSU, and the opportunity that Secretary Lan had found, Zhao Wei's class can take online classes and learn to play a traditional Chinese musical instrument—the cucurbit flute. The projector and children's cucurbit flutes were all donated by faculty and staff from SYSU. The headmaster said that children are quite excited about playing a musical instrument. In the classroom, with their cucurbit flute teacher's face projected on a screen, children were all attentive in learning to play. We saw Zhao Wei's face blushing as he practiced.

As a teacher, Lan was special to the children here, and he got on well with them. "I can talk with him like talking to my parents," said Zhao Wei. The local Village Secretary noted, "He would play with the children so that they wouldn't disturb their parents when the Secretary and other local officials were visiting families in extreme poverty. "

Guo was popular among villagers too. He proved to be more than just a Party Secretary in the village but also a family member. Stories of his magic tricks had become part of the local lore. Guo got along so well with children that even three-year-olds knew him. "He can do magic with a ring and chains!" recalled Zhao

Wei, who currently studies in the fifth grade. That is the first impression that came to his mind. But as for grown-ups, they hold even more affection towards their Party Secretary. They recount that on the first day, Secretary Guo warmly greeted villagers, waving his hand to say "Hi". But they noticed that he had a different accent, which meant he was not local. Was he a fraud? Or was he nuts?

Ultimately, it was his devotion to this place that earned him their trust and love.

We heard a lot about Secretary Lan from Zhang Guofeng, the grandma of a household of five, whose husband has a disabled leg. We met her in the Imperial Chrysanthemum Garden, where she works, picking tea leaves to earn some extra money for the family.

With a strong accent but a confident voice, she reported that she was glad that she no longer needed to travel a long way looking for work before tea-leaves'picking time. "Thanks to the Imperial Chrysanthemums Garden, I don't need to go out of the village to look for jobs. I can help in this garden, which doesn't require much physical labor. I can make money close to home and can take care of my family at the same time." The Imperial Chrysanthemum Garden was a hotspot during the holiday, and Mrs. Zhang's work is to sell tickets.

As China made it a national policy to support poverty-stricken regions by helping those in extreme poverty, new local industries are given a lot of support. Besides the herbal industry, the imperial chrysanthemums recently planted in the Imperial Chrysanthemum Garden was one of such industries. It has created more jobs and improved income for the impoverished population.

"Since my time had been freed up, I could enjoy dancing with my friends." Mrs. Zhang's face was beaming. "Secretary Guo did so much for us!" As an example, when he learned that they enjoyed dancing, he bought them speakers with his own money. They were just dancing for fun at the beginning. Later, with the support of Guo, who made sure they had transportation, they went to another village for a dancing competition. Though the team members were too busy to dance at the moment, she was sure they would pick it up again soon.

"We were unwilling to part with Secretary Guo. It's unbearable," said Mrs. Zhang, who, together with the villagers, made a silk banner, a gift that was also presented to Secretary Lan as a going-away present. It was Secretary Lan who came up with the idea of planting chrysanthemums, turning the land into a tourist destination, thus contributing to the increase in the villagers' income. The growing of chrysanthemum has provided jobs for gardening, selling tickets, and chrysanthemum-picking and drying to produce chrysanthemum drinks. The Party secretaries had done a great deal to help them: inviting experts to teach them to plant chrysanthemums and to finance the streetlamps. When Zhang's uncle was very sick, Secretary Lan helped to take him to the People's Hospital of Fengqing County. "My uncle was moved to tears," she recalled.

"All our thanks go to SYSU," said Zhang. "With Party secretaries dispatched from SYSU, the village has installed streetlamps. Without the support from SYSU, the village would have been in total darkness at night. Were it not for SYSU, how could all these changes take place?"

Another example of promoting new industry in Fengqing is the planting of *polygonati rhizoma*, which has a great value in the Chinese herbal medicine market and grows in Chinese provinces like Yunnan, Sichuan, and Guizhou.

But Hongtang did not start planting *polygonati rhizoma* until 2016, when Li Maochang, a former migrant worker in Hangzhou, returned home to devote himself to this new industry that 174 poor households were involved in. As a man with experience in planting herbs, he serves as the leader in the local cooperative for *polygonati rhizoma*. With the joint effort of several departments in the Fengqing government and equipped with a processing workshop financed by SYSU, this cooperative had begun to reap revenues after five years of growing. The local Village Party Secretary affirmed that this industry was helping to maintain the workforce in Hongtang.

The current Secretary Zhang Liangyou said, "After I arrived, I discovered that if you visit villagers in their houses, many of them would talk about Secretary Guo and Lan. As long as you sat with them, they would tell you what those people from SYSU have done to help the village." Consequently, our group of four students would stay for a night in the village to talk with villagers and experience the life and food in Hongtang.

Walking in the village, we saw comic artwork on the walls of villagers' houses; this was the work of Xiaolin, a famous cartoonist and faculty at SYSU, whose art had become very popular in the country. Thanks to Zhang Liangyou, who contacted Xiaolin and invited him to paint, Hongtang now possesses these beautiful decorations.

As it grew darker, we set off for the local lodging. On the way, surrounded by deep pits and tall trees on both sides of the narrow lane, we wandered in the desolate mountain darkness before we saw the first street lamp labelled SYSU—exactly as Mrs. Zhang Guofeng had told us.

A little further, we arrived at the lodging. Entering the living room, we saw photos of foreign teachers from the School of International Studies (from SYSU). We were quite surprised to find familiar faces there.

"Wow, is this Stephen? They have come here before?"

"They came on July 13th this year," recalled the hostess, Chen Yingqin. "I remember quite well." This was a special day for Hongtang villagers, as foreign teachers came to visit the village, which made it a piece of local news in the surrounding villages. Villagers were all eager to share what had happened on that day.

"People were saying that our village had great progress, and now foreigners were visiting Hongtang. Even police cars were here! They came to prevent traffic jams and make sure the road was clear."

"It was a great honor for me to receive people from seven different countries because I've never met any foreigner in my 20 years of catering," said Chen. "All people in Fengqing who use WeChat knew we had foreign guests! They saw it in our WeChat Moments."

"I never thought their visit would make Hongtang the envy of the neighboring villages," said Lan in the online interview three weeks before. "I feel extremely proud of it, as we enabled villagers to experience a great change of spiritual life using all the resources, excellent teachers, and officials dispatched in work teams."

The chat with Chen moved from foreign guests to Secretary Guo, whom the villagers all admired. They were all talkative when his name was mentioned. As the first Party Secretary from SYSU to Hongtang, Guo led a team of people to another village in Yunnan, called "Iceland's Natural Village" to investigate and survey the organic tea and to promote Fengqing's tea. People not only remember what he has done but also his hobbies.

"Guo loves singing," said a villager. On the day he was about to leave after one year's work in the village, people saw him off, following the traditional custom of "Da Ge" (written as "打歌" in Chinese), singing and dancing as a way of bidding farewell.

"Both villagers and Secretary Guo's eyes were wet," recalled Chen Yingqin. Every Party Secretary is looked up to by the villagers. When Lan was leaving the village, they saw him off too though it was raining that day. "We wish the secretaries will stay forever, instead of coming and leaving," said the Chens, "and we still keep in touch on WeChat."

After five years of development, the responsibility to alleviate poverty and promote wellbeing has shifted to Zhang Zhe, the current Deputy County Magistrate of Fengqing, and Zhang Liangyou, the current First Party Secretary in Hongtang Village.

"I hope I may serve as a bond between Fengqing and SYSU in delivering what they need," said Zhang Zhe, who pointed out that the next critical step is to consolidate and expand the achievements in poverty alleviation to the next stage of rural revitalization.

"The first step of realizing rural vitalization is to develop the local industries," said Zhang Liangyou. Therefore, his mission in Hongtang village is to expedite the development of main products, like tea and walnuts.

China has made it a national policy to dispatch officials to work in the countryside and bring knowledge and resources into the battle against poverty. As a resalt, it has not only reduced poverty but also strengthened the ties between the Party secretaries and the people. As Party Secretary Guo Xingyong said, though the dispatched secretaries and deputy county magistrates only stay for a period, but "A short time fighting for poverty elimination in Hongtang leaves you with a lifelong affection for this place".

The attachment is mutual. "Welcome home" will always be the greeting delivered to Party secretaries from SYSU, said the Chens.

SYSU has been supporting Fengqing for five years. So far, it has dispatched three secretaries and two deputy magistrates to this county. As President Xi Jinping declared in 2021, China has achieved the goal of building a moderately prosperous society in all respects and succeeded in eliminating absolute poverty. Now, we are marching toward the second centenary goal of building China into a great modern socialist country, which means that "Shaking off poverty is not the finishing line, but the starting point of a new life and new endeavor".

# Two Mountains and Two Hands: Sun Yat-sen University's Medical Support for the People's Hospital of Fengqing County

## TAN Xiaoyan

"I would like to end my speech by expressing my gratitude for the assistance from the affiliated hospitals of Sun Yat-sen University. In the future, please continue holding our hands, and together, we make our way forward," Dr. Li Chunguang said in our interview, his sunburned face glowing with sincerity.

His words brought me to tears.

Dr. Li is the epitome of what the affiliated hospitals of Sun Yat-sen University have contributed to the cause of poverty eradication in Fengqing County, a poverty-stricken area, located in China's southwestern Province of Yunnan. It is Sun Yat-sen University, to which we belong, a comprehensive university in China located in southeastern Guangdong Province, that has dispatched medical support. In its poverty alleviation effort, Sun Yat-sen University has also offered educational, managerial and medical support. On October 24th, 2021, to explore how this university was engaged, what effort were extended, who was helped, and what impacts there have been, we set out to this county to interview the locals and those dispatched by Sun Yat-sen University who are still contributing to poverty alleviation in Fengqing.

Our team included one teacher and 12 students, 6 undergraduates and 6 postgraduates. The students were divided into 3 groups, each with 4 students, responsible for interviewing the locals concerning education, medical service, and management support. My group was to interview the local medical staff.

Dr. Li was the Deputy Director of the Department of Ophthalmology at the People's Hospital of Fengqing County, Yunnan Province. In 2018, he went to an affiliated hospital of Sun Yat-sen University for further study.

"At that time, I was very impressed. The hospital was so prominent in ophthalmology, treating patients in many areas not only within China but also from Japan, South Korea, and across the whole of Southeast Asia. I was inspired and determined to study hard to be a better ophthalmologist." Dr. Li smiled, with a touch of shyness, gazing at us across the table. His determined eyes revealed flashes of an ambitious young man. After three months of studies under a cohort of experts, he came back bearing new expertise and performed multiple surgeries. He reported,"I am the only one who can conduct such an operation in Lincang City. Several patients from other areas even make light of long travel only to come here for treatment!" His eyes were sparkling.

Before meeting Dr. Li, we had interviewed the medical staff involved in poverty alleviation from the affiliated hospitals at Sun Yat-sun University. Among them, Dr. Zhang Xuanye (chief internist at Sun Yat-sen University Cancer Center) told us, "The affiliated hospitals at Sun Sat-sun University began sending medical staff to Fengqing County in 2019, to provide comprehensive medical support. Our entire team, including the three doctors here today, are part of the third batch of dispatched medical teams." She smiled and exchanged a look with her colleagues, Dr. Zheng Tingting (physiotherapist of the Department of Rehabilitation Medicine at the Sixth Affiliated Hospital of Sun Yat-sen University) and Dr. Zhang Jun (paediatrician at the First Affiliated Hospital of Sun Yat-sen University). They nodded and smiled.

Dr. Zhang continued, "Our team is composed of 14 medical staff members from 9 affiliated hospitals. Ours is the largest medical support team to date. We assisted the People's Hospital of Fengqing County in building an Oncology Department and a Women's Rehabilitation Department. In addition, more than 30 new medical technologies have been introduced to this hospital, benefiting the local patients and a medical staff numbering more than 800."

"Wow, more than 800! Such a large scale!" My team member Jingjing murmured. She had a broad smile, with black-rimmed glasses covering almost half her face. Another two partners, Xinqi, a relatively introverted girl with long, brown bangs hiding part of her eyes, and Yuanheng, a bespectacled boy with a handsome appearance, were whispering, nodding, and then looking back at Dr. Zhang.

"Our goal is to bring cutting-edge medical technologies to Fengqing County and to build a professional medical team that can handle major ailments so that the local patients don't need to travel to larger cities for treatment." Through her clear, detailed introduction, her confidence captured my attention. I pictured their devotion to the locals back then, and I hoped to see the fruit they harvested there in person.

Our first stop was Lushi Town (a small town in Fengqing County). We travelled from Guangzhou to Dali Autonomous Prefecture to Fengqing County, and finally, to Lushi Town, following the footsteps of the medical group, who had arrived here to conduct free diagnoses. Travelling from Fengqing County to Lushi Town, we were told this journey would cross two mountain ranges. As we looked out of the windows, mountain upon mountain passed before us while the bumpy road zigzagged through dense forests and heavy mists. The twists and turns and ups and downs threw me into projectile vomiting. After five disgorging episodes, I became increasingly appreciative of the medical group, who had to brave this bumpy road whenever local patients need them. This road, the only way to Lushi Town, is by no means safe and often puts passengers at risk. Sometimes, confronted by a sudden twist, our bus rubbed shoulders with a life-and-death moment. The curve, nearly 360 degrees, overlooked a drop-off of thousands of meters, absent guardrails or other protection when other trucks abruptly bore down. In those instances, I forgot the five times throwing up and simply prayed we could survive. At that time, I couldn't help imagining what the medical groups had gone through.

After three hours, we finally arrived at Lushi Town. Most habitations are dispersed among sporadic low valleys, several hundred meters lower than the roadway. As we rode on, we saw a few residents trudging, bearing large wicker baskets filled with corn or walnuts on their heads, their emaciated bodies straining under the heavy loads, their burdened spines bent.

This reminded me of what Dr. Zheng Tingting had told us. "Many of the local women suffer from backaches and postpartum conditions. The demand for rehabilitation is considerable. However, no rehabilitation-related department is in existence." Dr. Zheng thus planned to establish a rehabilitation department.

"I made a proposal, and then one doctor and three therapists from the Rehabilitation Medicine Department at Sun Yat-sen University were sent to the People's Hospital in Fengqing County. Together, we conducted women's rehabilitation clinical training sessions, teaching the local doctors rehabilitation treatment skills. Our effort paid off. The first Women's Rehabilitation Center was established in this hospital, which was equipped with advanced technologies." A smile lit up her face, and her clear eyes twinkled in her white-rimmed glasses.

Such a smile was also seen on Dr. Zhang Xuanye's face. The young and energetic doctor had served as the Director of the Department of Oncology in the People's Hospital of Fengqing County, and she was also the dispatched leader of the third medical team there.

"I still remember a special patient, Lu Guangdian, 70 years old. He had been diagnosed with advanced lung squamous cell cancer in the local hospital half a year ago. But he chose to go home without any treatment. In April, he came to the hospital again because the symptoms had worsened, and he couldn't bear the pain." Dr. Zhang's brows were knitted, her fair face stern.

"He then received my treatment plan—two courses of combined chemotherapy in the Department of Oncology. After that, his symptoms diminished and the tumor shrank. Henceforth, the patient finally began to trust the doctors, and he realized the anti-tumor treatment was not to end his life but to save him. His son told me, 'In the past, my dad firmly opposed chemotherapy. Every time, to make him go to the hospital, we had to 'coax' him. Now he feels much more comfortable, and he even comes on his own initiative.'" Dr. Zhang laughed, the stern expression replaced by a broad grin.

This echoes what Yang Chunlong, the director of the Department of Oncology at the People's Hospital of Fengqing County, had reported. "At first, few patients came to our hospital for treatment. That had changed since Dr. Zhang Xuanye came here. She brought a great deal of expertise, in optimizing our treatments. Thanks to her guidance, visits went from 20 to 80, or even to 100 per day. Finally, our Department of Oncology has transformed from being backwards to relatively advanced."

Dr. Zhang's help constitutes more than that. "Working in this county hospital, I find it more important to treat minds than bodies," Dr. Zhang paused. Jingjing and I exchanged a look. Yuanheng slightly opened his mouth but said nothing. Xinqi stopped typing and raised her head, looking at Dr. Zhang.

"In my communication with local patients and their families, I find most still have a deep-seated misunderstanding about tumors and cancer, 'If we have cancer, we can only go home to die'; 'chemotherapy will only make us die faster'; 'We just want to get a diagnosis and we will give up treatment if it is cancer'. That prompts me to reflect that it is most essential to correct such misconceptions."

To correct the locals' misconception that cancer equals death and convince them cancer is treatable, Dr. Zhang delivers lectures on the local TV channel. She shares with the locals that most early-stage tumors can be eliminated, and even advanced tumors can be responsive to treatment.

"The hospital can provide a great deal of treatment that can relieve patients' pain and prolong life. A tumor is not that terrible. What is terrible are misconceptions about tumors, blind fear of treatment and missing the best time to receive treatment."

We later watched the broadcast and observed her clear, fluent and logical diction. "Now, as misconceptions are gradually reducing, locals are more and more willing to receive cancer-related treatments."

Such misconceptions are not limited to cancer. Liu Liangping, a physician from Zhongshan Ophthalmic Center, Sun Yat-sen University, told us, "I have found that cataracts are quite common in this area. It is conducive to blindness and can even be fatal without timely treatment. However, I have heard many locals say, 'Having cataracts is not a big deal. It is unnecessary to receive any surgery unless cataracts are on the brink of causing blindness.' Hence, most local people wait until a cataract causes total vision loss. This amounts to a very bad misconception. Patients must receive early treatment, instead of letting the condition deteriorate."

On the day he attended our interview, we happened to witness his reception of a *jinqi*, a silk banner, delivered by one of his patients. After undergoing surgery conducted by Dr. Liu, the patient not only fully recovered from her cataract but also considerably improved her eyesight. She no longer had to wear spectacles, thus ending her 40-year myopia.

"Had it not been for the help from the affiliated hospital of Sun Yat-sen University, I would be blind now." With a glance at Dr. Liu, eyes sparkling, which added to her beauty, she reported, "I am so delighted to be back to normal life and work."

"After having heard her story, other cataract-suffering locals also flood into the hospital for surgery, even including the parents of the General Director of the Hospital," Dr. Liu added. He grinned, accompanied by a deep chuckle.

His child-like grin was contagious, reminiscent of the lovely, smiling baby's picture shown by Doctor Ji Yuanhong from the People's Hospital of Fengqing County. She told us how Dr. Zhang Jun had saved this premature baby. This reminded me of the day when we interviewed Dr. Zhang Jun. Doctor Zhang Jun was deployed to the People's Hospital of Fengqing County from June to August 2021. In a very gentle voice, Doctor Ji Yuanhong brought us to the life-and-death scene.

"I still remember that night. A less-than-800-gram infant was born, no more than 25 weeks in her mother's womb. Within two hours after birth, the baby was barely breathing and suffered from pulmonary bleeding. Other doctors and I saved the baby from pulmonary bleeding in time. Luckily, the baby survived and was discharged after three weeks, without any sequelae."

In her journal, Doctor Ji Yuanhong recorded the details, "It was 1:00 p.m. and we were still fighting. Everyone was sweating. The world was in dead silence, apart from the sound of the ward monitor ticking. I still have a clear memory of the day when the infant's parents held my hands tightly, sobbing, 'You have given our child a second life; you have given our family hope, and you have brought hope to the whole of Fengqing County. Thank you! Thank you! Thank you!' That always reminds me that my job is not just a job, but the hope of thousands of families."

A warm current flowed through my whole body. I couldn't help imagining such a moving scene, picturing that day, and that scene. Had it not been for Dr. Zhang's help, the infant may have died, and the parents would have lost a beloved child. In the video sent by the parents to Dr. Zhang, the parents were holding their adorable baby, smiling, happiness written all over their faces. My mind was brought back to what Doctor Ji Yuanhong had added, "During the critical period, Dr. Zhang was with the infant every day, carefully observing every sign, no matter how small. Every time there was a change in the baby's condition, she would communicate with us and inform the infant's family. After the infant got better and was discharged, Dr. Zhang still asked often the parents about the baby's condition via WeChat. The parents were extremely grateful and delivered her a silk banner."

I looked at the baby, the bright eyes, the reddish face, the round legs and the tight fists. It drove home the importance of Dr. Zhang's care. Through this infant,

I see also a doctor's caring, professional skills, and work ethic.

And she is not alone.

Behind her are many more professional, respectable medical staff members from the affiliated hospitals of Sun Yat-sen University. As Dr. Wang Shimei, a stomatology doctor at the People's Hospital of Fengqing County, put it as follows: "Those doctors from the affiliated hospitals of Sun Yat-sen University are extremely impressive. Our going to further study for half a year can't be compared to their one-month teaching. Besides skills, we also learned an outstanding tradition in daily work, a noble spirit and work ethic, as well as a rigorous and pragmatic work style. I still remember, they always said, 'Do not take habits as standards, but to take standards as habits.'"

That reminds me of what Li Hai, the President of the People's Hospital of Fengqing County, told us, "Dr. Zhou Jun has inevitably strove to provide effective, affordable medicine and meticulous care. Once, when Dr. Zhou Jun was about to eat, one of his patients had an emergency. He immediately left to observe the patient, and it was 9:00 p.m. when he finally had time to have a bite. Being too busy with work, he often missed meals. Once, he had attended a severely ill patient back and forth—before dinner, after dinner and before getting on the plane. It was not until he was sure that the patient's situation had stabilized that he finally boarded the plane."

I couldn't help but look around, finding my group members were nodding their heads, all in rapt attention to his speech. Speaking slowly, Li Hai lowered his voice and continued.

"Similarly, Dean Liu from an affiliated hospital of Sun Yat-sen University provided patients with a lot of humanistic care. He did ward rounds each day. If young doctors didn't carry it out properly, he would immediately point it out and ask them to think from the patient's position, saying, for example, 'What if they were your parents?' Currently, our hospital's doctors pay more attention to humanistic care. Those doctors set good examples for us. Thus, we are moving forward to become a 'Mini-Hospital of Sun Yat-sen University'." He smiled as he spoke, and so did we.

"With continuous endeavors, the current treatment level of our hospital has been greatly improved: 20 new departments and more than 50 new projects have been set up, and the result of these projects have filled in the gaps of our medical service."

This reminded me of the Women's Rehabilitation Center initiated by Dr. Zheng Tingting, who said proudly, "The People's Hospital of Fengqing County has now upgraded to a tertiary hospital."

After they had participated in the neonatal resuscitation skill training, such confidence and pride were also written on the faces of other medical staff from the People's Hospital of Fengqing County. The training was organized by Dr. Zhang Jun, who told us, "I observed that the hospital is relatively weak in neonatal resuscitation skills, and the neonatal asphyxia rate here is high." Therefore, she and Jiang Xiaoyun (a pediatrician from an affiliated hospital of Sun Yat-sen University) as well as other doctors conducted neonatal resuscitation skills training in this hospital. "It just took half a day to learn neonatal recovery skills, but it means saving a life in that first critical 10 minutes. After the training, all participants passed the test. They reported proudly, 'Now we can save more babies with the newly-learned skills!'"

This hospital has become a typical model. Li Hai said, "Now our medical staff are more proactive in attaining new skills. The whole hospital has a more potent learning atmosphere."

And it is far more than that.

"Even doctors from other county-level hospitals attend the lectures. In addition, patients from other distant places also come to our hospital to receive treatment." The Director of the Department of Oncology Yang Chunlong added.

All of these achievements are remarkable and unimaginable without help from the affiliated hospitals of Sun Yat-sen University. Behind this bountiful harvest is China's poverty-eradication policy, with the unremitting effort of over 400 personnel. The support work in the People's Hospital of Fengqing County is only the tip of the iceberg. Other places, be it in Yunnan Province or around the whole country, are all composing their spectacular chapters in China's poverty-reduction epic.

Our story will end here, but their stories continue. Those who have come back persist in giving support to the locals, either through WeChat or MDT (multidisciplinary diagnosis and treatment, participated in by local doctors and doctors from the affiliated hospitals of Sun Yat-sen University) or by other means. Meanwhile, there are continuous newcomers and others not mentioned here. Two mountain ranges can't separate bonded hearts, and two hands will always clasp each other tightly. Going forward together, Sun Yat-sen University has been holding and will continue to hold the hands of Fengqing people.

# 中山大学历年派驻凤庆人员名单

# 一线挂职干部名录
# Cardres Dispatched by Sun Yat-sen University

挂职云南省凤庆县副县长：

Deputy County Magistrates, Fengqing County dispatched by Sun Yat-sen University:

  2013—2015 年：郑　哲　Zheng Zhe
  2015—2016 年：朱志辉　Zhu Zhihui
  2016—2017 年：曹　新　Cao Xin
  2017—2019 年：余立人　Yu Liren
  2019—2021 年：王　克　Wang Ke
  2021—2023 年：张　哲　Zhang Zhe

驻云南省凤庆县落星村第一书记：

The First Party Secretaries dispatched by Sun Yat-sen University to Luoxing Village:

  2015—2017 年：麦伟立　Mai Weili
  2017—2018 年：郭兴勇　Guo Xingyong

驻云南省凤庆县红塘村第一书记：

The First Party Secretaries dispatched by Sun Yat-sen University to Hongtang Village:

  2018—2019 年：郭兴勇　Guo Xingyong
  2019—2021 年：蓝澍德　Lan Shude
  2021—2023 年：张良友　Zhang Liangyou

## "组团式"派驻凤庆县医务人员名录
## Doctors Dispatched by Sun Yat-sen University to Fengqing County

2019 年：
- 李永浩　Li Yonghao
- 邢　蔚　Xing Wei
- 蔡华雄　Cai Huaxiong
- 廖维立　Liao Weili
- 钟　娟　Zhong Juan
- 曹务腾　Cao Wuteng

2020 年：
- 张涤华　Zhang Dihua
- 罗年桑　Luo Niansang
- 耿登峰　Geng Dengfeng
- 林永清　Lin Yongqing
- 赖　菁　Lai Jing
- 孔亚楠　Kong Ya'nan
- 熊　斐　Xiong Fei
- 李明哲　Li Mingzhe

2021 年：
- 巴宏军　Ba Hongjun
- 张　军　Zhang Jun
- 曾　钢　Zeng Gang
- 湛海伦　Zhan Hailun
- 刘良平　Liu Liangping
- 张玄烨　Zhang Xuanye
- 李志鹏　Li Zhipeng
- 陈建宇　Chen Jianyu
- 胡晓文　Hu Xiaowen

曾映娟　Zeng Yingjuan
孙　莹　Sun Ying
郑停停　Zheng Tingting
黄张森　Huang Zhangsen
周　俊　Zhou Jun
马　飞　Ma Fei

2022年：
柯志勇　Ke Zhiyong
张　帆　Zhang Fan
吴杰英　Wu Jieying
余曦灵　Yu Xiling
任　超　Ren Chao
蔡伟鑫　Cai Weixin
范　翔　Fan Xiang
尤龙飞　You Longfei
李　娴　Li Xian
叶思康　Ye Sikang

## 凤庆历届支教团成员
## Volunteer Teachers Dispatched by Sun Yat-sen University to Fengqing

2014 年：
    刘友武　Liu Youwu
    扬　子　Yang Zi
    宋嘉颖　Song Jiaying

2015 年：
    蒋丽怡　Jiang Liyi
    杨彦鹏　Yang Yanpeng
    冯利影　Feng Liying

2016 年：
    徐述腾　Xu Shuteng
    陶　慧　Tao Hui
    陈　曦　Chen Xi

2017 年：
    陈佳敏　Chen Jiamin
    方　媛　Fang Yuan
    方仕杰　Fang Shijie

2018 年：
    钟　滔　Zhong Tao
    谢　杭　Xie Hang
    杨文锦　Yang Wenjin
    孙雨婷　Sun Yuting

2019 年：
    刘玲琳　Liu Linglin

叶惠珠　Ye Huizhu
李广涵　Li Guanghan
胡玉立　Hu Yuli

2020 年：
黄晓波　Huang Xiaobo
曾小晖　Zeng Xiaohui
梁伟诺　Liang Weinuo
冯思嘉　Feng Sijia

2021 年：
许锦涛　Xu Jintao
牛璐璐　Niu Lulu
吴雅婷　Wu Yating
刘超宇　Liu Chaoyu

2022 年：
卢彦询　Lu Yanxun
段亚娟　Duan Yajuan
刘云翔　Liu Yunxiang
刘淏天　Liu Haotian
蒋　彬　Jiang Bin
姜清越　Jiang Qingyue
李心琪　Li Xinqi
孔维祥　Kong Weixiang

# 潮州报道篇

　　这部分的三篇报道是潮州班学生根据在潮州期间的调研经历所写的报道,不仅包括调研内容,而且包括在调研过程中的所闻、所见、所思、所想。

## 重品茶香，重识潮州

### 丁可欣

广州南站 A14 检票口前，即将上车的旅客已排起了长龙。长龙边上，一群大学生提着大包小包，将一位戴眼镜的女老师团团围住。学生们有的东张西望，脸上是抑制不住的期待与喜悦；有的则认真注视着正在说话的老师，时不时地点头。

"同学们，从现在起，大家要认真观察和记录身边发生的每一件事……"女老师的声音温和又不乏果断，吸引了其他旅客的注意。检票口长龙中一位阿姨的目光在这群大学生身上游走，而后锁定了我：

"同学，你们这是参加什么活动？"

"我们是中山大学的学生，要去调研潮州文化。"

"噢，听起来挺有意思的。"阿姨和蔼地朝我笑笑。"看到你们一群年轻人，真好呀！"

我们这群年轻人来自中山大学国际翻译学院，调研潮州文化、积累写作素材是我们"创意写作与翻译"课程的一部分。我们有三个小组，分别调研茶文化、食文化、潮剧和潮绣；每个小组有四位成员，分别负责撰写英文故事、中文故事、小组报道和视频的中英文字幕。与我们同行的还有负责摄影与视频制作的魏东华老师和两位学生助手、课程助理符韵老师、来自潮汕地区的谢桂霞老师，被我们围住的是课程的主讲老师——戴凡教授。

赶了一天路。晚上，我们到了此行的第一站——韩山师范学院（下文简称"韩师"）。韩师地理科学与旅游学院开设了"创意旅游"课程，参与课程的学生近期对潮州文化做了一些调研，他们将为我们介绍他们了解到的潮州文化。

多媒体教室被灯光照得犹如白昼，两校师生们被几张大桌切割成几组。我和茶文化小组的其他成员——王茜、志高和一诺——与韩师负责介绍茶文化的三位小伙子同坐一桌。小伙子们都目光低垂，偶尔摆弄着桌上的纸笔。

"这是我们院三个害羞的男孩子。"旅游学院的老师打趣道。

问答环节时,同组的志高站了起来,挠挠头,问道:"潮汕地区的茶为什么叫工夫茶?"

那三个男孩子之一拿过话筒,说道:"因为潮汕工夫茶从泡茶到饮茶,每个环节都进行得非常缓慢,非常花工夫。"

在发展日新月异的今天,这样花工夫的活动还能在潮汕地区绵延不绝,足见潮汕人生活节奏之慢。

小组展示活动长达两个多小时,同学们介绍了潮州的茶文化、美食、建筑、景点等,其中大部分我早已熟知。我有些兴味索然,目光扫过身边聚精会神的众人,随后停留在谢老师脸上,她眼角弯弯、满面笑意地看着台上讲解潮州文化的同学。小组汇报结束后,我们离开韩师,前往位于步行街的客栈。我和一诺、志高走在步行街上,看着街上悠然漫步的行人、街边凉茶铺里喝着工夫茶的热热闹闹的一桌子人,不禁惬意地笑笑,心里感慨着:"不错,回家啦。"

好吧,必须坦白,其实我是潮汕土著。一般来说,潮汕地区包括汕头、潮州、揭阳三市,我在汕头城区长大。

"走吧,我们去吃夜宵!"志高提议,我和一诺点头如捣蒜。行至一家糖水铺,招牌上有醒目的"鸭母捻"三个字。

"鸭母捻,就是刚刚韩师同学介绍的潮汕美食。"一诺说道,"可欣,你觉得好吃吗?我想试一下。"

"我没吃过……"我汗颜,"试试吧。"

我不由得想起在小学旁做生意的手推车,上面总有"鸭母捻一碗5块钱"的牌子。我一直因为鸭母捻貌若汤勺的古怪形状而对它敬而远之,但想到韩师同学的介绍,鸭母捻吃起来其实跟汤圆差不多,我突然很想尝试。

"不错,好吃。"我们三人点了鸭母捻、土豆粿、菜头丸等潮汕小吃,吃得津津有味。

"我一直觉得,食物要分着吃才好吃。"志高感慨道。

"的确。"我和一诺点头。

第二天上午,我们参观了非物质文化遗产展览馆百师园和陶瓷博物馆。大家对陶瓷博物馆里各式样的陶瓷摆件赞不绝口。我和摄影师魏东华老师站在一个圆形的陶瓷盘摆件前,专注地看着盘子上精致的花纹。

"这里的陶瓷称得上是艺术品啦。"魏老师操着一口流利的广式普通话。

"其实我家里就摆着一件这样的盘子。"我突然记起来,有一件与它相差无几的艺术品,已在我家饭厅的玻璃橱柜里悄无声息地摆了许多年。

午饭后在街上散步。一路上都是低矮的民房和高大的绿树,偶尔有人用扫帚打扫房前的空地,爽快利落的摩擦声伴随着鸟儿叽啾,拨动着我的心弦。空气中是舒适的阳光的味道,有时候飘来几缕香火味,让我想起儿时在乡下度过的悠长暑假。

我和王茜站在一栋布满藤蔓的老旧居民楼前,阳光下的藤蔓青翠欲滴,像极了宫崎骏的动画电影中的场景。"我觉得这里适合定居。"王茜举起手机,拍照。我无声地笑了——这于我而言是常态的生活场景,却引得我的同学老师们拍照纪念。

时间回到一个月前,戴凡老师公布此行的目的地是潮州。听闻此消息,我心里是难以抑制的失落。我原本期待着可以去课程的另一个目的地——云南省凤庆县,了解全然陌生的文化。我不抱期待地踏上了这趟旅程,但此刻我看到了此行的新鲜之处——非潮汕人或许能比我注意到更多家乡的细节。

晚上,我们对韩师的几位潮汕籍的学生进行了访谈(见图1)。访谈地点在一座安静古朴的四合院里——严格来说,这种建筑在潮汕地区被称为"四点金"①。低矮的屋脊上是大片紫黑色的夜空。这里的路灯照明不似大城市那样强烈,因此,星月显得格外明亮。几位温柔的潮汕女孩子将她们与潮汕工夫茶的故事娓娓道来:

"我的家里人会要求我学会沏茶,虽然我现在的沏茶功夫还不到家。"

"只要有客人来,我们就一定会把茶壶打开,沏茶。从早上7点一直到晚上10点,只要客人还没走,我们的茶壶就不会熄火。"

"潮汕人饭后肯定会喝上一杯茶,如果不喝茶,生活就少了点什么。"

…………

她们所讲述的生活片段正好也在我的生活里日日上演。坐在面前的这些潮汕女孩子虽与我素昧平生,却因这些文化符号而与我有着大同小异的生活点滴。文化,这个笼统又抽象的词,突然间有了一些可以捉摸的形状。文化或许是一些共同的生活习惯、相似的生活记忆,将一群互不相识的人划归为一个群体。

"你们喝茶前真的会把21道泡茶工序都过一遍吗?"志高问。

---

① "四点金"是潮汕风俗的独特建筑,因其四角上各有一间其形如"金"字的房间压角而得名。

"怎么可能!"我坐在人群中偷偷地笑了。我突然意识到,这些我习以为常的文化符号,对于非潮汕人而言是全然陌生的。在我的大学宿舍里,新疆室友喜欢吃馕,东北室友喜欢囤粮,不同地域的人都有着自己熟悉的独特文化符号,而这些在外人看来非常新奇。

图1　课程师生与韩山师范学院外国语学院的潮汕籍学生在柏荫精舍交流茶文化

眼前的潮汕女孩子们,谈起家乡时眼角眉梢里是藏不住的笑意。我很想知道,平时我向身边的人谈起家乡时是否也有一样的笑容。

访谈结束后,韩师的柯敏老师向我们展示如何制作手拉壶,也就是潮汕地区泡茶用的茶壶。他从身边的桶里揪出一团泥巴,往高速旋转的木质托盘上猛地一拍,双手像抱着碗一样调整着泥巴。谈笑间,一个手拉壶便大致成形了。戴凡老师抱着手站在边上,乐呵呵地吆喝:"哪位同学想来尝试一下?茶文化组的同学先来试试吧。"

我暗自摇摇头,下意识将自己那双笨拙的手掩于身后,把自己藏在众人中。一诺从人群中探出头来:"我想试试。"

她学着柯敏老师的动作,将泥团干净利落地往托盘上一砸,双手触摸着泥巴,一个像模像样的手拉壶在她手里逐渐成形。众人惊呼:"可以呀,一诺!"

"一诺很有天分。"柯敏老师也忍不住称赞。

我默默佩服着一诺的天分和勇气,谁知下一秒,一诺手一歪,原本像模像样的手拉壶瞬间垮掉。众人爆笑,一诺也笑着摇摇头。直到后来人群散开,一诺仍坐在托盘前专心致志地摆弄着泥巴。

第三天,大巴车将我们送到了当地著名的茶树种植区——凤凰镇叫水坑村。一排多层小楼傍山而建,一楼是茶铺和会客厅,摆着好几个装茶叶的大桶、一张长长的茶几、几张塑料椅。懂茶的游客会在一楼品茶,无须茶商推销,自会被茶香征服而解囊。这天刚好遭遇"断崖式"降温,萧萧寒风仿佛能扎入骨髓,我们一行人裹紧单薄的外衣,紧跟着韩师的柯老师,他像一名经验丰富的领队一样带着我们往山里走。踏上山路前,我们经过一个开放式凉棚,只见两位村民坐在凉棚下的石桌前,抖抖簌簌地沏着茶,抖抖簌簌地邀我们喝茶,再抖抖簌簌地洗茶杯。大冷天里也要在外沏茶喝,喝茶这项活动在潮汕人心中的地位可见一斑。

说是已开发的山区,其实大部分路都没有铺台阶。众人小心翼翼地在石头中找落脚点,倒也别有一番风趣。山上没有指示标,全靠领队的方向感和记忆来寻找道路。走近茶田,每一棵茶树前都立着一根木杆,上端贴着黄色符纸样的纸片。难道潮汕地区迷信到这种程度,连茶树上都要贴驱邪的符纸吗?后来才知道,这些黄色纸片其实是涂了诱导剂的粘虫板,可以保护茶树免遭飞蛾啃咬。刚下过雨,崎岖的山路湿滑难行,我们顺着一片茶田边下山,在队伍前方探路的学铭同学回头惊呼:

"我的天呐!我们好像走到了别人家的屋顶上!"

"现在情况就是,我们可能只能从他们家的屋顶下山。得让人家上屋顶开门。"他补充道。

众人爆笑。谁能料想到爬山活动还能发生如此戏剧性的一幕。戴凡老师也兴奋极了,回头对我叮嘱再三:"这可能是你们 report 的 highlight 部分!要记录下来!"

下午,我们前去参观涌泉古岩茶庄。这是一处主打绿色健康理念的茶庄,其有机茶园"涌泉古岩"种植面积达 200 亩。众人围着茶庄老板黄寰,听他讲解茶园建筑设计的理念。这时,我瞌睡虫上身,索性坐在人群外的路边上,志高和王茜与黄寰先生交谈的声音逐渐离我远去。即将梦见周公之时,一个声音将我唤醒。我抬头,是一位农民打扮、干瘦黝黑的老奶奶。她指了指几步开外的小木屋,问我是否要去她家休息。我摇头婉拒,开始用潮汕话与她闲聊：

"姨，你住在茶庄里吗？"

她点点头："对啊，我平时在这里做田①。"

"那你平时每天都做些什么？"

"那可多了。大清早就要起来做饭，然后上山做田，一直到下午四五点，然后回家做饭，忙到晚上总是腰酸背痛的……"

后来，茶庄老板带我们到园内的制茶厂，向我们展示如何摇青（摇茶叶）、烘茶。我游离在人群之外，看到王茜在和符韵老师交流写作的思路。参观结束后，一行人零零散散地走出茶庄。

刚刚遇到的那位茶农老奶奶忽然叫住了我："到我那里喝杯茶吧。"她热情地招揽着，说话的乡音让我想起了我奶奶。

我怔住，连忙摆手拒绝，说我们赶时间，就不麻烦啦。

"我看你们也太辛苦了，连口茶都没得喝。"她叹气。

我们一整天都辗转于各座茶山之间。晚上，我们前往潮州城南中英文学校对潮剧从业者进行访谈。潮剧是潮汕地区特有的戏曲，也是广东四大剧种②之一。第一位接受访谈的是李英群老先生，一位已至耄耋之年的潮剧作家。老先生说话非常实在：

"……潮剧曾经辉煌过，但是现在受到外来思潮的冲击。年轻人不喜欢潮剧，我也很无奈。现在的年轻人学习、恋爱、赚钱都追求快，看一场潮剧要花太多时间，而且欣赏潮剧又需要门槛。但我对潮剧还是有信心的，因为潮剧跟工夫茶一样，已经刻在潮汕人骨子里了……"

潮剧正陷于低谷。喜欢潮剧的人在逐渐老去，而年青一代对唱戏和听戏都不感兴趣。老先生一番话说得我非常惭愧，因为我就是不喜欢潮剧的年轻人之一。从小接受普通话教育的我根本听不懂潮剧，而潮剧哀哀戚戚的唱腔和喧闹的大锣鼓声让我觉得吵闹。在我看来，在日新月异的现代文明前，潮剧和其他地方传统戏曲的没落是无法避免的。我急哄哄地追逐着影视剧的热点，理所应当地将潮剧抛诸脑后。潮剧于我而言，只是一段吵闹的背景音乐、一个逐渐离我远去的文化符号而已。

与我年纪相仿的青年演员刘樱妮在接受访谈时红了眼眶："我觉得最苦的时候是，别人都问我，潮剧已经没有人听了，你为什么还要唱呢？"国家

---

① 潮汕话，表示"耕田"的意思，这里指在茶山上劳作。
② 广东四大剧种分别是粤剧、潮剧、汉剧和雷剧。

一级潮剧编剧陈韩星则在呼吁守旧创新,说:"现在潮剧在尝试外请导演,越搞越不像话!"普宁市潮剧团艺术总监李丹丽还走在探索复兴潮剧的道路上,提出:"要培养出唱戏的好苗子。"

身处绝境,依然有人在坚持奏响这段背景音乐,行业中的每一个人都尚在尽自己最大的努力。潮剧于我而言有了更加丰富的内涵,我看到这个符号背后一张张真实的面孔、一个个虔诚的灵魂,看到一群人为了潮剧付出的努力、情感与思考。我的心中满是感动。

访谈结束后,青年演员刘樱妮为我们表演了一段潮剧。哀戚的唱词像流水一样涌出,几位师生当场湿了眼眶。表演结束后,谢老师接过话筒解释道:"我刚刚忍不住落泪,是因为我听到乡音,听到她唱的这个故事,心中有种很深的感触。"

我开始不安起来——身为潮汕人,我连她在唱什么都听不明白,更别提与之共情了。

后来,戴老师邀请我和另一位潮汕籍的同学分享我们的感受。摄影灯亮起,十几双目光突然间齐齐落在我们身上。我有些局促,提醒自己挺直腰背、板紧面孔,生怕一放松下来就会暴露出自己对潮剧的无知和偏见。身旁的潮汕人林涵同学口若悬河,谈的是对潮剧传承中守正创新的看法。我心中愈发不安,愧疚之情不断发酵。

"那可欣同学呢,你有什么感受?"众人齐刷刷望向我。

"我倒没有很多想法。"我不知怎的就开了口,心里的声音赤裸裸地走到了喉咙口,"就是非常感激有这样一群人在努力发扬我们的文化。作为一个潮汕人,我会默默关注和支持吧。"

第四天上午,我们参观了名瑞潮绣艺术馆,然后前往潮剧培训中心。潮剧培训中心是培养潮剧职业演员的中等专业学校,这里的学生都是十几岁的青少年。我们站在练功厅门口向内张望,看着几个孩子有模有样地摆着唱潮剧的架势。我还是头一次近距离地观察潮剧演员的训练生活,心中备感新奇,以至于后来大家都在与培训中心的负责人进行访谈时,我又偷偷溜回了练功厅,想看看这几个小孩子。

阳光被窗户切割,在走廊上投下长方形的光影。几个孩子穿着红色练功服和黑色束腿裤,站在光影里说笑打闹。他们见了我都很热情,好奇地询问我的情况,还邀请我去食堂吃饭。从闲聊中我了解到,这个学校只有10个学生——6个女孩、4个男孩;年龄最大的是一个19岁的男孩,已在这里学了3年戏；另一个女孩甚至已经学了5年戏。这所学校其实只是一栋6层高的楼，这10个孩子平时都住在学校，在这栋楼度过6年光阴后再进剧团工作。他们每天的生活非常简单，白天练唱戏、练身段，晚上学习普通话和戏曲理论。我看着他们明亮澄澈的眼睛，想象着若我和他们一样在这方狭小的天地与寥寥可数的几个人过着6年千篇一律的日子，会有多枯燥无趣。

我环视四周，老师们都不在走廊上。于是，我小心翼翼地问出了在心中打转的疑问："那你们都喜欢潮剧吗？喜欢现在的生活吗？"

"喜欢呀。"

"喜欢。"

孩子们回答得干脆利落，一双双大眼睛仿佛能看穿我心里的"小九九"。

离开潮剧培训中心后，这几个孩子的神情一直浮现在我脑海中。我萌生了一个想法，希望将来能够与他们重逢，看他们登台唱戏。如果说昨晚的访谈就像看一群潮剧老将在千军万马的包围中搏杀一条出路，那么今天这些孩子就像一群雏鹰，跃跃欲试地挥舞着羽翼未丰的翅膀。只要有人继续热爱潮剧、学习潮剧，潮剧就会生生不息、永不消逝。

第五天和第六天，我们参观了明德园、木雕馆与著名古村落龙湖古寨。明德园是中国工艺美术大师谢华的手拉壶工作室，园内装修古朴雅致，陈列着谢华大师精心打磨的手拉壶，有的浑圆如鼓起的肚皮，有的棱角分明、敦厚方正。谢华大师之子谢思博说，要学做一个能用于泡茶的手拉壶费不了多长时间，但要做出一个能被摆上展台的手拉壶，则要费好长时间构思、打磨。偌大一间陈列室，满满三面墙都是出自谢大师之手的展品，我一件件细看着这些艺术珍品。志高和王茜正入神地听着谢思博的讲解：

"君德壶，看着造型简约，做起来其实很费工夫，但是这是最实用的壶型。"

"提梁壶和方壶看着都很漂亮，但是用着并不舒服，这种壶型观赏意义大于实用意义。"

"水平壶是最传统的器型，有好几百年历史了。"

…………

参观完明德园，我和几位同学聊天，询问他们经过此行对潮汕地区的印象。森彦说："以前看网络上的视频，拍的是潮汕人在高铁站喝工夫茶。那时候我觉得也太夸张了吧，没想到是真的。"我笑笑。的确，每天我们从客栈步行至乘车处，一路上都能看到搬着小板凳围坐在茶盘边喝茶聊天的人，难怪王茜说，"我觉得茶对于潮汕人而言不只是一种饮品，更是一种文化，一种风土人情"。

是的，茶更像是潮汕人的精神食粮。

"不识庐山真面目，只缘身在此山中。"从前我身处于潮汕文化圈中，却对家乡文化的诸多特点毫无察觉；我一直被动接受着潮剧、潮绣等艺术文化的影响，未曾主动去了解其内涵。在这趟旅行中，我跟着一群对潮汕文化知之甚少的人，站在潮汕文化圈外部，建立起了对家乡文化的整体认识；而与潮剧行业从业者的交流更让我触碰到这些文化符号的血肉。这趟旅行赋予了我不同的视角，让我重新发现了家乡文化的美。

在潮州考察的几天，我一直在回忆从前自己对家乡的感情。这片生我养我的地方，有闻名遐迩的工夫茶，有令我骄傲的美食，有"加密"程度极高的方言，但每当我向别人介绍家乡之美时，心中总有几分迟疑。我无法忘记，某一次回老家时，家中阿叔跷着二郎腿躺坐在实木沙发上，叼着香烟吞云吐雾，而后起身去上厕所，回来后开始数落家里的女性，只因厕所打扫得不够干净；无法忘记家族中的长辈去世时，家族中人为了面子而大办丧事，花费了十几万；无法忘记妈妈每次在饭后闲谈中忆苦思甜时，常提到奶奶因为觉得她的生肖不吉利而阻挠她与我爸爸的婚姻。这些阴影一度笼罩住了家乡在我心中的光亮，直到踏上这趟旅途后，我才看清阴影背后的光。

我的家乡像一位耄耋老人，看过世事变迁，历经岁月积淀，却也因年事已高，有着腿脚不便的局限。老人家将满腹学识教给了我，我不应苛求他做一个永恒的圣人。这趟旅途过后，我重新拾起了对家乡的爱恋。

# 与潮州的相遇和别离

## ——食文化小组调研日志

### 张 婧

## 11月6日 广州南站

我、鲁晖和林涵坐在广州南站3A层的麦当劳。我们三人再加上黄森彦，是中山大学国际翻译学院"创意写作与翻译"课程的学生，组成了潮州食文化调研小组。刚从珠海坐了一小时的动车到广州，我们这时正在等其他师生一起坐下一趟前往潮汕站的动车。对于接下来的旅程和任务，我彼时还是迷惘大于期待。

本科四年级的林涵是我们小组唯一的男生，瘦瘦弱弱的，戴着眼镜，滔滔不绝地讲着自己来调研之前还如何如何忙着学校交响乐团的排练，我这才注意到他穿了一件印着"沉迷练琴"的白卫衣。鲁晖和我都是研究生，我在笔译班，她在口译班。在这门课出行前的见面分工之后，她每次遇见我都会热情地打招呼，让我觉得这个小脸长腿的女生非常大方善良。森彦没从珠海校区出发，在广州站和我们碰头。她绑着低马尾，穿着一件明黄的卫衣，朝我们点头打招呼时笑得有点拘谨。

这时，课程助教符韵老师从远处叫我们，我朝她点头，颇有种见到乡亲的归属感。"老师好！我们是食文化小组的同学，我是组长张婧。"

她亲切地招呼着，把我们带到主讲课程的戴凡老师所在的集合处。戴凡老师把头发盘了起来，背着标志性的黑色大双肩包，正和其他两个调研组的同学们笑着寒暄。我也凑过去打了个招呼，给老师介绍我们组的分工——我是小组的记者，森彦负责英语写作，林涵负责中文写作，鲁晖负责字幕。

这时，广州新华学院的魏东华老师和两个摄影助理也到了。魏老师个头很高，背着一堆器材，乐呵呵的。临检票之前，魏老师提议我们在候车厅里拍一张合照。于是，我们一行人浩浩荡荡地在检票口旁准备拍照。虽然其他旅客好奇的眼光令人尴尬，但我突然意识到自己属于这个大团队，刚开始的懵懂和刚见面的尴尬随之被抛到脑后，我对即将开始的行程有了期待。

## 11月6日　潮州古城

潮州是美食之都，到潮州的第一餐引起了我和组员们十足的期待。作为食文化小组成员，我们一直既庆幸又不敢表露，怕引起其他组成员的"嫉妒"：一到吃饭时间，我们就理所当然地坐在最佳位置品尝美食。事实上，调研前我和组员们对潮汕美食的了解只局限于牛肉丸，所以对每一餐都充满了新奇感。随着一盘盘精美的菜肴上桌，众人都埋头吃饭。突然，有人幽幽说了一句："我们是不是忘记拍照了？……"我连忙停下筷子，对哦，我们研究食文化的，在这里的每一餐难道不都是我们的调研对象吗？正当我彷徨无措之时，隔壁桌传来消息说森彦已经拍照留存，于是，我的愧疚感就随着猪肉冻细嫩的口感一同滑进了胃里。

吃到尾声时，一道晶莹剔透、橙白相间的菜品被端上桌，只听林涵说道："来了来了，潮汕菜最有名的甜品，'甜过初恋'！"我才记起他好像来自潮汕地区——看来我们组有"专家"指导了。

"这是……那个……叫什么来着？对！'翻沙芋'！"同桌一直强调自己正宗潮汕人身份的谢桂霞老师补充道。

"啊，这是'糕烧芋'的。"旁边接待我们的韩山师范学院（下文简称"韩师"）的李煜老师说。谢老师立马点头说，"对对对。"看着林涵和谢老师这两个常年在外的潮汕人对潮汕菜那种熟悉而又陌生的样子，我深感家乡的文化也不是理所当然就能留在记忆里的。

这盘糕烧番薯芋，又叫"金砖银砖"，卖相极佳：番薯金黄，芋头银白，被切成正好能一口吃下的大块，表面均匀裹着晶莹的糖衣，色泽通透，撒上白芝麻、绿葱油，点缀得色香诱人。一口咬下，香甜爽口，芋头和番薯软糯粉嫩的口感被甜蜜的糖浆衬托得更加浓郁。李老师介绍说，潮汕宴席的一个特色就是"头甜尾甜"，寓意从头甜到尾。转盘转过两轮，我们面前的"金砖银砖"就没了，我和林涵对视一眼，从彼此心虚的眼神中看出来：我们都多吃了一块。

晚饭后，我们来到接待单位韩师听其"创意旅游"课程的学生对潮州美食、茶、潮绣、潮剧等方面的潮州文化调研报告。这是我们第一次与韩师的师生见面，宽敞明亮的智慧教室里每个人都朝气蓬勃、热情大方。报告持续了三四个小时，让我印象深刻的是，这些同学报告说潮州美食注重养生，小吃与民风民俗密切相关。旅游学院的高级营养师黄武营老师告诉我们，潮州菜之所以能成为粤菜代表，就是因为下了功夫，匠心满满。这使我们小组对潮州美食更期待了。

报告结束的时候已经接近10点半，回民宿要经过潮州古城的牌坊街。这个钟点不算早也不算晚，街上稀稀拉拉几个人，只有我们食文化小组的几个同学步履匆忙。牌坊街的灯落寞地亮着淡淡的黄色，好像在计较着有人来了却不好好欣赏似的。

突然，我看到路边有一家小店挂了写着"潮汕牛肉丸、凤凰浮豆干、萝卜糕"的招牌，便想起韩师同学说到的小吃凤凰浮豆干，是将炸豆腐配薄荷叶和蒜泥醋一起吃的。一开始听到这种搭配时，我就觉得口感层次会很丰富，但林涵这个潮汕人没太大热情，其他人也提不起兴致。我动员大家："我们美食小组的，不得尝尝潮汕小吃嘛！"

鲁晖第一个响应，她从最具代表性的牛肉丸尝起；林涵操着潮汕话老道地点了一份萝卜糕；森彦选择了潮汕的糖水海石花，并对我的选择表示质疑："豆干？加上薄荷？一听感觉就很'黑暗'啊。"但我还是选择相信我的第一感觉，毅然决然地让阿姨给我做一份浮豆干。

店主阿姨乐呵呵地在不足几平方米的小厨房里忙前忙后，很快端上了三碟小吃。我一一品尝：萝卜糕香酥，牛肉丸弹牙，海石花鲜甜。就在众人交口称赞之时，我的浮豆干也上桌了，金黄的豆干被摆在有白色花边的吸油纸上，和旁边翠绿的薄荷叶、红色的蒜泥醋一起装在泡沫盒里。我手忙脚乱地蘸酱，又夹上薄荷叶，试着把它们一口吃下去。豆干皮酥肉厚，豆香浓郁，配上天然薄荷的清香味、蒜泥醋的酸辣，清爽甘甜，中和了豆腐炸过之后的油味，一口咬下去层次感丰富，让尝过多地小吃的我觉得相当惊艳。

森彦见我一边被烫一边坚持继续吃下一口的样子，表示自己也可以勉为其难地尝一块。我喜出望外，紧盯着她，见她努力把薄荷叶和豆腐夹在一起，然后飞速掠过醋酱就往嘴里塞。

她面无表情地咀嚼了两下，随后眼睛一睁，神情一凝，我就知道，"真香"时刻到来。果不其然，她扭扭捏捏地说了一句"还不错……"，随后又很自然地伸手想要再夹一块。我急忙阻止，表示她要是不承认好吃，就不能再夹了！一番打闹之后，她终于坦承，自己之前的偏见在浮豆干对味蕾的强势进攻下，显得多么浅薄。她还准备在朋友圈大力推销宣传一下。林涵在旁边慈父般地微笑，大有一副"我早知如此"的态势。

"我就说肯定会很销魂！"他十分得意。

在牌坊街一路吃吃喝喝，不知不觉已经11点半了。林涵突然说了一句："好辛苦啊！食文化小组深夜11点半还在调研潮州美食，真的很辛苦呢！"

"哈哈哈哈哈哈……"

森彦立马发了一条朋友圈，配上林涵的文案和令人垂涎的照片，顿时招来在校同学们在评论区"哀鸿遍野"。

潮州美食那么多，食文化小组的工作真是既繁多又甜蜜呀！

## 11月7日　枫春海鲜大排档

结束了上午名瑞潮绣艺术馆的行程，我们早已饥肠辘辘，终于在12点多的时候前往潮州老字号枫春海鲜大排档，享用"韩公宴"。我们有幸采访到该店老板、潮州市餐饮协会会长张生。"韩公宴"是他受韩愈研究资深学者曾楚楠之托，在2019年韩愈治理潮州1200周年之际，结合韩愈诗词研究，与研发团队做出的一系列佳肴。

为一个古代文豪设计一系列菜谱，如果放在其他城市，我可能会觉得过于大张旗鼓，但是放在潮州，就一点也不奇怪了。历史上，韩愈治潮虽不过八个月，但却使得远离中原的潮州移民摆脱身份焦虑，在地理边缘成功构建了文化正统性。潮州人对韩愈的尊崇是写在骨子里、刻在文化基因里的：有占地百亩的韩文公祠，有名为"韩江"的母亲河，有叫"韩山"的山岭。难怪记者陈一鸣说潮州是一座"灵魂蒙着包浆的古城"[1]。

张先生在餐前特意腾出时间，介绍了自己做餐饮的渊源和"韩公宴"背后的文化（见图1）。"上班了，上班了！"鲁晖提醒道。于是，我开始用手机录音，森彦用笔纸记录，鲁晖把笔记本电脑放在腿上，噼里啪啦地打字，林涵则全靠脑子强记。就着不断给众人续上的凤凰单丛茶，张先生开始娓娓道来。

张先生说自己其实也是半路起家，之前是做建筑的，但是吃得多了，也就吃出门道来了。"韩公宴"体现了他对潮州美食和文化的钻研：韩愈抵潮后作的《初南食贻元十八协律》，写潮州海鲜"章举马甲柱，斗以怪自呈。

---

[1] 陈一鸣：《潮州：一座灵魂蒙着包浆的古城》，见"南方+"客户端网站（http://static.nfapp.southcn.com/content/202105/26/c5316724.html）。

图 1　师生在枫春海鲜大排档听张生会长介绍"韩公宴"

其余数十种,莫不可叹惊",写菜肴蘸料"调以咸与酸,芼以椒与橙"。因此,枫春海鲜大排档与学者曾楚楠合作,根据韩愈的相关诗作,研究出了14道菜,既有引自韩文公的"白灼章举",也有跟历史故事相关的"芦菔瑶柱";有传统家常的"翻沙香芋",也有高端隆重的"赤龙卧茵"。按张先生的话说,"韩公宴"是集文化、历史、传统于一餐的代表性潮菜。

几样菜品吃得我们心满意足。"芦菔瑶柱"是传统名菜,一般称作"护国菜"。羹汤勾芡出白绿太极,按位每人一盅。一开始我只觉得颜色鲜艳,摆盘奇特,但是一勺舀进嘴里,白萝卜被切成丁的鲜甜和干贝的浓郁融合在一起,滑若凝脂,口齿留香。甚至在回到中山大学后的一个多月里,森彦还在微信群里怀念这道菜的滋味。这时,林涵才道出了只有本地人才知道的秘密:"我猜这道菜用了水蟹熬汤,然后把第一滚的生汤加入锅底。"

"但是我查资料,就只说了番薯叶和菇。"森彦质疑。

"配方不可能公开,以我在家做菜10年的经验,这道菜里面必有与蟹有关的要素,还有干贝。"

我那时才明白,看似简单的一道菜,背后却如此讲究,不愧是潮州美食。

我还注意到"韩公宴"的餐具跟其他饭店略有不同：整套陶瓷餐具呈紫灰色，其中取菜盘被设计成一个书简的样子，与其代表的文化底蕴遥相呼应；上有波纹凸起，精美异常，而颜色又很朴素，不至于让人只顾餐具而忽视美食。回想起刚才张先生在接受采访的时候，说自己承包了一个陶瓷厂，自己设计、生产餐具，不由得佩服他做餐饮的用心。这也代表了很多潮州人对美食的态度：不论是呈现佳肴的人还是品尝美味的人，都视之为艺术。

"韩公宴"的匠心不只体现在餐具上，还体现在食材的选择、蘸料的搭配、师傅的技艺上。"我们都选最新鲜的食材，成本无疑就变高了。同时，潮州菜一个很重要的特点就是注重健康和养生，所以在选择的时候也要注意营养搭配。"张先生介绍道，"还有酱料也是，正宗的潮菜每盘菜都会配相应的酱料，比如，这盘蚝煎和龙虾虽然都是海鲜，蘸料就不一样。"

张先生又说："不像其他菜系，我们做潮菜的师傅做了10年都不敢说自己是大厨……所以学做潮菜是个非常漫长的过程。"

潮汕人不仅美食门道多，对喝茶的神圣感让我这个来自茶叶之乡的福建人都自惭形秽。昨天就听韩师的黄武营老师说潮汕工夫茶的"工夫"即下功夫之意，今日一见果不寻常，连几克茶叶都要提前称好。聊天过程中，张先生的助理不停地进行观察，谁的杯子空了就往谁那里添茶。茶杯核桃般大小，一口就能喝完，像鲁晖这种平时没有喝茶习惯的湖南人都因为他们的热情而喝了好几杯。据说，重要的宴席要喝两次茶，开头喝一次，中间或结尾还要视情况再喝一次。

张先生十分坦诚，当被问到做餐饮给自己带来了什么的时候，他回答首先是带来了经济收入，没有经济收入什么也做不了。我想起之前在拜访潮绣大师李晓丹母女的时候，看到隔壁店铺的老板捧着一本名为《发财》的书在看，顿时觉得潮汕人的追求不是飘在空中的理想，而是扎根在生活这片土壤中的务实需求。

## 11月7日　柏荫精舍

晚上，我们和韩师外国语学院的几位潮汕同学在月色下进行了一次交流。来这里之前，我对这次交流的期待值并不是太高，感觉可能就是大家简单聊天而已。直到我们围坐在一起，在露天的花园里，潮汕的同学们一个接一个分享潮汕的茶文化、饮食、潮剧等对自己从小到大的影响，我才意识到我们这次调研真正的意义。

在潮汕土生土长的女生们，有的说自己从小跟着爷爷奶奶听潮剧，在乡里时总是要挤进人群去看潮剧表演；有的说自己从小就学喝茶、泡茶，不管去哪里上学，都要带着茶具，小时候喝的茶很淡，长大之后越喝越浓，还要带领全宿舍一起喝；有的说自己每年在祭祀的时候都帮着妈妈做传统的潮汕红桃粿；还有的说自己小时候总是期待着每个月农历初一和十五跟着家人一起烧香拜神，在香火缭绕下其乐融融。

听着她们充满深情的叙述，我仿佛经历了一场深入的沉浸式的文化体验：月光洒在我们脸上、身上，恍惚间，她们分享的故事好像把我带到一个个充满烟火气息的潮汕家庭里，仿佛我也出生在潮汕这片土地上，受到了潮汕文化的滋养。于是，我们对潮汕独特、强大且历久弥新的文化有了理解，也是第一次直观地感受到调研的意义，就像后来戴老师在总结的时候说的："在别人说起潮汕的时候，我们也会不自觉地开始捍卫这里的文化，毕竟经过这么多天各种方式的深入调研，我们好像也属于这里了。"

## 11月8日　凤凰山

我们一大早来到凤凰山的茶厂茶山，探究茶叶的生长和制作过程。爬山途中，由于一条道路被锁住，我们不得不转向一条不知道通往哪里的小路。小路陡峭窄小，刚下过雨的泥土松动湿滑，又是下山路，走起来时不时会被盘根错节的树根绊到，大家仿佛都是连滚带爬下山的。让我觉得很感人的是，团队里的同学们都非常贴心，互相照顾。

因为豪爽易相处，森彦被我们称作"彦哥"，她大步流星地在最前面开路；潮绣潮剧组的 Momo 看起来小巧文静，但每到一段有点危险的下坡路都要伸手牵我，令我担心笨手笨脚的自己会害得她一起滚下去；第一眼看起来酷酷的摄影组女生澄澄，扛着笨重的摄影器材还一直回头关心其他人；鲁晖更不用说，经过多天的相处，细致体贴的她已经有了"鲁妈"的外号，她帮我拿了一路的伞，都腾不出手来扶着树干了。还有林涵这个瘦弱的男生，早就冲到我们前面替大家探路，还主动帮忙拿各种器材。爬了一趟山，我们对彼此的了解也更加深入。

到了凤凰山，不尝尝正宗的凤凰浮豆干简直难以平息我们小组对其深切的喜爱与回味，何况一天前韩师旅游学院的柯敏老师就提醒我们："等到你们吃了真正的凤凰浮豆干，就会知道这儿卖的……"

果然，凤凰浮豆干外皮香酥滚烫，包裹着多汁的豆腐，鲜香的黄豆味和当地独有的散发着清新薄荷味的"草仔"① 相呼应，令人仿佛能感受到凤凰山清澈的山泉水。如果说上次在牌坊街初次吃的浮豆干还只是"含苞待放"，那么凤凰山的浮豆干则是这道菜彻底绽放的风味，就连自认吃了无数浮豆干的林涵都被折服，事后回忆起来也只能频频认可柯老师说的"真的不一样"。原来，做凤凰浮豆干用的是凤凰山土生土长的带有微微薄荷味的"草仔"，而不是我之前以为的普通薄荷。事实证明，很多美食只有在当地才能保留住最真实的风味，虽然凤凰山坐落于潮州，但出了凤凰山，在潮州市区做出来的浮豆干风味也截然不同了。

## 11月9日　韩师潮菜基地·实践

这天我们又来到韩师，这次去的是中国潮州菜研发和人才培养基地。进去之前，我迫不及待地穿上老师发的厨师服，腰间绑上黑色围裙，最后戴上带檐的条纹厨师帽，一个厨师学徒就这样诞生了。等我跑了一圈跟同学、老师们合照完，真正的厨师逮住了我，告诉我很多地方都没穿规范：袖口没折起来用纽扣固定住；围裙最上端也没有折两圈、塞进去再绑起来；最重要的是长发没有盘起来扎到帽子里。

进到基地，看到一排排整齐锃亮的料理台和身着厨师服的老师同学，顿时有了点神圣感。这次我们学的是潮州宴席和家常菜里很经典的"虾枣"，因为其球状的外形，所以有"团团圆圆"的寓意。我一听要处理海鲜，还是带壳的，顿时一个头两个大。果不其然，韩师的老师教我们先把冻虾剥壳，用菜刀在虾背上划两刀去虾线。仅这个过程就耗费了我们组几个厨房"小白"的大部分能量。戴凡老师和我们一组，她全程紧张，眼睁睁看着其他组娴熟的动作，表示不会做菜的自己压力很大。几个人好不容易把虾壳、虾线料理好之后，台面已经是一片狼藉。接下来又是拍虾胶这种高难度工序，一时间雪白的虾肉飞溅。跟我们一组的王茜虽然也不会做饭做菜，但是她很快掌握了窍门，做得又快又稳。直到我看到她手上的伤口，才知道她在剥虾时被虾头的尖刺扎到了。我们每个人都轮流到案板前用菜刀侧面把虾肉又拍又旋又拖，张牙舞爪了好一阵，才把虾肉打出胶质来。接下来又是一顿低温炸

---

① 凤凰山上长有一种当地人称为"草仔"的小草，青绿色，小叶略圆，高二三十厘米。这种小草在凤凰山区几乎随处可见，摘后放到嘴里一尝，除有一股淡淡的薄荷味外，还略带苦味。

煮，复炸了两三遍，虾球终于呈现出诱人的金黄色。

原来，在饭桌上再普通不过的炸虾丸子，烹饪工序都如此复杂。就像王茜说的，想到厨房里的景象是这样繁忙辛苦，以后到饭店吃饭再也不会催人上菜了。

## 11月10日　韩师潮菜基地·品味

距离结束潮汕之行只剩下两天了，临别前一天，韩师旅游学院的陈菁院长请来中国烹饪大师吴前强和苏培民为我们展示高端潮菜技艺。我们小组不等厨师展示就准备好做记录。这么多天以来，我们已经习惯把每一餐都当作"上班时间"，每次吃饭都是既期待，又担心——期待品尝美食，担心自己沉迷美食，漏掉细节。彦哥拿着不离手的棕色皮质小本，时不时记下几个关键词；鲁妈负责全程录像；林涵全靠记忆，时不时提出一些鞭辟入里的问题。我拿着从摄影组向澄澄那里"打劫"来的相机，拍几张大厨潇洒的身姿，同时不忘录音工作。

几位大厨在透明的玻璃窗后面忙碌着，雪白色的烹饪服上一枚鲜艳的国徽代表了"中国烹饪大师"这个级别，我的崇敬之情油然而生。吴前强大师作为国家级烹饪大师、广东省非物质文化遗产潮州菜烹饪技艺传承人，向我们展示了一些古法粤菜的烹饪技艺，包括雪山金丝燕、双梅扣猪手、蜜金瓜芋泥等高端菜品的烹饪手法。

其中，蜜金瓜芋泥让我印象深刻。大厨向我们介绍说金瓜就是南瓜，采取的是最古老的"蜜浸"做法，接近之前"金砖银砖"的"糕烧"方式：用糖腌制两天两夜，将水分通过蒸发完全去除，再用蒸发的原汤熬煮南瓜，用文火收干，全程不加一滴水，南瓜才会格外香甜软糯。还有双梅扣猪手，把猪手拆得精细完整，煮得胶质感十足，老少咸宜；酸梅与潮州家家户户都会腌制的咸梅相互融合呼应，加上一点红枣柔和两种梅子酸咸的口感，还可以活血，体现了潮汕菜讲究食疗健康和营养搭配的特点。

就像戴老师在晚上的总结会上说的那样，"之前都没注意过这些菜品是如此充满艺术感，了解了个中细节后就充满了神圣感和尊敬，因为我们懂得了背后的辛苦和心思，就不会随意对待大厨们精心准备的每一道菜"。每个行业和领域都充满了艺术，而我们此行最大的意义就是去发掘它，记录它。

## 11月10日 民宿

第二天就要离开潮州，戴老师在今晚开了一个小小的总结会，聊聊我们此行的收获和感悟。具体的内容我已经不太记得，但是有一句话引起了我们强烈的共鸣，那就是"经过将近七天的深度调研，我们似乎已经对这里的文化有了一定的发言权。当有人提起潮州的时候，我们也会像本地人那样，去纠正一些不实的传言或者有出入的理解；或许感觉已经融入了这片文化，会在回去之后忍不住寻找它的踪影"。

戴老师还分享道，她经常需要做实践项目，所以她很明白影像和文字的重要性。下一次就算我们来到潮州，也难以如此深入体验、了解当地的文化，更不会和同一群人一起经历。这种经历一生只会有一次，如果没有做记录，记忆慢慢随时间湮灭就太可惜了。由此我回想到这几天每每有小活动，临近结束，魏老师团队都会组织所有人合照一张。之前我还觉得天天拍合照，拍来拍去好像都一样。但是现在我却觉得，每一张合照、每一个视频的地点都不一样，人们的心情也都不一样。而我们作为调研小组，每天早出晚归，回去之后精心写作，不可能是单纯为了获得学分，取得成绩，而是为了一辈子只有这么一次的体验，为了纪念与潮州的相遇，为了回味所有留在这里的人和记忆。

## 11月11—12日 宿舍楼下

最后一天的最后一程，我们在潮汕站依依不舍地分别，戴老师还有工作，所以把我们送到车站就要返回潮州。我们一个个轮流和她拥抱，有些事情和心情好像只能停留在潮州。我也抱得格外紧，生怕在珠海再见，这些可爱的老师和同学就和在潮州时如此放松的他们不一样了。有一些别离，不是和同一个人说的，而是和某一个时间的人说的。

最后，森彦又如同来时和我们在广州站会合一样，在广州站和我们分别。等我、林涵和鲁晖三人到达宿舍楼的时候，已经是将近半夜12点了。同住榕园的林涵正和我们告别，鲁晖突然叫住了他。

我一愣，随即反应过来：之前我们无意中发现鲁晖的生日是1999年11月11日，林涵的生日正好是1999年11月12日，一个是研究生，一个是本科生，生日却只差了一天。如此的缘分和巧合，让人不得不相信我们的相遇真的是命运的安排。

鲁晖说："我今年的生日在赶任务和车上度过了，希望你可以好好过个生日。"

"确实确实！"我附和道，给鲁晖使了个眼色。于是，我们默契地在宿舍楼下给林涵唱起了生日歌。2021年11月12日，零点零分，在珠海17度的寒风中，在我和鲁晖不在调上的生日歌声中，在林涵有点尴尬又有点腼腆的微笑中，我们小组的调研画上了一个圆满的句点。

回想起来，从一开始在车上的懵懂、期待，和老师、组员们尚有些生疏的交流，到之后大家纷纷从中找到乐趣——这种乐趣是潮汕文化带来的，是和同学老师自在相处、相互体谅带来的；是沉浸于这六天的深度体验带来的；是我们一起品尝美食、参观潮绣、感受潮剧带来的。

潮州对我们所有的味觉、听觉、触觉感官大举"入侵"，又温暖包裹。我们几个组员回去之后，仍会想念我们最爱的"金砖银砖"和浮豆干。彦哥说自己已开始天天泡茶，那是"潮州DNA入侵"的结果；林涵期盼着学校北门那家正宗的潮汕粿条早日重新营业，他在朋友圈说道，"关于故乡的亮面和暗面都变得更加清晰"；而我则感觉这种记忆和文化对自己文化背景的侵袭，被妥帖安置在了内心某个角落，当有相应的场景唤起时，就能够引发潮水般的回忆，因为我们身上从此都有一个地方属于潮州。

# 潮州纪行

谭学铭

## 序　如是我闻

越为吴灭后，越王子孙离散、南迁，勾践后裔无诸于粤东自立为王，与当地海丰县古越人结合，潮汕文化随即开始生根。隋开皇十一年（591），义安郡改称"潮州"，取"在潮之洲，潮水往复"之意。承此悠悠历史，潮州文化自成一脉，潮州人民发展出了潮绣、潮剧、工夫茶等独具地方特色的文化形式，潮州也成为南方一大文化重镇。北宋陈尧佐曾有诗云："海滨邹鲁是潮阳。"潮州文化地位之高，可见一斑。

然则书中只言、他人片语，对潮州文化之精妙绝伦，虽有所耳闻，仍觉知之尚浅。中山大学国际翻译学院的戴凡老师开设了"创意写作与翻译"课程，她亲自组织、沟通，与潮州韩山师范学院（下文简称"韩师"）的旅游与地理学院·潮菜学院达成合作，为选择此课的学子提供前往潮州进行社会实践的机会，让学生们得以真切感受这片土地所承载的历史与文化。机缘之下，我选上了这门课，于2021年11月6日自珠海前往潮州，参与了六天的文化之旅。

课程将潮州文化中的饮食文化、茶文化、潮剧与潮绣作为研究对象，将学生分为三组，分别负责深入调研、学习其中一个方面。我被分到潮剧与潮绣组，与张笑言、莫艳池和马嫦君三位同学一起开展调研工作。

五日之行，我们采访了潮绣与潮剧的各路名家，见识到了大家们不世出之才华，也听到了他们关于文化与传承的肺腑之言——或忧虑，或愤懑，或坦然。相遇与交流带来了想法的碰撞，观点的交汇促成了思维的灵光。我自以为，此行之后，自己对于潮州文化之美、文化传承之艰有了更深刻的体会与看法。我想，该记录下遇到的大师们，以答谢他们为我带来的启示，使他们对潮州文化的热忱不会湮没在历史的尘沙之中。

三藏十二部经，皆以"如是我闻"作开宗明义之辞，以表佛法皆承佛祖，是佛前所听所受。以此为序，谨表记事如实之意。

# 潮 绣 篇

## 1. 老师

"老师"这个称谓用在潮绣市级非物质文化遗产传承人李晓丹女士身上，绝不仅仅是一个用以体现艺术家地位的尊称。

初见李晓丹老师，是在她和母亲的作坊门口。她身着白色的旗袍，长发过肩，端庄典雅，美丽而知性，颇有大家闺秀之范。她领我们进了作坊，作坊四周的墙上挂满了各式各样的潮绣作品，有龙凤图、金龙图、飞鸟图等，都是潮绣中较为常见的图案。李老师一边带我们参观，一边介绍母亲卓桂芬与我们认识。老人家是潮绣省级非物质文化遗产传承人，针技精湛，墙上的作品大半出自她之手。随后，李老师走到旁边的桌台上，小心地用两侧的塑料包装盖好正在绣制的作品，再拿出另一份作品，一层一层地拆去包在绣品外的塑料袋封膜，将它放在桌台上——那是一幅金龙鱼图。

"垫高绣是潮绣独有的技艺，这让潮绣和其他绣种不同，其他绣种的绣品都是平面的，我们的是立体的。"李老师耐心、详细地讲解，她一边解释，手指一边在栩栩如生的金龙鱼图上滑动，指向她要讲的技法部分。"你们看这个鱼肚子，它里面是用棉花填充的，棉花的大小一定要适中，否则鱼腹就会凹凸不平。所以，光是为了处理棉花，就要花绣娘很大的功夫。"她用手指按了按鱼腹，让我们感受鱼腹里的棉花被填充得多么充实与恰当。

"而这个鱼鳞，是我妈妈用垫边的手法绣制的。所谓垫边，就是用很薄的宣纸折起来，用金线固定在布上，形成线条感。"她把食指弯曲，顶在拇指上，比划出垫边的宣纸的样子，然后又拿出一块垫边的底料给我们看。

从交谈中得知，原来我们并不是唯一一批向她学习的"学生"。李晓丹老师在工作之余，也会给韩师美术专业的学生上潮绣课。说起学生们，李老师又拿出一个袋子，里面装满了扇子。

"这是我给他们布置的作业。在我一个学期的课程之后，这些有艺术功底的孩子们已经学会不少潮绣的针法，于是，我就让他们自己绣一幅图。我一直坚持刺绣要有主题，于是就布置他们围绕'建党一百年'这个主题去绣。"

李老师拿出一把扇子，左边是一列火车，右边是一面鲜红的党旗，下面绣了"初心"二字。"你们看这份作业,这列火车后半段是绿皮火车,前半段车头的部分是高铁'复兴号',以体现我们改革开放这些年的发展。"老师夸奖着学生的创意,眼睛看向手中的扇子,笑意也逐渐在脸上荡漾开来。

"你们再看这把。"扇子正面是一个舞狮头,极尽喜庆,她又把扇子转了一转,背面舞狮头的位置也绣制了图案,是一团火与篆书的"安宁"二字。"这个孩子比较有天赋,她学得比较快,我就教了她垫高绣和两面绣的技艺。你们看这把扇子的绣制工艺就比其他扇子复杂得多了,是蛮优秀的一份作业。"随后,李老师又给我们看了其他几份作业,喜悦自豪之意溢于言表。

看着李老师的讲解,我暗暗出神。我想起了素为潮州人民所敬重的韩愈著的《师说》,称颂老师的伟大。或许在潮州文化的传承路上,韩师的学子们可以从这位绣娘身上感受到"传道受业解惑"的师道之风。

## 2. 师傅

"潮州有几个是真正做潮绣的,我看一眼就知道了。"身为潮绣国家级传承人,对于自己精耕多年的手艺,康惠芳老师是自信的,也是带着傲气的。访谈中,戴凡老师说,她认识一个朋友,在潮州办工坊,教授年轻人潮绣。康老师将信将疑,戴凡老师把存在手机里的绣品照片给康老师看,她眯着眼,端详了一下手机里的图片,随即笑了起来,不再置评。

在问及潮绣传承问题时,康老师说:"你给我三十几个年轻的小姑娘,来我这里绣一个月。他们有没有天赋,能不能成,我一看就知道。从这三十几个里,挑出几个好料子,再跟我学几年,这样潮绣才可能有人接班,才可能传承下去。如果像学校那样偶尔上几节体验课,根本不行。"

在她三楼的工作室里有四位绣娘。康老师说,她们从没出嫁就跟着她学艺,如今她们已经带着孩子在工作室做刺绣了。

康老师谈及她唯一一位20岁左右的学徒时格外动容:"她是少有的好料子,她肯跟我学,我在手艺上就倾囊相授。"我们参观工作室时,康老师特地走到她身边,再次向我们介绍:"这就是我一直跟你们说的,我最看重的徒弟。"

她看着小绣娘做工,看了一会,不知道是对徒弟说还是在对自己说,喃喃道:"有的时候我看到你绣不好,我就急,说话也不分轻重,因为我真的希望你绣好。对于刺绣的技艺,我确实是毫无保留的,希望你能理解啊。"

但是,师傅也会有师傅的苦恼。实用工艺的模式在这个时代多少有点步履维艰。我们询问康老师的第一个问题,就是潮绣的传承情况。康老师没有回答,反而把问题抛回给我们:"你们上午在明德园,看到有人做潮绣吗?你们在牌坊街一路过来,看到有人在做潮绣吗?"

我们摇了摇头,康老师说,这就是潮绣的现状。

后继无人,是康老师反复强调的问题。戴凡老师问她,要留住这些学徒,又要经营这么大的店面,生活来源怎么办?康老师说,她做的婚纱不愁销路,有一个公司来下单要做一百来朵牡丹花,一朵近万元,收入根本不是问题。问题是,她没有那么多人手,做不出那么多嫁衣,也做不了那么多牡丹。

采访将歇,戴凡老师对康老师说:"如你所说,潮绣的传承问题目前没有解决,这让我们都对潮绣的未来备感担忧。"康老师此时也只有苦笑,一时无语。她望向窗外,只见太阳西沉,日至黄昏。

## 3. 大师

蔡民强和儿子蔡中涵是与我们潮绣组进行访谈的最后两个人,父亲蔡民强是国企潮州刺绣厂的前厂长,儿子则是曾在美国留学的海归。不同的经历,让父子二人对传承有着自己独特的见解。

在市场化的浪潮中,潮州刺绣厂变成名瑞集团,我们拜见两位老师的地方,便是名瑞集团的潮绣艺术馆。在一幅 20 世纪 80 年代绣制的金龙图面前,蔡中涵老师为我们介绍了金龙绣制的工艺。经过前几次访谈,我们对潮绣垫高绣等工艺早已熟悉,因此并没有感到很惊奇。但他随后就聊到了潮绣的传承问题:

"我常跟别人说,什么是'非遗','非遗'就是非常遗憾。大家要知道,'非遗'制造,就是落后生产力,就是被淘汰的生产力。手工业,是必然被工业淘汰的。我一直不认同所谓'不要让"非遗"走进博物馆'的观点。事实上,该成为历史的,就应该要成为历史。在此后的各种创新,你可能会运用到'非遗'的元素,但是'非遗'的文化要素可以被市场吸收,'非遗'自身独有的一整套技艺和工作流程则必然会消失在历史的长河里。"

话如惊雷,我猛抬头。"但是,有一些东西是没办法用工业价值去衡量的,那就是艺术性。我们没办法挽留潮绣的工艺,但我们可以保持潮绣的艺术性,使其变成艺术精品。这也是这个艺术馆存在的理由。"

接着,蔡中涵老师为我们展示了馆中的吉光片羽。

劈丝工艺是潮绣中的典型技法，而在这博物馆中，这一工艺的表现力得到了极致的展现。有人物绣，用四分的丝线绣制的齐白石像，远看有如工笔画，画工精细，近看有如照片，栩栩如生。而最妙之处在于，人移步之时，齐白石像的眼睛也会随人而动，画如有灵。有风景绣，远看有如水彩画，色彩斑斓，而近看则同样移步换景，左右高低，不同的观看角度，光影、层次皆不相同。更有巨型国画绣，高近两米，长近五米，远看即是一幅大型水墨画，近看光影粼粼，尽是劈丝所制。

参观时，蔡民强先生也来到了展厅。老人家精神矍铄，身披一件棕色背心，背着手为我们讲述名瑞集团的历史和画作的由来。蔡先生深谙艺术理论，多年来精益求精地在现场指导绣娘的绣制，艺术馆因而有了精美绝伦的艺术品。这些艺术品让各路领导驻足久看，让"他们的日程安排统统超时至少一倍"，也能在世界巡回展示。"去年去了纽约，今年本来要去卢浮宫，但因为疫情没能成行。文化局说，我们这些是国宝级的作品，是对外宣传的重要展品，要我们至少一年展出两次。"

参观结束，我们走到楼下名瑞集团的迎宾厅。迎宾厅极尽宽广，显得富丽堂皇。一侧墙上的浮雕写着习近平总书记考察潮州时的一句话："潮汕文化是岭南文化的重要组成部分，是中华文化的重要支脉。潮绣、潮雕、潮塑、潮剧以及工夫茶、潮州菜等都是中华文化的瑰宝。"另一侧是名瑞集团的商店，店内山水、花鸟的绣品琳琅满目，远看之下，宛如工笔画的艺术沙龙。

离开前，我们在迎宾厅合影留念。一时神游，想到楼上的藏品与楼下的布设，我不由得慨叹：所谓"大师"之风，今日知矣。

# 潮 剧 篇

## 1. 理想主义者

宪宗年间，韩愈上《论佛骨表》，惹龙颜震怒，被贬谪至潮阳。韩文公在潮阳励精图治，为当地百姓传颂千年，事迹被写在了一部又一部的潮剧里。韩昌黎的理想主义也由此深深地刻在了潮州人的文化血脉之中。

对潮剧大家们的访谈，被安排在城南中英文学校的会议厅里。到场的有潮剧编剧李英群老师、潮州文化研究中心的陈月娟老师以及百花潮剧团的青年演员刘樱妮，评论家陈韩星老师和普宁潮剧团艺术总监李丹丽老师则以视频形式参与。

李英群老师年逾八十，在陈月娟老师的搀扶下进入会议厅。他曾写了无数脍炙人口的曲目。一聊起潮剧，他便热情洋溢，仿佛回到了年轻的岁月之中。

李老说："很多人说我是潮剧的大师，但我其实不懂潮剧，我还远远没有踏入潮剧的门。潮剧博大精深，与潮州关系关联紧密，谁要是懂得潮剧，谁就已经是半个潮州文化的专家了。"老人家谦逊，说自己只是"闲间冲茶人"，但他对于潮州的农村与潮剧的情况，从最受潮州农民喜爱的剧目到乡下潮剧团的实际运作，都能娓娓道来，如数家珍。

文化发展的方向是讨论文化传承不可避开的问题。李老认为，潮州文化就是生活文化，潮剧的剧本改编要适合当地人的口味。

他说："《柴房会》这一曲本，本子是外来的，发生在饶平。改编成潮剧以后，大家都说，李老三是我邻居家的叔叔吧？从李老三身上，我们能找到属于潮州人的独特优点和缺点。《柴房会》把潮州文化融汇得出神入化，让观众从头笑到尾，这些都是吸引人的地方。所以我一直说，潮剧能够做到让人笑，就已经不得了了。"李老曾写下诗句赠予一同创作的友人，也是为自己的努力做注脚："几十年来当戏囚，修书一千谓之求。"

聊及创作问题，李老说的皆是趣闻逸事，自己也不禁莞尔。但对于比李老年轻10岁的陈韩星来说，创作问题则是更为沉重的——或许是因为，他比李老更了解当下潮剧团的运转情况。

他开口便带有几分愠怒："既然咱们今天是一个座谈会，我也就不妨把话说得直白一些。为什么'非遗'文化一定要发展？很多潮剧团外请导演，这些导演不懂潮剧，用所谓吸收了其他地区因素的方式，把潮剧弄得都不像潮剧了。"关于潮剧题材，他如是说："潮剧不写大人物，不写大题材。潮剧这么多年来的曲目没有群英会，也没有武戏，潮州也没有过武状元。可见，当下一些剧目创作的要求实际上是不符合潮剧内在发展逻辑的。"关于潮剧当下的发展，他的矛头更是直指"文化创新"："我认为，潮剧近10年内都不应排新剧，而应把旧戏排好。只改传统戏，我们自己排好传统戏。"

刘樱妮一直默默地坐在会议厅的一侧。这个与我们年纪相仿的女孩化了妆，做了美甲，和我们所见过的同龄女生别无二致。与李英群和陈韩星两位老师的访谈结束后，她为我们表演了一段潮剧，是《春香传》的一个"狱中歌"唱段。她站到会议室的前面，寻得一处空旷位置，随着手机开始播放乐曲，她将头微微抬起，仿佛在看向坐在远处、高处的观众，然后右手捏成兰花指，便唱了起来。戏中，春丽不从恶官之命而下狱，在狱中控诉冤情，哀叹命运。樱妮眉头微皱，唱腔哀婉，双手随唱腔而摆动，虽着常服，亦可见水袖翩翩。一时间，这个看似时尚的年轻女孩，带观众们领略了极致的梨园风华。唱段罢了，她向在座众人鞠躬示意，全场掌声雷鸣，随行的谢桂霞老师祖籍是潮汕地区的揭阳，更是为重闻潮剧而悄然落泪。

临行前，莫艳池学姐采访樱妮："学戏路上，最大的困难是什么？"樱妮答道："练功是辛苦的，但是我已经习惯，这些苦倒也无所谓。但是我不能接受别人说，为什么潮剧没有人听，你还要继续学。"言至后半，她已几近哽咽。

"潮阳不远明月升，旅馆中忧愁聚在心。这时间怨不得伴虎即君，刚直秉性我也不怨自身。"这是《蓝关雪》里的唱段，也是几位潮剧人的真实写照。或扎根乡土，或坚持传统，或为了热爱一往无前。如韩愈一般，李英群老师、陈韩星老师与刘樱妮怀揣着理想，努力在黑暗中为潮剧这项濒临失传的艺术点上自己的火光。

## 2. 现实主义者

在潮州市潮剧团门口，迎接我们的团长郭明城老师穿着一身宽松的西装，戴一副黑边方框眼镜。访谈前，郭老师带我们去了二楼的练功房。女生练功房里，一位老师正在教四个女孩运水袖；男生练功房里，三位男生在学习基本步法，一个穿着戏服的男生在对镜排练。

郭老师简单地为我们介绍了戏剧团的情况：四层楼的学院，学生并不多。随后，他招呼我们到楼下的舞台前落座。被问及潮剧传承的难处时，他娓娓道来："潮剧的学成要足足三年。要调整好嗓音的话，时间就更长。所以，学习好的孩子就不会学这个，经济条件好的孩子也不会来。"对于潮剧的局限，他也直言不讳："剧种的没落来源于语言的没落。以前我们上课都用潮州话，现在都说普通话。"谈及未来，他说："潮剧是不会灭亡的，只是质量会下降，因为我们生源不够。在我成长的那个年代，潮剧团是在申请者里挑选的，现在我们应收尽收。"

访谈过半，老师提议让学员为我们表演几段潮剧。学员们依次登台（见图1）。那个身着戏服的男生最为熟练，唱的是《梁祝》中的一段。他在台上步伐稳健，水袖的挥舞也恰到好处，表演可谓有板有眼。但是，郭老师只是静静地看着,表演结束后,鼓掌也颇有应付之意。待学员们离去,他叹了口气,说:"这个男生的嗓音和功夫还有待提高啊。"

图1　潮州市潮剧艺术培训中心的学生在表演潮剧

我们为郭老师的严格感到诧异,但他并未就此打住。"我们以前都是从小练的,底子扎实,要求必须练了嗓音才能上台。这个男生来我们剧团的时候已经快成年了,基础本身就不牢。"

我们问了很多问题,郭老师一一给出了回应。时代变迁、经济压力、方言使用频率变化、年轻人的审美转向、时尚变迁,种种原因导致了潮剧的困境。郭老师对此心如明镜,与我们谈起时,也一一做了分析,但他脸上始终没有情绪的波动。

这时,戴凡老师问道:"你们是怀着怎样的心情在从事这份事业?"

这正是我的困惑所在——即便是初来乍到的局外人,也能感觉到施展不开的无奈与困苦,一个常年生活在其中的人,又如何能始终保持平静?

郭老师没有给出直接的回答。他说:"无论是什么心情,我们都会继续做下去。"他顿了顿,又说道:"如果生源不好,我们心情就不好,那我们怎么生活下去呢?"

我终于明白,所谓现实的局促,并非没有在郭老师身上留下刻痕,他只是已经习惯与现实共处了罢。看着端坐在沙发上与我们平静交流潮剧未来的郭老师,我想到了荷马史诗《伊利亚特》中的凡人英雄赫克托尔。谁不知道阿喀琉斯是海洋女神忒提斯的爱子,全身刀枪不入?只是,如果因为对手身为神子便惶恐、焦虑,特洛伊的未来又由谁来守护呢?如果因为现实的困难而情绪上涌,那潮剧的未来与传承又由谁来守护呢?

由此,我对郭老师的敬意油然而生。在心中,我举盏:敬现实,敬坚强。

## 跋　珍珑棋局

行文至此,当有收束。此行之中,所遇之人,大抵已落笔纸上,唯有一事,仍未交代清楚,那便是作为观察者的"我们"该如何审视这段旅途。

《天龙八部》里,逍遥派掌门无崖子设珍珑棋局,棋局中劫中有劫,既有共活,又有长生,或反扑,或收气,花五聚六,复杂无比。苏星河设擂后,各路高手前来破局,也纷纷败下阵来。窃以为,潮绣与潮剧,亦如此珍珑棋局。

坦白来讲,至少对我而言,"文化传承"四个字的分量,更多的是政治课本里的几段话语。至今仍能记得高中政治课本中的若干表述:文化要批判地继承,文化要在继承的基础上发展,发展的过程中继承。哲学的观点是凝练的,但直到来潮州,我才意识到,现实的问题远远不是哲学抽象的规律所能解决的。这一路,我们与各种大家交流,他们用各自的方法守护着自己所爱的文化。我逐步意识到,传承与发展之间或许是存在矛盾的。工业化的浪潮改变了当代人的审美与消费习惯,失去了市场的文化产品,谈何发展?有时,文化创新也意味着削足适履,文化传统的核心与精髓在这一过程中往往会流失,失去了精髓的文化传统,又谈何传承?

来潮州后,自以为被各位老师对潮州文化的热爱牵引着入了局。可是,对潮州文化了解得越多,我便越觉得传承与发展的矛盾,凭我的见地难以寻得两全之策。我手握弈子,却迟迟不敢将其放入棋盘。

但是，我想起，访谈之余，戴凡老师购买了康惠芳老师的一幅潮绣作品，既是爱其精美，也是解囊支持。而莫艳池学姐在采访刘樱妮的过程中，听到她对于潮剧的爱与倔强，忍不住落下泪来，也为这个年轻演员送去了些许安慰。她们都尝试着在这局上落下了一子，这自然与破局之着仍有距离，但多少可以鼓励坚守在潮州文化传承第一线的人们的士气。

我意识到，自己有些过度悲观了。即便是珍珑棋局，也并非无解。虚竹胡下一子却盘活全局，珍珑棋局由此得解。现实中，天津相声曾经亦濒临失传，后有郭德纲组建德云社，既振兴了相声，也无损其精华。或许，我们即便不知道方向，也可以努力地尝试一下，为破局尽绵薄之力。

那么，回到最初的问题，"我"能做什么呢？我想，我或许可以效法苏星河。无崖子设的珍珑棋局自己解不开，便记录棋谱，广招天下英豪贤才以破局。韩愈云："文以载道。"我未能寻得破局之道，但我愿记录下途中所见诸位大师的努力，以让更多人得以了解潮州文化的困境，等待有人能提出破局的一着。

# 潮州故事篇

　　这部分的三篇作品在访谈和田野调查的基础上,分别讲述了潮州班学生所了解的潮州茶文化、食文化和潮绣、潮剧故事。

# 潮州茶事

## 王 茜

2021年，11月8日，上午11：49。

广东省东，潮州城北，凤凰山上，茶树丛中。

中山大学"创意写作与翻译"课程主讲老师戴凡，随行老师谢桂霞，韩山师范学院（下文简称"韩师"）的老师柯敏，课程小组成员们。

手机屏幕上显示的时间、百度地图的经纬定位和周遭熟悉的面孔并没有给人多少现实感——我们在屋顶上，不知道谁家的屋顶上。

为探寻潮州文化，课程师生从珠海市出发，逾五小时路程后抵达潮州市。自清早踏上山路，我们一行人穿行茶树丛中，一路跋涉至此，却不知茶山出口何在。

"真的要从别人家屋顶下山吗？"课程组里为数不多的男生之一——俞志高睁大了眼睛，不敢再向这离奇的出口迈出一步。他摇着头谨慎地向后退了几步，歪着脑袋看向其他同学。

食文化组的张婧原本叉在腰上的手这时伸出来试图挡住止不住大笑的嘴巴："一群人突然从别人家屋顶上冒出来吗？哈哈哈哈哈哈！"爽朗的笑声从她指缝里飘出来。

"天哪！这是什么《天降奇兵》的穿越情节！"鲁晖的手扶在我的胳膊上，一边弯下身去伸手捶打着小腿肚，一边抬起头向屋顶两侧张望着。

"这是什么'九又四分之三屋顶'①吗？从茶山穿越到现实世界的入口？"开往霍格沃茨魔法学校的列车轰隆隆地驶过我的脑海，我甩甩脑袋四处打量着。

呈阶梯状的茶田中，一排排近人高的茶树整齐地列队在仅能通过一人的小路一侧。茶树颇以山中土著自居，纵容树干高处的枝叶野蛮地向旁侧伸展。满山翠绿的枝叶中零散地立着略高于茶树的竹竿，竿头擎着一张张A4

---

① 类比"九又四分之三站台"，英国魔幻小说《哈利·波特》里的地点，每年霍格沃茨特快列车会自此开出。

纸大小的黄色粘虫板，庇佑着一山攀云饮雾的绿色生灵。

跟茶山上郁郁葱葱的茶树挤在一起，我们远没有这些绿色植物那么自在。身边的张婧使劲拽了拽两边衣领，瑟缩着把外套拉链拉到下巴尖，试图阻挡无孔不入的寒气。我轻轻跺了跺脚，把脚底松软的棕黄色砂土踩实，从地上捡起掉落的乳白色茶花使劲嗅着，残存的茶花香气和薄荷汽水般的寒意一同钻进鼻腔。我盯着脚边的一排排茶树，总觉得会有揣着怀表会说话的兔子从什么地方蹦出来。

"那么到底该从哪里下去呀？"戴凡老师一手揽了揽围巾，向身后的迢迢山路望去。不远处的山顶被笼罩在尚未散尽的白雾里，看起来没打算给出什么确切回应。

"难不成……难不成我们真的要原路返回吗？"队伍里探出一颗戴着黄色毛线帽的脑袋，潮绣潮剧组的莫艳池以往常一样温和的语气轻声问道。

"不会的，不会的！"潮州本土人柯敏老师扶了扶肩上的摄像机，大手一挥走过来，说："我知道茶山的出口，我带你们下去！"边说边迈着大步从队伍最后赶上前来。

柳暗花明，出口就藏在屋顶旁一个不起眼的转角里。穿过百香果藤蔓遮挡着的小路，走下略显陡峭的石板台阶——我们又重踏在扎扎实实的沥青路上了（见图1）。

图1 "创意写作与翻译"课程师生在凤凰山

沿着坡度很大的山间干道，我们来到当地茶农家中。甫一进入仓库，众人皆为满室馥郁茶香而惊呼，觅食小兽般伸长脖子，耸动鼻尖，四处嗅闻，那是鲜嫩叶尖的活泼清香混合加工成茶后的厚重醇香。黑而高瘦的茶农招呼我们落座饮茶。

　　"我知道有些人很讲究的，比如，茶叶泡20秒就要拿出来。你们有没有这种说法呢？"看着对面的茶农一壶热水浇下去，戴凡老师扶了扶眼镜，颇为严谨地问道。

　　"我们没有这么多讲究，泡下去就直接喝了。"

　　"请问'鸭屎香'是什么意思呀？"茶农身后是摆满一墙的各种类型茶罐和茶叶包装，肉桂香、蜜兰香、桂花香、夜来香、黄栀香……志高指着其中一个茶罐上"鸭屎香"的标签问道。

　　"是不是跟'猫屎咖啡'的名字差不多啊？"同为茶文化组成员，陈一诺探身过来在我耳边小声嘀咕，我努努嘴巴表示赞同。

　　"就是一种单丛茶的香型。"茶农泡茶的手没有停顿。

　　"那为什么叫'鸭屎香'呢？有没有鸡屎香呢？"志高继续追问道，手中仍握着纸笔，凝神侧耳等待茶农的回答。

　　"没有鸡屎香。"茶农抬起头来笑呵呵道，"有一个说法是，以前有茶农种出来的茶叶有特别的香气，怕被别人知道后偷走茶树，就说这香味是鸭屎香。"听闻茶农解释，课程师生无不一脸恍然。虽这一说法难辨真假，但由此大家再不必担心茶叶与鸭屎有甚瓜葛。

　　从高山寒雾到泥壶滚水，茶叶经几重辗转几番流离，我们一一寻去。

　　黄寰先生眉头轻蹙，嘴唇抿起，腰间靠着直径一米多的竹笪箩，两手手肘抵在笪箩边缘，双腿略微弯曲以保持稳定，全身力量协调一致，竹笪箩以稳定的频率和幅度依序向各个方向倾斜着上下抖动。旋转，滚动，跳跃，落下，竹笪箩里茶叶在跳舞。

　　"摇青是为了让茶叶碰撞，破坏茶叶的细胞壁，开始发酵过程。"

　　凤凰山北麓的涌泉古岩茶庄园里，制茶世家出身的茶园主人黄寰先生正为我们展示制作茶叶的全过程。在涌动着青草气的制茶间里，他伸手捞了几把竹笪箩里摊晾着的茶树嫩叶稍做观察，又置于鼻前轻嗅一番。我们一众师生围在黄先生身边仔细观察着，戴凡老师也学着他的动作，伸手捞起一把茶叶细细端详。"好香啊！"她睁大了眼睛感叹，从手里的一捧茶叶里抬起头来。

"你也闻闻。"鲁晖把手里的一捧茶叶从鼻下移开,打量了下我手掌的宽度,小心地在我并拢的手掌上方松开手,茶叶轻轻降落在我的手中。鲜叶香气自掐断的细嫩叶梗直冲入鼻。

黄先生用手轻抚过笤箩中当日采的嫩叶,准备开始下一阶段。他脱掉工整的外衣,撸起衬衫衣袖,双手抄起铺着一层嫩绿茶叶的竹笤箩,站起身稳了稳腿脚,调整好握笤箩的姿势,稍一发力,竹笤箩就自如地运作起来。

我目不转睛地盯着从笤箩中心翻腾到边缘的茶叶,转动的笤箩依次向水平面上的各方向微微倾斜一下,茶叶轮番翻转到最外层,滚动过笤箩每寸边缘,腾起后再落回笤箩,竟没有一片掉落在地。

黄先生轻松自如的模样惹得众人蠢蠢欲动,都撸起了袖子想小试身手。作为茶文化小组成员,我率先从黄先生手中接过了大竹笤箩。

"这么重!"我惊呼。黄先生的手刚一撒开,大笤箩就猛地朝我的右前方倾过去,满笤箩茶叶眼看就要倾撒在地!站在对面的一诺眼疾手快地抬起倾斜的笤箩,惊得我握着笤箩边缘的手沁出了汗水。纵使我展开双臂也无法环抱住的大竹笤箩,这时满载一大堆水分充盈的嫩叶,应该有近20斤重了。单是端起笤箩就是难题,何谈摇青?在黄先生手里如折扇般轻巧的竹笤箩却是我"不能承受的生命之重"。

好不容易摆正姿势,我铆足手臂力量试图转动这个大家伙。等笤箩开始转动了,大团茶叶还是稳稳地待在笤箩中央,只一小部分茶叶懒洋洋地随着大笤箩晃了一晃。我手上再用些力气,茶叶就开始狂飙疾走。我慌忙向反方向转动笤箩,几乎动用了全身力量,从大腿、腰腹、胳膊到嘴唇、眼角都挣扎着出一份力气。

笤箩应保持与胯骨同高吗?手臂弯曲还是伸直?顺时针转还是逆时针转?上下方向摇还是左右方向摇?怎么把中间一团茶叶摇散开?又怎么把快要掉落的茶叶归置到笤箩中央?我一边艰难地回想着刚才黄先生摇青的动作,一边紧盯着笤箩里不听使唤的茶叶,好像这茶叶会由我的意念驱使似的。眼看茶叶就要脱天漏网,黄先生及时上前解围,并给大家讲解摇青的动作要领。

我长长呼出一口气,甩动着酸软的手腕,退到小组成员身后。

"下一个步骤是杀青。"黄先生拍了拍卧于墙角的长筒状金属设备。"这是滚筒杀青机,通过高温防止茶叶过度发酵。现在机器在预热。"

"达到多少度才能把茶叶放进去呢?"站在杀青机旁的茶文化组组员丁可欣问道。

"这个温度要看情况而定。今天只给大家演示一下大致过程,温度不作严格要求。"黄先生边说边把手伸进杀青机的滚筒。"现在170摄氏度,不是很烫。"

"170摄氏度?你的手伸进去居然不会烫伤!"戴凡老师吃惊地问道。

"我的手很粗的。"黄先生笑着向围在身边的同学摊开手掌。

可欣扶了扶眼镜,目不转睛地观察着黄先生的手上动作,又问:"您是在调温度吗?这个过程要多久呢?"

"这个像炒菜调大小火一样,中间要调温度的。一般要焖炒四分钟左右。"

"大家可能闻到一点茶叶味了。今天只是快速地给大家演示流程,本来要炒得更久。今天摇青不太充分,茶叶含水量还太高。平时一般要摇青五六次,直到茶叶发酵。茶叶看起来是红边绿腹的,发酵过后味道才会更香。"黄先生一边解释着,一边从杀青机滚筒里抓起一把茶叶,问:"要不要试一下?"

"我来试试……哇!好烫!好香呀!捧在手里很舒服。"戴凡老师接过黄先生手里冒着热气的茶叶,趁着刚出滚筒的茶叶余温还未散尽,传到身边的艳池手中。"来,小心点。"

烘烤过的茶叶失了新摘下时的清脆,叶片变得薄而柔软。

"哇!是天然的清香!现在还不是乌龙茶的味道,而是绿茶味!"接过茶叶的艳池鼻尖差点埋在茶叶里,她闻了又闻。

黄先生把竹笸箩放在滚筒口前,按下按钮,茶叶便一股脑落回笸箩中,转眼进了揉茶机。

黄先生铆足力气推了一把揉茶机,转盘样的机器就依着惯性一圈接一圈地运作起来,状如锅底的圆筒把茶叶结结实实地压在下面的金属盘上,因烘烤而变成黄绿色的嫩叶开始打卷。

"这种没有卷起来的,是不是比较老的叶子?"一诺探头望着揉茶机里的叶片。

"对,现在这个季节的叶子都比较老了,这种已经揉成条的是比较嫩的。"黄先生捏起一条已经成卷的嫩叶向大家展示,说:"这些不嫩的叶还是片状的,很容易就能分辨。"

"原来嫩叶和老叶区别在这里。"一诺点点头,又问:"那卷不起来的茶叶就没有味道吗?"

"外形不好看,味道是一样的。只是生产高端茶叶时一般会把这种挑走,有些嫩叶也要剪掉茶梗。做成茶之后，这些片状的价格会便宜些，也可以用来提取茶多酚。"

揉好的茶叶即将进入烘茶阶段。"以现在的状态估计要烤15分钟，烘到茶叶大概七成干的时候，拿出来再结块，自然风干一段时间后，过差不多两个小时再推进去完全烘干，然后再把茶叶打散……这样做出来的是比较粗糙的初制茶，而生产精制茶还有很多步骤。"

来自华北平原中部小县城的我并非全无饮茶经验，但未曾料想过从鲜叶到新茶竟需如此精细繁复的工艺，小小叶片在沸水中伸展跳跃之前竟需经这番锤炼。

自幼时每至城郊外婆家，总有一壶热腾腾的日照绿茶候着来客。一张经年日久的小方木桌，夏天被摆在对着院门口的天井阴凉处，冬天被置于炉火烘暖的炕席上，一把浅砖红色瓷质大茶壶稳稳立于搪瓷茶盘，茶盘余处摆六七只与大茶壶同质同色的弯柄小茶碗。茶壶大肚细肩，一侧有细长壶嘴，一壶足可斟满五六个鹅蛋大小的茶碗。一小把茶叶进壶，半个上午就过去了。

而潮州人喝工夫茶，泡茶饮茶所用器具大有不同。隐于牌坊街深处的手拉壶展馆明德园，是中国工艺美术大师、俊合号手拉壶作坊第五代传人谢华的工作室，其子谢思博为我们讲解了潮州人泡饮工夫茶的器具和方法之独到。思博其人看起来人近中年，体格颇为健壮，戴一副眼镜，一口普通话潮味甚浓。引众人入室落座长木几旁，思博即着手泡茶。

"潮州人喝的是工夫茶，工夫茶现在已经是国家级非物质文化遗产了。"思博这边煮上水，那边开始整理件件茶具。得其名于"大耗工夫"，小壶小盏的工夫茶冲泡斟饮的确费工夫。

"是'功夫'还是'工夫'？"在全国各地见过各式称呼，向来严谨的一诺向思博求证。听闻"功夫"，我总忍不住想象身着白袍、须发飘逸的老者打完一套24式太极拳，盘腿坐下来品茶的场景。

"是'工夫'，潮州人喝的就是精细的工夫。"思博笑着抬起头答道。各处虽名称不一，但潮州人对此却笃定无疑。"一套完整的茶具有七八件……这个吗？这是煮水用的砂铫。这些都是茶具，羽扇、竹夹、茶壶、茶杯、杯垫……"思博的手指落在桌上或卧放或挂立的各式茶具，一个个茶具名称听得围坐一旁的同学们不禁啧啧称奇。

"哇！这是茶具还是玩具啊？"坐在思博对面的戴凡老师和谢桂霞老师一同凑近来端详。这是一套装在透明玻璃箱中的极微型茶具，茶壶不过拇指指甲大小，茶杯不抵茶壶一半大小，轻薄精巧得令人敛了手脚，只敢隔着玻璃瞧着。

"这也是正经的茶具，也能泡茶，这个茶壶壶嘴能倒出水。"思博打开玻璃箱，捏起最小的茶壶，放在戴凡老师的拇指指腹上比量着。我屏气凝神地凑上前去，生怕一呼一吸间就能掀翻这纤薄的器物。

热气腾起，手边茶壶茶杯已备好，思博微微侧身，桌上茶具全然呈现在众人眼前。茶壶已加好茶叶，热水入壶后，一通热水又结结实实地浇在壶盖上，沿壶身瓢泼而下，流入茶盘，壶中茶叶煎煎又熬熬。片刻后，思博将一壶茶水倒掉，再次往壶中加水。他解释道："第一泡用来洗茶，我们是不喝的。"

"潮州人喝茶用三个杯子，三个杯子摆成一个'品'字，喝茶的往往不止三个人，这三杯茶就需要喝茶的人互相谦让了。"思博边说边把茶水均匀倒入面前几个杯子里。

我想起之前黄寰先生的介绍："以前各条村都有一个驿站，每个驿站都有一个算是茶台的地方，大家商量事情就去驿站喝茶慢慢谈。商量事情三个人才好办，两个人商量容易斗嘴，三个杯子还有投票的功能，两个人是没有办法投票的。如果吵起嘴来，倒茶喝茶的空当也好让人琢磨下一句怎么讲。"

走神间，思博手边已经摆好几排茶杯。"今天人多，我们就不讲究这么多了，平时都是只倒三杯的。"思博斟好茶水，起身弯腰依次将茶杯双手奉于茶桌一侧的各人。

"器为茶之父。"思博说着，领我们走进一间宽敞的制壶室。潮州人泡饮工夫茶用的是朱泥手拉壶。制壶室里，几位制壶匠人在转盘上摆弄着形状各异的黄色泥团。"手拉壶是用手工拉坯法在转盘上用手拉出茶壶造型，做出来的茶壶壶身没有任何接缝，这一点是别的工艺做不到的。"

"这壶用手拉好就算成功了吗？"戴凡老师盯着在制壶师傅手中形态、花纹不断变化的泥团问道。

"这个拉出来的是壶身，拉好之后放着阴干，之后要修坯，后面还要加上壶盖、壶嘴、壶把，最后才放到窑里烧制，烧好的壶是朱红色的。"思博指着制壶师傅手里的黄色泥团解释道。

"制作成功率高吗？"戴凡老师继续问。

"潮州手拉壶用的朱泥跟其他泥不一样。朱泥很容易在烧的过程中出问题，成品率很低。就算前面的步骤全都万无一失，要是后期烧制出问题，前面的工作就白费了，这种情况总是有的。"

在偌大一间茶具展室里，思博开始讲解各式工夫茶具的功用。他指向进门右手边展示台上的一款壶，说道："这款叫'飚壶'，它的风格很现代，设计灵感是一台跑车。像那把太极百岁壶，就是专门展示制壶技术的，壶身线条一气呵成。"

离展室门口最近的侧边展台上陈列着几款稍显朴素的茶壶，在一众造型别致的茶具中并不显眼。"这个是经典的壶型，叫作'思亭壶'。'思亭'从清代制壶大师陆思亭的名字而来，这种矮梨壶非常实用；这把'君德壶'也是非常实用的。"思博依次托起茶壶，向大家展示几款基本壶型。他说："比较经典的还有'水平壶'，流传下来有几百年历史了，也有人叫它'孟臣壶'。这些壶现在都使用得很广泛了。"

思博表示，为大力推广潮州手拉壶，近年来，潮州制壶匠人做出了诸多努力。"传统的潮州壶都比较小，一般只能倒三杯。后来为了向全国各地推广潮州壶，我们根据各地喝茶习惯对茶壶做了一些改进，来适应不同地区顾客的需求。比如，把茶壶容量做大一些。这是因为有些地方喝普洱、白茶、铁观音之类的茶，用潮州壶冲就太小了，这些壶能容纳的茶可能都倒不满人家一个杯子。但是在潮州喝凤凰单丛茶用这种壶很合适，因为单丛这种茶不能一次喝太多。"潮州手拉壶工艺精湛至此，却并不像宜兴紫砂壶、景德镇瓷壶那样广为人知，所以当地匠人自发进行改良，以符合更多元受众群体的需求。

"我们不只有经典壶型，也会根据生肖设计对应主题的壶，猴年出猴壶，马年有马壶，在壶中加入动物元素来创新。"

"这些表面光亮的是水磨壶。研发水磨壶是为了开拓东南亚市场，东南亚的顾客比较喜欢这种质感。比如，泰国经销商会买这些壶回去做水磨加工，像揭阳做玉一样，把外面磨掉，露出里面的颜色，水磨出透亮的光泽。"

"这种方壶的壶型是非常漂亮的，但是用手拿起来会不太舒服，这种主要是作观赏用。我们做这个提梁壶也是尽量做出最大气、最漂亮的壶型，不太考虑实用功能的。"

思博站在几款造型相当别致的壶具前，在我们的惊叹声中逐一介绍。"在潮州传统工艺里，手拉壶是有实用性的。潮州的木雕、潮绣一般只作观赏用途，实用性比较低，手拉壶工艺就不一样。"

一路随行的韩师的柯敏老师是拉得一手好壶的制壶匠人，他的手拉壶工作室"柏荫精舍"隐于市井深处。为了解潮州人日常生活中的饮茶文化，我们与韩师外国语学院的同学们聚于柏荫精舍，饮茶闲聊。

一盆热水端上来，柯敏老师起身挽了衣袖开始工夫茶的第一道工序——洗杯。冒着腾腾热气的水中，将一个茶杯平放于盆中，他的拇指和中指轻执另一杯的杯口和杯底，使手中杯的杯口与盆中杯的杯口垂直，两指稍用力，手中杯即开始快速转动，其杯口在盆中杯的水中巡过几遍。只手翻飞间，小小工夫茶杯被洗得仔仔细细。

"热水不烫手吗？"座位离柯敏老师最近的张婧迎着热气发问。

"烫是烫的，习惯了就好。"柯敏老师的语气和手上洗杯的动作一样从容淡定。我盯着柯敏老师手上令人眼花缭乱的动作，心想不知经过多少次热水洗礼才造就这样一双灵巧的手。

潮州人对茶有一种理所当然的钟情，简直令人觉得潮州人生而具有泡茶饮茶之天分。但在我等异乡人看来，潮州人津津乐道的"上门吵架也要先泡一壶茶"的嗜茶精神实在有趣得离奇。

"茶在我家其实是很重要的一部分。家里人要求我们学会沏茶，虽然我现在的功夫还不到家。只要有客人来，我们就一定会拿出茶壶泡茶，可能会从早晨7点就开始喝茶，一直到晚上10点，客人不走，茶壶就不凉。"

"我只会烧点热水泡泡速溶茶包。"鲁晖拍拍我的腿，凑到我耳边小声嘟囔着，"我都不知道家里的茶叶放在哪里。"不常待客的我对此也知之甚少。

"茶对我来说不仅仅是'茶米'，更是一种精神食粮。我来自潮州市凤凰镇，那里以产茶闻名。从小我的生活就和茶紧密相关。小时候，我会和父母一起去采茶，帮父母做茶，我们就是以茶为生的。我还记得高中有位老师说过，一个凤凰人，无论他/她去到哪里，无论他/她走多远，他/她的生活都会和茶有关。"

"饮茶其实也是一种商业往来方式。像我爸爸他们谈生意，就会一起喝茶，一边喝茶，一边谈生意。"

"我的印象中，潮州人喝茶要有三个杯子，放在一起成一个'品'字。这三个杯子是有讲究的，喝茶的可能不止三个人，所以需要互相谦让。比如，在座各位同学喝茶，就要在老师们之后。"毕业自中山大学、如今生活在潮州老家的林悦师姐也向大家分享了多年的饮茶体验。"潮州有句俗话叫'茶三酒四玩耍二'，意思是说，喝茶最好是三个人，喝酒四个人，玩耍两个人。喝茶有一点非常好，就是可以避免尴尬。几个人坐在一起，特别是有陌生人在场，找不到话题，气氛尴尬，你总可以说一句'喝茶'，然后洗茶、泡茶的过程就可以消磨时间，泡得差不多了，脑子里也想出话题了。人越喝茶越精神，话匣子也就打开了。"

"潮州人泡工夫茶，可以有21道工序。大家或许听过其中几道，像'茗倾素纸''烫杯滚杯''关公巡城''韩信点兵'这些招式……"作为柏荫精舍的主人，柯敏老师讲起潮州工夫茶艺如数家珍。

"21道工序？那什么时候才能喝上茶啊？"张婧回过头来吐了吐舌头。

"泡茶也可以很随意的，像散打一样，没有那么多规则，只要打赢就好。"柯敏老师笑着解释道："不是非要学会21道工序才能泡茶。最简化的程序是先烫一下茶具，把茶具的温度提高，把茶叶放进去。第一泡用来洗杯子，第二泡就可以喝了。潮州人想喝茶，用一个小杯就能喝。"

茶水不断，语声不绝，柏荫精舍门前巷口众人惜别时已是午夜时分。

"这一晚上听下来，潮州真是男女老少都爱喝茶啊！现在如果能喝杯热乎的工夫茶就好了！"鲁晖裹紧外套走在我旁边感叹着。

"可不是吗！潮州人血管里流的都是工夫茶！"我挽着鲁晖的胳膊向前走着，一个劲直点头。

像过去六天一样，客车停在牌坊街入口对面，我们忙不迭地在20秒的绿灯时间里小跑着穿过入口前的十字路口，与夜色一道向牌坊街深处走去。抵达客栈时已是处处灯火，这是我们在潮州的最后一夜。洗漱过后，我拿起房间置物台上红色塑封的小包凤凰单丛茶包仔细端详。出了潮州地界，全国各地怕是再没有什么客栈会备着凤凰单丛茶了。瞥见置物台下墙边的一团白色物件，我蹲下身去打量，下是大肚广口的小瓷罐，上是平底弯边的瓷托盘，那托盘上倒扣的，正是工夫茶杯。茶叶归于热汤，旅程近于尾声，不知潮州城外何日再见凤凰单丛。

# 潮州随想：食味之极在纯粹

林 涵

　　18岁后，因求学故，我在珠三角定居。每与好友出去吃饭，几经商议后选择潮汕牛肉火锅，作为潮汕人的我总免不了自动晋升一桌之厨。朋友们往往信任我娴熟得像刻进DNA里一样的操作，其间或无觥筹交错，但众宾往往必欢。

　　不久之前，一位熟人跟我讲，他的潮汕朋友在牛肉火锅面前手足无措，什么都不会，有时他甚至怀疑这朋友是个假潮汕人。潮汕饮食的精妙或许在此可见一斑：牛肉与汤锅"几上几下"的关系，看似朴实无华，要是没有细心留意、亲身实践过，亦参不透这半尺方寸间的美味玄学。火候少了，肉不出味；火候过了，肉质僵硬；不同部位，秉质不同，因"材"施"火"，方得好味。场面每及到此，总是牵扯出一些关于故乡的片段。

　　今年秋末，我因修习中山大学国际翻译学院"创意写作与翻译"课程，到潮州一周调研地方文化。在牌坊街的一条横巷里住下，巷中新营的民宿鳞次栉比。我们小组的任务是调研潮汕食文化，对于我这个本地人来说，一踏进潮汕地界[①]，"食文化"就已经环绕不绝了。

　　我住的民宿门口有一家只做早餐的肠粉店。第一晚住下时，我还没意识到这夜中巷口紧闭的铁门意味着什么，只当是一户人家。我自幼对声音极其敏感，翌日清晨被隔了两层楼的窗下细细碎碎的声音吵醒。推窗一看，已然炊烟腾腾，食客络绎不绝，手表的指针停在6点18分。看来老板已经在夜半之中悄悄地磨好了第二天的肠粉粉浆了。肠粉粉浆隔半天便始趋变质，故每一个做肠粉的厨师都要知道当天自己大概能卖出多少份，并据此磨相应分量的粉浆。熟悉的方言从小店的各个角落传入我的耳朵，食客无一例外是本

---

[①] "潮汕"并非行政区划概念，而是以是否通行潮汕方言为根本标准划定的一个在文化上紧密联结的地理区域，在行政区划上从东至西包括粤东的潮州、汕头、揭阳三个地级市。本文作者为汕头市澄海区人。本文所有注释皆为本文作者自注。

地人，且多为穿着得体的老阿姨，想必来此是她们晨练之前的必备流程。

说到肠粉，我小时候第一次到潮州去的是饶平，记忆已模糊不清，唯记得吃了一家"老字号"肠粉店。店比一般的饮食小店破旧得多，木门爬满铜锈，座椅也破如残垣，其实跟所见这家相去不远；但肠粉确实美味，且四元钱可得一大碗汤，汤中加入瘦肉、肉丸、猪肝、虾肉等，几小片芹菜浮于清汤之上，食材新鲜，味道把控得刚好，很是鲜甜。清汤之美味秘诀往往在食材之鲜，无他。

肠粉原是广府食物，传入潮汕地区之后，潮汕各地厨师又因"口"制宜，根据潮汕不同地区的口味，调整内馅与佐料，将其逐渐本土化，开创了新流派。时至今日，潮汕肠粉已扎根到每一个潮汕人的味蕾之中。潮汕肠粉"三足鼎立"：就酱汁而言，潮州肠粉以入盘姿态显眼的花生酱为标志；汕头肠粉酱汁最少，只由酱油和"菜脯麸"①组成，但该组合咸香非凡；揭阳肠粉酱汁几乎与汕头肠粉相同，但味道较清淡，量却更多，摆于盘中，肠粉体如湖中大屿。就馅料而言，无非鸡蛋、瘦肉、虾肉、蚝、豆芽、生菜等而已，不置其他调料，以亦无重味的粉皮包住各食材原真的味道。其他为入口之时锦上添花的事情，何不交给精心准备的酱料？

食材加工过程以保持原真性为第一要义，结合酱料之精调，从而达到提取食材纯粹味道的理念，这是潮菜区别于其他菜系的一个关键点。此次调研期间吃了一次"韩公宴"，其总负责人张生大师为了纪念韩愈治理潮州1200年，在2019年带领团队研发了潮菜宴，希以此尽量完整地展现和宣传典型的潮菜。其含14道菜，菜品名参考或结合了韩愈初到潮州时所写的述赞潮州食材丰富的《初南食贻元十八协律》②一诗中之词句。其实，14道菜里的各种食材，从绿植瓜蔬到荤肉海鲜等，无一样使我感到陌生。此宴最大的亮点莫过于酱料碟比菜盘还多：每一道菜都使用不同的酱料，有些菜品不止搭配一种酱料。酱料多以普通调味品特调而成，而食材的制作过程多求简以保原真。例如有一道菜"小象拱冰"，"小象"无非新鲜象拔蚌一只，而"冰"

---

① "菜脯"，潮汕方言对萝卜干的称呼。萝卜称"菜头"，晒干为脯。"菜脯麸"乃是将萝卜干切成丁并用植物油炒制成的调味品。

② 诗云："鲎实如惠文，骨眼相负行。蠔相黏为山，百十各自生。蒲鱼尾如蛇，口眼不相营。蛤即是虾蟆，同实浪异名。章举马甲柱，斗以怪自呈。其余数十种，莫不可叹惊。我来御魑魅，自宜味南烹。调以咸与酸，芼以椒与橙。腥臊始发越，咀吞面汗骍。惟蛇旧所识，实惮口眼狞。开笼听其去，郁屈尚不平。卖尔非我罪，不屠岂非情。不祈灵珠报，幸无嫌怨并。聊歌以记之，又以告同行。"

则是鸡蛋清中加入少许纯牛奶，入油鼎文火焯熟，一熟即捞出，因此成色光滑丝润。

"纯粹"如果只能登大雅之堂而不在市井之间，那多少有造作之嫌，但事实却并未如此。调研期间，与非潮汕人的食文化组组员们在子时已过的牌坊街上散步，买了一点凤凰浮豆干①吃，我特别叮嘱要夹一片新鲜薄荷叶再蘸特制的酱料吃。组员小黄一开始不解，觉得这样的搭配很奇怪，按我们说的做了之后，除一些表示感叹的汉语词汇和复读机一样的"真香"之外没说别的。豆腐本无奇香，是新鲜的薄荷叶和特调的酱料为豆腐的香味烘云托月。

记忆中的牌坊街尚未开发到如我此行所见巷陌已然栉列民宿的程度，此番一来，倒骤有日月新天的既视感。牌坊街仍是老样子，但每走几步就看到几家新开的装潢漂亮的小店，心中隐约觉得其与复原陈列的古老牌坊和痕纹深浅的青石砖路有些格格不入。不过吃的东西倒还是老样子。有街巷的地方就有逡巡着叫卖糕粿、豆花、草粿②的老伯。只是时过境迁，老伯也不复以口吆喝，而是将录音喇叭系在木色的小推车上，小推车所到之处，吆喝声也如影随形，小推车后角的红色塑料零钱桶上飘扬着绿蓝二色的付款码卡片。

关于故乡的记忆总是与食物相关。自记事起，我常在城与镇之间来往。我和父母住在城区，奶奶住在村里一方并不宽大的老房子里。老屋院子里的桑葚长势甚好，邻居的小孩常去采摘，父亲常打趣说，再这么摘下去，今年的桑葚酒就酿不成了。我家有酿果酒的习惯，以镇上或隔壁镇上不知从何年何月就开始酿酒的酒坊老板的高度数纯米酒为底，以各种当季水果为料，如桑葚、青梅、青葡萄、龙眼等。新鲜的果子经过清洗、加工、入酒、密封的步骤，隔之几月或经年，则可饮享，往往甘醇。家酿果酒因底酒本烈，故性亦稍烈，但没有欧洲烈酒那种直击喉头的淋漓与刺激，多的是入喉后酒味和果味对味蕾反应的轮番调取。别家别户自然也有相似的酒酿存在，关键在于，酿酒所用的果子一定要是本地当季的新鲜水果，尤以采摘下来立即处理的为最宜，否则入酒之后，植物果实本身的香气和汁液之精华散发不出来，果酒也就失去了其存在的意义。

---

① "豆干"，潮汕方言中对"豆腐"的称谓。"浮"是豆腐的做法，即将豆腐加入滚烫油锅炸熟，由于豆腐外脆里嫩，入油锅后浮于液面之上，故潮汕人称此法为"浮"。"凤凰"，地名，指潮州市潮安区凤凰镇。

② 潮汕小吃，做法和成品均类似龟苓膏，但原料不同。

村里还常有那种走街串巷卖糕粿的老人。小时候会去买"风吹饼"。"风吹饼"乃是特薄特脆的煎饼,由于形体极薄,仿佛风一吹就折,因而得名。圆形"风吹饼"色泽淡黄,在幼小的我眼里像极了月亮,轻咬一口,就好像真的尝到月亮的味道,滋味甜而不腻,确似早春轻风拂面。

奶奶早些年有豢养禽畜的习惯,养了两只猪和几只母鸡,有时到了"做节"①前,还会买两只鹅养着待宰。汕头澄海的狮头鹅闻名遐迩,这要归功于澄海几乎每镇每村都有养殖户承包池塘养鹅,小户少说也养有几十只,超大户饲上千只不在话下。澄海村镇养鹅成风与鹅一直是潮汕人祭祀的重头供品密不可分。潮汕人的理念是,理所当然要将人间的美味进贡给神明和祖先。

"做节"的前一天,各家各户往往都会宰杀一只成年鹅,在灶台上或院子里支起一口大铁锅,旺盛的柴火直冲云霄。将新宰的整鹅放入锅中,辅以生抽、老抽等调味酱料,川椒、八角、南姜等香料或药材,以及符合各家口味的各种小调味品。几个小时之后,通体棕色的卤鹅出锅,香味远传。祭拜结束之后享味时,一般将其连皮带肉切成薄片,再蘸上煮制时原初的卤汁,食客能感受到卤味渗进皮肉的每一处细节。

"做节"的时候,做红粿桃②更是常事。以面粉和少许淀粉等为原料,加入少许深浅不一的红色植物汁液,打发成面团以成粿皮。内包或甜或咸的馅料,甜者多为豆沙、芋泥,咸者多是以肉丁和蔬菜炒制的饭团,或半咸半甜谓之"双拼"。最后用"粿印",即是塑形的模具,塑造成形似逗号的"粿",然后入鼎蒸炊,或炊后再煎制至外皮酥脆。红粿桃不仅是一种祭拜神明祖先的标准供品,更是食味层次丰厚的佳肴:不论是炊制即食还是煎制再吃,都可以感受到从内到外多重而统一的口感。甜者自不必说,丝滑热流,入口即化;咸者入口,米香面味、荤素交织,如精妙的弦乐四重奏一般。

一年一度的"营老爷"③也是我早年印象深刻的场面,丝竹锣鼓,鞭炮不断,数不完的热闹堆积在短短几天之中。"营老爷"一到两天前的晚上就要去"大宫",即村中礼神的大庙里敬神祭祖,此间红粿桃等粿品、最大最漂亮的卤鹅、平躺在贡桌后的巨大乳猪等,是最鲜明的标志。有些地区或村镇还有"赛大猪"仪式,即是每家都要以整猪为祭品,比一比谁家杀来敬神

---

① "做节",潮汕方言,即传统节日时,潮汕人需要礼敬神明、祭拜祖先,以节日的重要程度为标准,规模从小到大不等。
② 由于潮汕方言的分化与流变,"红粿桃"在潮汕部分地区又称"红桃粿"。
③ 潮汕方言。"营"通"迎";"老爷",潮汕方言中对神明的称呼;"营老爷"即游神赛会。

祭祖的猪最大最肥，这往往代表了此家之人财力何厚、敬意几诚。

"营老爷"当天，村里的老人各携丝竹锣鼓组成行进乐队，配合木雕的神明塑像和以潮绣技法制作的大型旗幡在村寨之间行进，是为迎神仪式。队伍经过的各家各户都会在自家门前放响一串长鞭炮，热烈迎神"落天"[1]，有些人家的鞭炮长得挂在二楼屋檐，地上还绕了好几圈。在潮汕民俗信仰中，各神在农历新年前需回天界开"年度工作会议"，做保佑百姓、造福当地的政绩述职报告，而农历新年过后，就又必须回人间供职，继续护佑一方土地。因此，神明"落天"时，人们必须盛大欢迎。

每村"营老爷"的时日几乎都在农历正月或二月，但日子一般不同。到这一天，村落之间亲朋邻人会互相邀请到本村参加"营老爷"。而"营老爷"的重头戏，其实依然在于吃。当游神队伍欢驰完毕之后，这一天剩下的事情就是宴请宾客。潮汕话将吃席称为"食桌"，其意绝非要你把桌子也当食物吃了，而是一桌全席；潮汕人素有"十二样菜桌"的说法，以虚数"十二"述一席之丰盛，有时候并非真的凑齐12道菜，但必须吃到你腹中妥帖，心情舒畅。尤记得家父一位旧友在宗族和社会关系中均德高望重，每一年都是从正月初一一直被请"食桌"到正月廿九，一个月下来，仅是吃卤鹅的量少说也有七八整只。

愈发觉得我同故乡之间的一切联结更多地是维系在"吃"这件事上了。我不常回乡，有很多偶然或必然变得陌生的要素在我的生活之中变得愈发清晰，但唯有我的口与胃，对潮菜的执念实比入木三分的墨痕再深两三分。粤菜固然精彩，只是若何时我感觉食欲不振或腹中不适，什么都不想吃，最终还是要去吃一顿潮菜。中山大学珠海校区北门外有一位揭阳大叔开牛肉粿条铺，虽然一直都是流动摊贩，但在所有的流动摊贩里，他几乎是人气最高者，潮汕人、非潮汕人从日中到子夜，络绎不绝，我自然也是他的老主顾。

近日，流动摊贩因某些原因而暂停营业，我认识的潮汕人和非潮汕人无一不想念他，还好他历经月余终于找到了新的店面，又重新营业，客皆大喜。潮菜之所以让我觉得口与胃直至心中都十分倚赖，或许关键就在于它的纯粹。正宗牛肉粿条的汤底是别无他物的，只有牛大骨数条，加盐熬制，成品汤汁色泽淡雅，嗅来与喝下都唯感醇厚牛味。牛肉和牛丸在牛骨汤中焯熟即捞起，但粿条是绝不可在牛骨汤中烫熟的，非另起炉灶支一清水锅来对付

---

[1] 潮汕方言中，"落天"意为"从天上下来"。

它不可，否则粿条的米面成分与牛肉牛骨汤的荤性混淆，将两败俱伤。

"纯粹"其实就是一种宗旨，不论食物的组分如何复杂，必须保证每一组分的原味发挥到极致。或许我的胃对"纯粹"的识别与记忆是深刻且排他的，这也或许就是潮菜某种诱人的长久魅力所在。

对"纯粹"的极致追求，不仅是个别现象。我的一位同村人在中山大学珠海校区南门外的城中村开食档。数年以来，每从清晨开店到深夜打烊，都很难闲出一双完整的手，不过店面也已从以前二三十平方米的小单间变成了有大厅和包厢的大排档。过去的一年，我见证了他试图研发潮菜与其他菜系的融合料理，最终宣告失败的过程，觉得吃起来荡然无潮菜感觉、非心中之所想。于是，他重新规划，把大排档改为纯正的潮汕牛肉火锅店，生意火爆好几倍，估计天天笑着睡。

城中村人来路繁杂，餐馆菜系百家齐放；五湖四海的城中村人，终还是为潮菜所征服。我的这位同村人数年来还一直在做烤鸡外卖，且从不打潮汕人的旗号，已久被周边食客尤其学生们奉为"永远的神"；然而潮菜是没有烤鸡的，但我确信他制作烤鸡也运用并融入了潮菜的技艺与宗旨。

前些日子，我拜访了一位已是高校教师的同门学长。在他简朴的办公室里，主宾二人对坐，学长娴熟地操作着工夫茶具，并拿出了一盒"地豆方"与我共享。"地豆"在潮汕话中意为花生，因其果实生于地下，开壳而见豆身而得名。潮汕人为食材取名，有时往往比顾名思义更加简明扼要。"地豆方"是将花生与糖混合炒制，再经过几道工序制成的形体长方的小吃，糖分将花生的豆香衬托得更加醇浓。夏日灼炎，不大宽敞的办公室里，空调散出凉风，二人以"地豆方"就着工夫茶闲坐畅聊，突然发觉这场面与感觉像是在故乡的某个下午也曾有过，口中眼前，仿是童年即景。

我还认识一位顶级咖啡师，年纪五十有余，同丈夫经营一家专门做手冲咖啡的咖啡店，客户多在一次试饮后频顾，"除却她家不是啡"。她跟我说："我做了二三十年的咖啡，来喝我们家的咖啡的人没有一个不夸的，就是你们潮汕人最难对付！潮汕人的嘴太刁了，有时候真搞不懂你们的味蕾是什么做的。我但凡知道顾客是个潮汕人，冲咖啡的时候觉得操作有一点不够完美，都要重做，不敢出品，怕砸了自己的招牌。"

仿佛潮厨们的匠心就藏在 DNA 里，誓要把手中新鲜的食材变成精细的艺术品。甚至对于厨师自己来说，完成这样的艺术品，首先乃是"为悦己者容"，而后才有"众宾欢也"。潮州调研之行有一细节使我印象颇深。在韩山师范学院观摩国家级潮菜大师做菜（见图1），其中有一食材是金丝血燕。

他的做法是将其用纯净水焯熟并滤出汁液即其精华，但正是这个简单的步骤，他同助手一直边做边讨论，检验滤出的原汁如何如何，需不需回炉再造。反复十数次之后，他紧锁的眉头终于得到放松，绽开欣慰笑颜，眼神像极了一名对构图、配色、笔触等追求完美的画家，在对作品局部暂时感到满意之后终于长舒一口气。

图1　学生们在韩山师范学院潮菜基地观摩国家级大师烹饪

或许我对牛肉火锅"几上几下"精细娴熟的把握，是我多年来受到潮菜纯粹的熏陶、内化后的外显。潮菜从里到外透露着的"纯粹"，首先是人之本心的纯粹。它是家酿甘醇的果酒里蕴藏着的对自己味蕾和生活质量的追求；是村里叫卖的"风吹饼"，物如其名地薄如蝉翼的表象之下，饼匠企盼村人给予认同与信誉的本质；也是在"做节"时祭拜神明和"请人食桌"的卤鹅、红粿桃、大猪等反映的潮汕人对于非敢渎神和宴宾之道的严格准则。

其次是菜品本身及厨匠对待菜品制作的贯穿始末的纯粹，是一种无论如何都要保证食材新鲜，并以恰如其分的酱料搭配衬托出食材原真纯粹韵味的理念。关于这种纯粹的艺术性，你不仅可以在大雅餐府精致的宴席上尝到，也完全可以在市井街巷的豆腐坊中、肠粉店里找到。此外，它更是一种可延留、难消散的纯粹性。

美不过是一瞬间的感觉,唯有真实才是永恒的。潮菜之所以让潮汕人和非潮汕人都流连忘返,正是因为它纯粹得真实,也真实得纯粹,因此是常可追忆的、挥之不去的。姑且不表我一个在潮汕生活了18年的人对潮菜波澜起伏的执念,组员小黄在调研后两个月的昨天又问:什么时候再去吃凤凰浮豆干?

至此,脑中唯余今秋潮州随行的一位韩山师范学院与我同龄的老师说的话,便引此论以作结语:"我觉得我们潮汕人有一种特别的生活哲学,我们把几乎全部的精力都投入在'吃'这件事上了。"她教授的课业亦与潮汕文化相关。此言之绕梁,与食一顿潮菜后口中震荡着的回味同久。

## 遗憾·不再遗憾

莫艳池

名瑞潮绣艺术馆里,蔡中涵的洪亮声音在宽阔的展厅里回响。眼前这个年轻男子身着休闲套服,体态端正、言辞流利,正向我们讲解橱窗里一幅龙凤潮绣作品(见图1)。他时而伸手指向橱窗,示意我们观察某个绣品中的垫高细节,时而注视我们的摄像头,露出礼貌的笑容。

图1 蔡中涵先生在名瑞潮绣艺术馆向师生介绍潮绣作品

"想请问一下,潮绣不同于苏绣或其他绣种,那它最大的特点是什么?"我张了张嘴,心跳微微加速,提出了困惑我多日的问题,几秒后抬头迎上蔡中涵的目光。

蔡中涵转头看向我,说道:"我们都知道,中国的四大名绣是蜀绣、苏绣、湘绣以及由广绣和潮绣构成的粤绣。四大名绣在丝线、针法的使用上都有异有同。由于现代交通的发达以及中西方文化的融合，这四大名绣其实逐渐演变成你中有我、我中有你。苏绣以鱼为主，湘绣以老虎、狮子为主，蜀绣以熊猫等动物为主，而潮绣则主要以龙凤为主。潮绣和其他绣种最大的区别是其垫高的技艺。'垫高'是一种能使物像形成立体效果的工艺技法，绣前先用纸丁、棉絮在需要垫高的图案上做立体造型，而后在上边用金银线、丝绒线施绣。你会看到很多潮绣作品中都有垫高的部分……"

随着蔡中涵的话音，同学们纷纷看向橱窗里婚纱主题的潮绣作品：有的做成了鱼尾裙的样式，有的做成了镂空款，有的做成了中国传统旗袍的样式，白色的婚纱在模特摇曳的体态下显得格外浪漫。此时，每一幅作品在暖黄灯光的照耀下，都充满了生机与活力。

"蔡中涵是从美国留学回来的。"身边不知道谁传来了一句嘀咕。我再次抬头，细看眼前这位艺术馆负责人，年轻的他话语间透露着丰富的学识，他的观点也让我耳目一新，与此前我们采访的康惠芬老师以及李晓丹老师截然不同。

李晓丹老师是非物质文化遗产潮绣技法市级传承人，她将剪纸的元素融入了潮绣作品中，开拓创新，创作了《红船启航》《井冈山会师》《开国大典》等作品。李老师在接受采访时，神采飞扬地谈及自己的母亲。"我的妈妈最擅长绣的是人物。我可以给你们展示一下她的作品。"说罢，她便拿出了一幅被折叠得整整齐齐的绣品，外层包裹着多张塑料纸。她轻轻将绣品摊开放在桌子上，绣品上的人物一个个地呈现出来：一群身着五颜六色衣服的女孩正在互相交谈。"这是红楼梦中一个很经典的场景。你们看，每个人脸上的表情都是不一样的，都是我妈妈一针一线做出来的……"晓丹大师对自己母亲的敬佩之意溢于言表。在被问及潮绣的传承时，她告知我们，目前她在韩山师范学院担任潮绣老师，不过，她坦言，暂时没有更多的精力去培养自己的接班人，只想做好当下的作品。

康惠芳老师是非物质文化遗产潮绣技法国家级传承人，2015年被授予"联合国文化大使"称号。与康老师进行访谈的那天，我问了同样的问题："康大师您好！我们是中山大学国际翻译学院的学生，此次来潮州主要是想实地调研，了解潮州茶文化、饮食文化以及潮绣和潮剧的发展。我想请问一下，您觉得潮绣与苏绣或其他绣种最大的区别是什么？"

"我就问你一个问题，你知道什么是潮绣吗？你见过潮绣吗？"康老师身体靠在椅子上，双腿交叉叠放着，一只手搭在膝盖上，一只手搭在椅子把手上,两眼直直地看着我,脸上看不出什么表情。

我顿住了,往右边看了一眼课程负责人戴凡老师,再转头看了一眼同伴,握住麦克风的手不由自主地往回缩了一下。"呃,好像见过。前几天在百师园博物馆,当时看到一个女师傅在绣着一幅……"我的声音越来越小。

康老师突然发出了一声笑,打断了我的话,说道:"你看,除了在我的展馆,你还能在其他地方见到这么多潮绣作品吗?应该很少了吧?现在,除了我,还有多少人在从事这个行业呢?我敢说,整个潮州,没几个了!"说罢,康大师看了我们几眼。我不自觉地避开了她的目光。

戴凡老师开口:"据我了解,也有一些潮绣爱好者,他们自发组织起来,定期举办一些工作坊活动。这也算是一种努力吧。"

"谁?你给我看看。是不是真正的潮绣,我一看就知道。"

戴凡老师掏出手机,找了好几分钟,终于翻出了一幅刺绣图。康大师只瞥了一眼,便大笑起来。我和其他小伙伴面面相觑:这是什么意思?

"我只能说,这完全就是小学生写作文的水平,连入门都不算!"

康大师不再笑,语气忽然变了:"很少有年轻人愿意从事潮绣这个行业了。我就问问你们,你们会愿意花一整天在这里做刺绣吗?我跟政府说,我有钱啊,我出钱,请一批年轻人来我这里学刺绣。就学一个月,一个月我便知道谁是一块好料子。条件是,被我挑中的人,要留下来跟我学。现在跟我学潮绣的绣娘中,有的是出嫁前便跟我到现在的;有一位小姑娘跟你们年纪差不多,很有天赋,我就把她留了下来。她是一块可以好好培养的料子!至于她以后会不会继续留下来从事这一行业,就说不准了,现在的年轻人选择更多了!"

随后,康老师领着我们去到顶层的绣坊工作室。这个工作室虽然不大,但是整齐地分成了三列,每列摆了三到四个工位,每个工位上都有一个潮绣专用的架子,上边放满了不同颜色的针线。我左右环顾,一眼就看到角落里一个最年轻的扎着高马尾的女孩。

"她就是那个小姑娘吗?"我低头向同行的君君问道。然后,君君和我一起慢慢地走近那个女孩。女孩感受到了我们的靠近,抬头礼貌性地冲我们微笑了一下,手上的针线却没有停下。

"你很喜欢潮绣吗?"我轻轻问。

女孩低着头,继续摆弄着针线,一秒已经穿了好几次针线。她轻声回应:"呃,也没有很喜欢,就是家里人让我来试试,就当一份工作嘛。"

我们还没来得及继续交谈,大部队已经随着康老师下楼了,我们也只好匆匆紧随，以至于我都忘记询问女孩的姓名了。

后来，康老师在一楼展示厅带我们参观了她绣有孔雀、牡丹花、锦鲤等的作品，还有一幅作品绣的是习近平总书记的寄语。

原来，2020年习近平总书记考察潮州古城时，康老师在广济楼现场为习总书记介绍了潮绣刺绣针法，并当场演示了潮绣技艺。习总书记对康老师说："你们是中华民族几千年文化的传承人。感谢你们做出的贡献。"这一席话被康老师做成了刺绣，装裱起来，挂在展馆的一楼。她向我们介绍这幅刺绣时，眼里仿佛泛着泪花，声音激昂，充满了坚定和自豪。

灯光下，藏在她眼角下的细纹和弯弯的眼袋让我有些动容，这双眼睛，想必一生都只专注于她心中的方布和丝线吧。

临别时，康老师意味深长地拉起我的手，说了一句："谢谢你，小美女。"我和康老师对视了一眼，会心一笑，被她握紧的手也用了点力。最后，我们一起看向了镜头，留下一张大合影。

在我看来，康老师是坚守传统、捧着一颗炽热的心培育下一代的代表，而李晓丹老师则是在传承的基础上寻求创新的潮绣传承人。相比于她们，蔡中涵先生可能是在对潮绣的传承中持开放态度的代表。

我的思绪忽然被蔡中涵的声音打断，他的那句掷地有声的"所谓'非遗'，就是非常遗憾"又在我脑海里响起，不断地碰撞我此前接受的观点和态度。我怔怔地看着蔡中涵以及眼前琳琅满目的潮绣，有些不知所措。

我还没来得及好好整理脑海中的思绪，蔡中涵便带着我们继续参观。我们走近了一个展台，那里摆放了十几件潮绣做的潮剧服装。

"潮绣也常用于潮剧服装。现在，几乎没有地方能像我们这里这样保留这么多潮剧服装了。大家看到的每一件服装都代表着潮剧中不同的角色，每一个角色都有其特点。"蔡中涵的话让我想起了之前李英群老先生说的话："潮剧讲述的是老百姓的心声，所以深受老百姓喜爱。"

脑海中又浮现出前一天晚上李英群老先生的身影。前一天晚上，为了解潮剧在潮州的发展情况，我们邀请了李英群先生做采访。他出生于广东揭阳，定居于潮州古城，是潮剧作家和编剧。那天晚上，他在潮州文化研究中心的陈月娟老师的搀扶下，步伐缓慢地走进城南中英文学校的会议室。他身形消瘦，有较明显的驼背，戴着灰色的帽子和黑框眼镜。

"我是搞潮剧的，普通话不太好。要是今天讲得不好，那肯定是因为要讲普通话。"老先生开场的幽默感一下子拉近了与我们的距离。随后，李老先生和我们分享了许多他与潮剧的故事。"我以前下乡，在农村遇到了很多有趣的事情，后来我就把这些故事写到潮剧里。一眨眼，从事这一行业也几十年了。现在，看的人少了，我们都很少排新戏了……"从他的介绍中，我们了解到，潮剧不同于其他剧种的特点是丑角类型多。李老先生仿佛对潮剧中的丑角有着特别的执念，说："我不参与表演，但你看我这模样，演的话也肯定是个丑角！"

潮剧与潮绣一样，都是非物质文化遗产，而且都面临着难以传承的困境。被问及如何看待潮剧未来的发展与传承时，李老先生顿了几秒，缓缓说道："看懂潮剧是需要基础的。现在是'快餐'时代，年轻人们都太忙了，都忙着奔小康。"他说完之后，大家都陷入了沉默。

在当今时代，"唱戏"不再是热门的工作出路，而"看戏"也不再是常见的娱乐方式，那些仍在坚守传统的年轻人成了与当下追求潮流的趋势格格不入的一种特别的存在。那天晚上，在李英群先生的分享结束后，青年演员刘樱妮给我们演唱了潮剧《春香传》中的片段"狱中歌"。

《春香传》是由王菲先生根据上海同名越剧移植改编的潮剧。它讲述了18世纪后期，朝鲜淑宗时代，南原府艺妓月梅的女儿春香在广寒楼前邂逅当地使道子弟李梦龙，两人互生爱慕，却受到李梦龙之父的谴责。恰好李父升迁到京城汉阳任中堂，梦龙与春香被迫分手。此间，新任的南原使道卞学道强娶春香不成，便以"谋叛造反"的罪名，将春香施以酷刑下狱。春香忠贞不屈，被判死刑。时梦龙已任巡按御史，得讯后急赴南原查办了卞学道，与春香团聚。故事讲述的恰好是春香在狱中面临酷刑的片段。

手机里音乐响起，只见樱妮姐姐神情专注，开口便是如泣如诉，眼里写满了忧伤，又带着坚定，将那股对爱人的思念、面对恶霸势力的宁死不屈表现得淋漓尽致。

我和在场的大多数同学虽然都不懂潮汕话，但都被她的表演深深打动了。我的眼眶湿润了，抬头看到戴凡老师也红了眼眶。一时间，大家都沉浸在饱含深情的潮曲中。

我鼓起勇气举起了手，向樱妮姐姐提出了一个问题："请问你在学习潮剧这条路上遇到过最困难的事情是什么？有没有哪一刻让你觉得坚持不下去，想要放弃？"

谁知我这一问，竟惹哭了樱妮姐姐。"我觉得最困难、最坚持不下去的时候，就是不被身边的人认可的时候。他们，包括我的父母，都会说，'你为什么要学这个？有什么出路？'。每每听到这些话时，是我最坚持不下去的时刻。"

她的话一字一句地落在我心里，令我动容。那一刻，我对面前这个女孩涌起了一股深深的敬意，为她的勇敢喝彩，被她的坚持打动。

当晚采访过后，我的心情有些沉重。作为一名非潮州人，我对潮绣和潮剧的了解都不深，没有资格去评判这两项艺术的现状，但我却在短短几天的参观、采访中，对这两种艺术产生了深深的怜惜与敬畏。

不过，从蔡中涵的博物馆走出来后，原来沉重的思绪似乎轻松了一些。戴凡老师说："看到这些艺术被以这种形式保存下来，仿佛我们的不安与焦虑得到了安放。"她的话也给了我很大启发。也许，真的如蔡中涵所说，所谓非物质文化遗产代表的是落后的生产力，是注定要被淘汰的。但我们也在这个淘汰的过程中，看到了依然坚守着传统的康老师，依然对潮剧怀着热忱的李老先生，也看到了融合时代特色不断创新的李晓丹老师，他们都在用不同的方式去呵护心中的热忱。

离开潮州的前一天，我们参观了龙湖古镇。在古镇狭小的小巷中，我偶然遇到了一位正在听潮剧的老婆婆。老婆婆的家只有一个房间，房间的尽头摆放着一张床，床底下塞满了各种杂物，而另一边则放满了衣服。她在家门口端着小锅，洗着米。在一张轻微掉漆的黑色小方桌上，摆着一台黑色收音机，里边正在播放着潮剧。我听不懂潮剧讲的是什么内容，只觉得收音机里的声音格外动听，充满了人间烟火。

我莫名地被眼前的一幕打动。不管是潮绣，还是潮剧，它们其实永远都不会消失，它们一直存在于每一个潮州百姓的生活中，乃至生命里。

# Reports of the Teochew Field Trip

In this section, the three reports constitute narratives concerning a field trip to Teochew City, Guangdong Province, covering the students' visits to a range of locations and their reflections on their experiences.

# Nice to Meet You Again, My Tea and My Hometown

## DING Kexin

At Gate A14 of Guangzhou South Railway Station, a long queue of passengers had lined up to board the train. Alongside the queue, a female teacher was surrounded by a group of university students with luggage, some glancing about with expectation and joy, while others were gazing at the teacher, who was speaking and nodding from time to time.

"Guys, from this moment on, everyone should carefully observe and note down everything around us," the teacher said.

The group drew the attention from other passengers. An old lady wearing reading glasses was in the long queue at the boarding gate. Her eyes swept around the group and stopped at me:

"Hi! I was wondering what you are doing. Is it an activity or what?"

"We are students of Sun Yat-Sen University, heading to Teochew to investigate Teochew culture."

"Oh, that sounds interesting," she smiled kindly. "It's so good to see a bunch of young people like you."

We, the bunch of young people, came from the School of International Studies at Sun Yat-Sen University. We were taking the Creative Writing and Translation course and needed to collect writing materials by investigating Teochew culture. We were divided into three groups: tea culture, food culture, and Teochew opera and embroidery. Each group had four members respectively responsible for composing an English story, a Chinese story, a group report, and Chinese and English subtitles for the video we made during the investigation. In our group of Teochew tea, the one in charge of photography and video production was Wei Donghua, who was assisted by his two students. We also had Fu Yun, the course assistant, and Prof. Xie Guixia, a Teochew native. The teacher who was speaking to us was Prof.

Dai Fan.

We spent the first day en route. In the evening, we arrived at the first destination of our journey, Hanshan Normal University (hereafter "Hanshi"). The School of Geography and Tourism · School of Teochew Cuisine at the university had a course entitled "Creative Tourism", and the students of the course had just completed some research on Teochew culture. These students would give us the first glimpse of Teochew culture.

The multi-media classroom was illuminated by blazing lights. Groups of teachers and students were allocated to several large tables. Members of the tea culture group—Wang Xi, Zhigao, Yinuo and me—sat with three young men in charge of introducing tea culture. The students all lowered their eyes and occasionally played with the paper and pen on the table. Even their teacher made fun of them, "They are quite shy." During the Q&A session, Zhigao, scratching his head, stood up and asked, "Why is the tea in Teochew called Gongfu tea?"

One of the three students took the microphone. "Because it takes a lot of time to make Teochew Gongfu tea and drink it. ①" Unhurried activities like tea-drinking endure in the Teochew area, demonstrating the spirit of Teochew life.

The introduction lasted for two hours. Frankly, it was nothing new. I was a little bored. I glanced at the attentive people around me, at Ms. Xie, a Teochew native, who was gazing with rapt eyes and a smile at the student on stage explaining Teochew culture. After the introduction, we left Hanshi and I went to the inn on the Pedestrian Street. Strolling along the Pedestrian Street with Yinuo and Zhigao, reviewing dawdling passers-by and tea drinkers lingering over Gongfu tea in the herbal tea shop, I couldn't help saying, "It's so good to be home." Well, I must confess that I am also a Teochew native. Teochew area includes Shantou City, Teochew City and Jieyang City. I grew up in Shantou City. "Let's go eat something!" suggested Zhigao. Yinuo and I nodded. We saw a dessert shop, identified as "*Yamunian*" (written as "鸭母捻" in Chinese).

"*Yamunian* is the Teochew cuisine introduced by the Hanshi students," Yinuo recalled. "Kexin, is it tasty? I want to give it a try."

---

① In Chinese, Gongfu means time.

"Have never tried it..." I felt embarrassed. "But I want to now."

*Five yuan for a bowl of Yamunian.* I remember that those were the words on the stand beside my primary school. But I have always steered clear of it because of its strange shape. Recalling that the Hanshi students just said *Yamunian* tastes like *Yuanxiao*, I wanted to try it.

The three of us were soon lost in Teochew desserts.

"I've always felt that food tastes the best when shared," said Zhigao.

"Exactly." Yinuo and I nodded.

The next morning, we visited the Master's Park, an exhibition hall for intangible cultural heritage along with a ceramics museum. In the ceramics museum, everyone gushed over various styles of ceramic ornaments. Mr. Wei, the photographer, and I stood before a round ceramic plate, studying the exquisite patterns on the plate.

"These ceramics are works of art," said Mr. Wei.

"There's a plate like that in my home." I envisioned the object set unobtrusively in its glass cabinet.

After lunch, we all took a walk. Along the way, we saw low houses and tall green trees. Occasionally, someone swept before a house. The crisp sound, accompanied by birds' chirps, stirred my heartstrings. The smell of sunshine in the air and a few wisps of burning incense reminded me of the long summer vacation I spent in the countryside when I was a child.

Wang Xi and I were standing in front of an old residential building wrapped in vines, which shone in the sun like those in Miyazaki Hayao's animated film. "I think it's good to settle here." Wang Xi took pictures with her smartphone. I smiled—an ordinary life scene for me had my classmates and teachers snapping photos. Let's go back a little bit. One month ago, Prof. Dai announced that the destination of the course was Teochew City. I was devastated. I had anticipated going to a new place and learning a kind of culture utterly new to me, but the reality turned out to be the opposite. I embarked on this journey with low expectations, but now I began to notice interesting points in it; people from other places might notice details I would pass over.

In the evening, we interviewed several Teochew students at Hanshi. The interview was held in a quiet and simple quadrangle courtyard, called "*Sidianjin*" (written as "四点金" in Chinese) in the Teochew area. On the low ridge stretched a great patch of purple night sky. The streetlights here are not as intense as those in big cities, so the stars and moon are particularly bright. Several Teochew students sedately related their stories over Teochew Gongfu tea:

"My family is asking me to learn how to make tea, although I'm not skilled yet."

"As soon as a guest comes, we would prepare the teapot and make tea. From 7:00 a.m. to 10:00 p.m., we won't turn off the electric teapot if a guest is still there."

"Teochew people are sure to have a cup of tea after dinner. If they don't, they will feel that something has gone awry."

...

These everyday narratives of tea were second nature to me. These Teochew young women sitting in front of me, although strangers to me, live the same kind of life as I did because of this cultural symbol. Culture, a general and abstract word, was producing some elusive shapes at the precise moment. Culture may indicate common living habits and similar life memories, which bind a group of people together, even though they don't know each other.

"Do you go through all the 21 tea-making processes before drinking tea?"

"Come on! That's impossible!" I was laughing within. These cultural symbols, which are old hat to me, are completely strange to people from other places. Just like in my university dormitory, my Xinjiang roommate likes to eat naan, while my roommate from the northeast likes to store food. People of different regions bear their own sets of unique cultural symbols, which strike outsiders as novel.

When talking about their hometown, the Teochew students in front of us can't hide their smiles. I wondered if I wore the same smile when I spoke of my hometown to the people around me.

After the interview, Ke Min, a teacher of Hanshi, demonstrated how to make a teapot. He pulled out a mass of clay from a bucket. Cradling the clay as if holding a bowl, while talking and laughing with us, he finished the teapot. Beside me, Prof. Dai shouted: "Who wants to have a try? Come on! Guys from the tea culture group should have a go!"

I shook my head, covering my clumsy hands, and hid in the crowd. Yinuo poked her head out and said, "I want to try."

She imitated Mr. Ke, plopping the clay neatly on the tray. Then she pressed it between hands, and a decent teapot gradually took shape. The crowd exclaimed, "Wow, you are doing it so well!"

"Yinuo is very talented," confirmed Mr. Ke.

I admired Yinuo's talent and courage, but the next second, Yinuo's hand tilted, and the pot collapsed. Everyone laughed and Yinuo shook her head. Until the crowd dispersed, Yinuo sat before the potter's wheel, engrossed in playing with the clay.

On the third day, the bus took us to a village on a tea mountain. Narrow, multi-storey buildings were situated in a row near the mountain. On the first floor, which served as a tea shop and reception hall, are large barrels of tea, a long tea table and several plastic chairs. Tourists who are regular tea drinkers will taste it on the first floor. Without any promotion by tea merchants, they will be conquered by the fragrance of tea and willing to buy.

The temperature had plunged, and a bleak, cold wind cut to the bone. Wrapped tightly in our thin coats, we followed the local team leader toward the mountains. Before we set foot on the mountain road, we came to an open shed where two local villagers, shuddering like us, made us tea at the stone table beneath the awning and then washed the teacups. Even in cold weather, Teochew natives drank tea in the open. We could see how important tea is for Teochew natives.

Although this was said to be a developed mountainous area, we ran out of steps and had to search for footholds in stone. There were no signs on the mountain, so we had to rely on the leader's sense of direction and fuzzy memory. In the tea field, there is a wooden pole in each tea tree, with a piece of yellow paper pasted on the top. Is the Teochew area so superstitious that even tea trees are pasted with runes? Later, I learned that these yellow pieces of paper are sticky insect boards coated with inducers, which protect tea plants from moths. Finally, we went up and down the mountain from a tea field.

"Oh my God! We seem to have walked onto someone's roof!" Xueming, who was making his way at the head of the team, turned back and exclaimed. "Now we may have to get down off the roof. That is, we have to let the family get up here and open the door for us," he added.

Everyone laughed. Who could have expected such a dramatic scene? Prof. Dai was also thrilled. She turned back and told me again and again, "This can be the highlight part of your report! Do record it!"

In the afternoon, we went to visit Jiaming Tea Estate. It is an organic tea farm covering 200 hectares. My classmates gathered around the owner of the tea garden and listened to his introduction to its architecture. At this time, I was sleepy, so I sat on the roadside beyond the crowd. The voices of Zhigao and Wang Xi and the tea garden owner faded away. As I was drifting off, the voice of an old woman woke me up. I looked up and saw a thin and dark figure in farmer attire. She pointed to the cabin a few steps away and asked me if I wanted to go to her home to rest. I shook my head politely and began to chat with her in Teochew dialect.

"Yi[①], do you live here?"

She nodded. "Yes, I am a farmer here."

"What do you usually do every day?"

"Quite a lot. I have to get up early in the morning to cook, then go up the mountain to work in the field until four or five in the afternoon, and then I go home to cook. My back always hurts in the evening."

Later, the owner of the tea garden took us to the tea factory to show us how to process tea. I drifted away from the crowd and saw Wang Xi exchanging ideas on writing with Ms. Fu Yun. After the visit, we walked out of the tea house. The old woman farmer stopped me.

"Come to my place and have a cup of tea," she said, her accent reminding me of my grandmother.

I waved my hand and declined, saying that we were in a hurry.

"I think you work too hard. You don't even have time to have tea." She sighed.

We spent the whole day wandering in the tea mountains. In the evening, we interviewed professionals in Teochew opera, which is a unique opera in the

---

① A way to call old woman in Teochew dialect.

Teochew area and one of the four famous operas in Guangdong. The first person to be interviewed was 80-year-old Li Yingqun, a senior writer of Teochew opera.

"Teochew opera was once brilliant, but now it has been impacted by foreign cultures. Young people don't like Teochew opera these days, but I can do nothing to help. Today's young people pursue efficiency, be it in learning, in love or in money-making. Teochew opera takes too much time to watch, and it needs a threshold of patience. But I still have confidence in Teochew opera, because, like Gongfu tea, it has been engraved in the bones of Teochew natives."

Teochew opera is at a low ebb. Its fans are getting older, while the younger generation is not interested. I felt quite ashamed because I am one of those young people who don't like Teochew opera. Having received Mandarin education since childhood, I can't understand Teochew opera at all, and its music stroke me as sad and noisy. In my opinion, in such an era of rapid changes, the decline of Teochew opera and other local traditional operas alike is inevitable. I pursued blockbusters and television dramas and ignored Teochew opera. For me, it is just a kind of noisy background music and a cultural symbol gradually fading from sight.

Liu Yingni, an actress at my age, blushed during the interview.

"I think the hardest time was when others point out that no one is listening to Teochew opera, so why am I still singing?"

Chen Hanxing, a well-known Teochew opera critic, has been calling for the revival of traditional Teochew opera, saying, "Now people have invited directors from other fields to innovate Teochew opera, but that's a ridiculous thing to do!"

Li Danli, the Artistic Director of Puning Teochew Opera Troupe, is exploring the ways to revive Teochew opera.

"We should cultivate young talents in this field," she said.

In such a desperate situation, there are people who try to keep the heritage, and people who are still in the industry are doing their best.

As for me, Teochew opera has now gained a richer connotation, behind which I see real faces, ardent souls, and all the efforts, emotions and thoughts of a group of people contributing to the development of Teochew opera.

After the interview, Liu Yingni performed a bit of Teochew opera for us. Sad lyrics poured out like running water. Several teachers and students wept on the spot. After the performance, Prof. Xie took over the microphone and explained,

"I just couldn't help crying because I heard the local accent and the story she sang. I have confidence that Teochew opera will go on. "

I began to feel uneasy—as a Teochew native, I couldn't even understand what she was singing, and could make no connection like Prof. Xie.

Later, Prof. Dai invited me and another Teochew student to share our feelings. I could feel a dozen pairs of eyes falling upon us. I felt stiff, and I reminded myself to keep my back straight. I was afraid that once I relaxed, I would expose my ignorance and prejudice against Teochew opera. The Teochew student beside me expressed conservative yet positive views on the inheritance of Teochew opera. I could feel my guilt fermenting, I grew more and more anxious.

"What about Kexin? How do you feel?"

In unison, everyone looked at me.

"I haven't considered it deeply," I opened my mouth somehow, and the voice in my heart came through.

"I'm very grateful that such a group of people are trying to carry forward our culture. As a Teochew native, I will pay attention and try my best to support it. "


On the morning of the fourth day, we visited the Teochew Embroidery Art Museum, then the Teochew opera training center, a secondary school which specializes in training professional actors. The students there were teenagers. We stood at the door of the practice hall, and watched the children performing Teochew opera. It was my first time to observe opera actors in training. Later, when everyone interviewed the person in charge of the training center, I snuck back to the practice hall to have a closer look at the children.

The sunlight, filtered by the window, cast rectangular light and shadow on the corridor. Several children, dressed in red practice clothes and black-legged pants, stood in the corridor, laughing and joking. When they saw me, they became very talkative and eager to know about me. They invited me to the canteen for dinner. While chatting with them, I learned that there are only ten students in this school, six girls and four boys. The oldest was a 19-year-old boy who had been there for three years, another girl for five years. After spending six years in the school building, which has six floors, the ten children are very likely to work in the troupe. Their daily life is simple. They practice singing and dancing during the day and learn Mandarin and opera theory at night. I looked at their bright and clear eyes and imagined how boring it would be to live with a few people for six years in this small building.

I glanced around to make sure there were no teachers in the corridor. Then I quietly asked the question that had been circulating in my heart:

"Do you all like Teochew opera? Are you happy with your life?"

"Yes, I like it."

"Yes."

The children answered neatly. Their big eyes seemed able to see what I was thinking.

After leaving the Teochew opera training center, I couldn't help thinking of those children. I hoped that I might meet them in the future and watch them sing on the stage. If the interview last night was like watching a group of Teochew opera veterans, besieged by thousands, trying to fight their way out, these children I saw at the school are like a flock of eagles, eager to flap their fledgling wings. As long as someone continues to love and learn Teochew opera, it will live and never fade away.

On the fifth and sixth days, we visited Mingde House, an exhibition hall for tea pots as art, and then Longhu Village. Mingde House is the teapot studio of Xie Hua, a Chinese master in this field. There is a myriad of teapots carefully polished by Mr. Xie, some as round as bulging bellies, and some with clear edges and corners. The professional maker of teapots said that it doesn't take long to learn how to make a practical teapot, but it takes a long time to conceive and polish one that can be called an art work. In such a large showroom, three walls are full of teapot exhibits. Like the emperor looking over the maidens, I inspected these art treasures one by one. Meanwhile, Zhigao and Wang Xi were listening to the explanation of the teapot master and the garden owner.

"The *Junde* (written as "君德" in Chinese) pot, which looks simple, actually takes a lot of time to make, and it is the most practical pot type."

"Both the *Tiliang* (written as "提梁" in Chinese, meaning with a long handle) pot and the *Fang* (written as "方" in Chinese, meaning square) pot look beautiful, but they are not practical. They are more beautiful than practical."

"The *Shuiping* ( written as "水平" in Chinese, meaning level) pot is the most traditional type, with a history of hundreds of years."

After visiting Mingde House, I chatted with several students and asked them about their impressions of the Teochew area. One of my friends said, "I used to watch videos on the internet, which showed Teochew natives drinking Gongfu tea at the high-speed railway station. At that time, I thought it was too exaggerated. I didn't expect it to be true."

I smiled. Indeed, every day, when we walked from the inn to the bus station, we could see idlers sitting on small benches around the tea tray, drinking tea and chatting. No wonder Wang Xi said, "I think tea is not only a drink here but also a culture and a local custom."

Tea is more like some kind of spiritual food for Teochew people.

In the past, immersed in the Teochew cultural environment, I had been unaware of the many features of my hometown culture. Nonetheless, I had been passively influenced by its art and culture, including Teochew opera and embroidery; still, I had never bothered to understand their connotations. During this journey, I followed a group of people who knew little about Teochew culture, and I had stood outside the Teochew cultural circle to establish an overall understanding of my hometown culture. Communication with professionals in the Teochew opera industry allowed me to get to the heartbeat of these cultural symbols. This journey provided me with a different perspective and helped me to rediscover the beauty of my hometown culture.

These days, I have been reevaluating my feelings for my hometown. In this place where I was born and raised, you will find the renowned Gongfu tea, distinct cuisine, and a unique dialect. Still, whenever I introduce the beauty of my hometown to others, I would hesitate somewhat. I can't forget that once when I went back to my hometown, I saw my uncle, smoking cigarettes on the ornate hardwood, his legs crossed, get up to the toilet, and came back scolding the women for a toilet that was not clean enough; I can't forget that when my grandpa died, our family spent more than a hundred thousand yuan on the funeral to flaunt our wealth; I can't forget that my grandmother was unhappy with my mother marrying my father simply because her zodiac was said to be "unlucky". These shadows once shrouded the light of my hometown in my heart. Until I embarked on this journey, I didn't see the light behind the shadow. My hometown is like an old man over eighty years old. He has seen the changes in the world over the years, but he is also limited by his ageing body. This old man taught me a great deal. I shouldn't expect him to be a saint. Thanks to this journey, I have picked up my love for my hometown once more.

# Meeting and Parting with Teochew: The Research Journal of Teochew Food Culture Group

ZHANG Jing

## Nov. 6th, Guangzhou South Railway Station

Lu Hui, Lin Han, and I were sitting at the McDonald's in the Guangzhou South Railway Station. The three of us, plus Huang Senyan, classmates of the Creative Writing and Translation course, made up the research group of Teochew food culture. Having just taken a one-hour train ride from Zhuhai to Guangzhou, we were waiting for the next train to Teochew. At this moment, I remained more bewildered than excited about the journey ahead.

A fourth-year undergraduate and the only gentleman in our group, Lin Han, looking thin and frail and wearing glasses, spoke endlessly about how busy he had been with the school orchestra rehearsals prior to this trip. Since our first meeting in the course, Lu Hui, a graduate student like me, would always greet me amiably every time she saw me. Senyan, wearing a bright yellow sweatshirt and smiling reservedly, is from Guangzhou, which is why we met directly at the Guangzhou South Railway Station.

At that moment, Ms. Fu Yun, the assistant teacher for the class, called out to us. "Hello, teacher!" I replied. "We are the food culture group, and I am the group leader, Zhang Jing." She brought us to the gathering place, where Prof. Dai Fan, the leading course instructor, with her hair up and carrying the iconic big black backpack, was smiling and exchanging pleasantries with the other two research groups who were also part of the Teochew team. I also went over to say hello and informed her of the division of labour in our group: I was the reporter; Senyan was in charge of English writing; Lin Han, Chinese writing; and Lu Hui, subtitle maker for the video we would make.

Before we left, Mr. Wei Donghua, the photographer and his two assistants from Guangzhou Xinhua College also arrived. Mr. Wei was carrying a lot of phototaking equipment. Before checking in, Mr. Wei suggested that we take a group photo, and so we gathered together for a photo in front of the boarding gate. That was the moment when I felt belonging to this big team, and the initial awkwardness of the meeting was discarded, leaving me with a sense of anticipation for the upcoming trip.

## Nov. 6th, Teochew Old Town

Teochew is a city with great food. The first meal primed my group members and me to greatly anticipate each tasting experience. As the food culture group, we were simultaneously glad and apprehensive to reveal our enthusiasm for the fear of arousing other groups' "jealousy". Whenever it was time to eat, we were seated like royalty at the table. With exquisite dishes arrayed before us, we buried our heads in food until one group member murmured, "Have we taken any pictures of the dishes?" I dropped my chopsticks. Right! Shouldn't all meals be our research subjects? As my distress mounted, words from the next table that Senyan had taken pictures and kept them for record helped to make my guilt for failing to meet my responsibility as the team leader vanish like the plate of tender pork jelly at the tip of our chopsticks.

At the end of the meal, a crystal clear, orange and white dish was brought to the table.

"Here we go, the most famous dessert of Teochew cuisine!" Lin Han said, taking the role as a local Teochew guide. Mr. Li Yu from Hanshan Normal University (hereafter "Hanshi"), who sat next to me, said, "This is '*Gao*-roasted taro'."

This *gao*-roasted sweet potato and taro, also called "golden brick and silver brick", tasted excellent. The pale golden sweet potato and silvery taro, diced into large pieces to be eaten in a single bite, are coated in transparent crystal sugar, sprinkled with white sesame and green onion oil. Every bite is crispy, while taro and sweet potato are soft and tender within, accentuated with syrup that makes its flavor all the more intense. Mr. Li said that one of the characteristics of a Teochew banquet is "head sweet, tail sweet". That is, the first and last dishes should be sweet, meaning sweetness from the beginning to the end. After the lazy Susan made its two rounds, the "gold and silver bricks" in front of us were empty.

After dinner, we visited Hanshi, the host institution, to listen to a research report on Teochew food, tea, opera, embroidery and other aspects of Teochew culture by students of the Creative Tourism course. This marked the first time we met with students and teachers of Hanshi. Everyone in the bright and spacious classroom was energetic and enthusiastic. During the three-hour report, I was struck by the extent to which Teochew cuisine focuses on health and by the fact that its snacks are deeply intertwined with folklore and customs. A senior nutritionist from the School of Geography and Tourism · School of Teochew Cuisine at Hanshi, Mr. Huang Wuying, informed us how Teochew cuisine, a representative branch of Cantonese cuisine, features superlative effort and craftsmanship. While preparing us for the next step in our research, this report allowed our group to increase our understanding of Teochew cuisine beyond the well-known and stereotyped "Teochew beef ball" to a deeper spiritual and cultural openness.

By the end of the presentation, it was close to 10:30 p.m. Our food culture team walked along the Paifang Street located in the old city of Teochew. The street was sparsely populated at this hour, and most of us were in the mood for a stroll.

A sideboard on a stall on the side of the road read "Teochew beef balls, Phoenix floating Dougan, Turnip cake". I remembered the *Fenghuang* Fried Tofu, which is Phoenix floating Dougan, was strongly recommended by students in the Hanshi division. I immediately mobilized everyone, "We, the food team, must try the Teochew snacks!"

Lu Hui was the first to respond to my call, and she tried the most representative snack, beef balls; in Teochew dialect, Lin Han ordered a turnip cake; Senyan chose the Teochew sweet dessert and questioned my choice, saying, "Dried tofu? Plus mint? It's so weird." But I trusted my intuition and resolutely asked the vendor to sell me fried tofu.

In a small kitchen, the owner cheerily labored, while enthusiastic Teochew folks around us proved eager to introduce us outsiders to the unique local snacks, the crispy turnip cakes, plump beef balls, and sweet jelly.

While the crowd was praising their cuisine, my fried tofu arrived in a foam box: golden with green mint leaves and red garlic vinegar. I dipped one in the sauce and mint leaves, attempting to gobble them all in one bite. The dried bean curd's crispy skin and thick, rich bean flavor, combined with the natural mint fragrance and the spicy and sour garlic vinegar, were refreshingly sweet and the combination neutralizes the oiliness of the fried tofu.

Seeing me eating joyfully, Senyan was persuaded to try a piece. I was overjoyed and watched her as she struggled to fork the mint leaves and tofu together, then dunked it in the vinegar sauce, and shoved it into her mouth.

She chewed twice without expression, but I could see her eyes widen a little. She said, "Not bad", and reached out for another piece, a move I hastily impeded, insisting that if she didn't admit its good taste, she couldn't take any more! After baulking waggishly, she fully confessed how shallow her previous prejudices were and pronounced that she was ready to recommend it to others in the group. Lin Han, with a grin, oversaw how everyone received their baptism into Teochew cuisine, saying, "I told you it would be soul-crushing!"

By then, we noted that 11:30 p.m. had crept up on us. Lin Han said, "Ah! Such hard work." Before I could ask what he meant, he added, "The food culture team is still researching Teochew cuisine at 11:30 p.m. at night—how arduous!" Senyan sent a WeChat Moment, with Lin Han's words and mouth-watering food photos, and the comment section is immediately filled with "Woes" from students on campus. With so many types of food in Teochew, I felt, the work of the food culture group was as sweet as it was demanding.

## Nov. 7th, Fengchun Seafood Restaurant

After wrapping up our morning session in the museum, loaded with knowledge of Teochew embroidery culture, we were starving and headed to the long-established Teochew Fengchun Seafood Restaurant for the Hangong[①] Banquet for lunch. We were fortunate enough to interview the owner, Zhang Sheng, President of the Teochew Catering Association that was just established. At the request of Zeng Chunan, a senior scholar of research, for the 2019 Symposium for the Cele-

---

① Hangong refers to Han Yu, a master of classical prose in the Tang Dynasty (AD 618—907).

bration of the 1200th Anniversary of Han Yu Governance of the Teochew, Hangong Banquet comprises a series of delicacies Zhang Sheng designed with his R&D team, coupled with research on Han Yu's poetry.

To design a series of recipes for an ancient literary figure might feel like too much fanfare if it transpired in other cities. However, in Teochew, it doesn't sound strange at all. Historically, Han Yu governed Teochew for just a few months, but it allowed Teochew immigrants far from the Middle Kingdom to be free from identity crisis and successfully built a geographic cultural orthodoxy. The reverence Teochew people have for Han Yu is engraved in their bones and in their cultural genes, as exemplified by the Han Wen Gong Temple, which covers an area of 100 acres; by the mother river called Han River; by a mountain called Hanshan, which is where Hanshi is located. No wonder it is said that Teochew is an "ancient city with its soul covered with history and culture".

Before the meal, Mr. Zhang Sheng took the time to introduce us to the origins of his catering and the cultural heritage behind the Hangong Banquet.

"It's time to work!" Lu Hui shouted, and I started recording on my phone while Senyan followed with pen and paper; Lu Hui set her computer on her lap and typed; Lin Han relied entirely on his brain.

Mr. Zhang said he used to be a builder who went to restaurants a lot, as the more food he tasted, the better he understood it. Hangong Banquet reflects his study of Teochew cuisine and culture: while Han Yu was in Teochew, he wrote about various Teochew seafood. Therefore, Fengchun collaborated with scholar Zeng Chunan to develop 14 dishes along these lines. According to Mr. Zhang, Hangong Banquet is a representative Teochew meal that combines culture, history with tradition.

We were delighted with several dishes, including a traditional dish known as the "protector dish". The soup is thickened with a white and green Tai Chi pattern, one small bowl for each person. At first, I only thought the color was bright and the presentation peculiar. Yet, as I scooped a spoonful of soup into my mouth, the sweetness of the diced white radish and the richness of the dried scallops blended, smooth as gelatin, leaving a fragrant tang in my mouth. Even after over one month back on campus, Senyan was still talking about the flavor of this dish in the WeChat group. Lin Han revealed the secret that only locals know, "I guess this soup is boiled in water crabs, before the coating is skimmed."

"But I checked it out online, and it only says there are fava leaves and mushrooms," Senyan questioned.

"The recipe can't be made public. Based on my ten years of cooking experience, I guess there must be crab and dried scallops in this dish," Lin Han added.

Lin Han's words made me realize that seemingly simple fare could mean a lot of work behind the scene. No wonder Teochew cuisine is famous in Guangdong!

I also noticed that the Hangong Banquet tableware differed from those in other restaurants. It was purple-grey, and the dish was designed like a booklet, echoing the cultural heritage it represents; with ripples, it was exquisite; yet the color was plain so as not to attract more attention than the food. I recalled that Mr. Zhang had just described during the interview how he contracted a ceramic factory to design and produce his tableware. This is emblematic of the attitude of many Teochew people towards food: both those who make it and those who taste it, treating it as a kind of artwork.

The craftsmanship of Hangong Banquet is not only reflected in the tableware, but also the selection of ingredients, the matching of dips, and the skills of the chef. Just as what Mr. Zhang said, "We choose the freshest ingredients, which inevitably raises the cost. At the same time, an extremely important feature of Teochew cuisine is to focus on health and wellness, so we also pay attention to nutrition. Authentic Teochew cuisine will be paired with the right sauce for each dish, such as these two plates of oyster and lobster, which have dips that contrast with the seafood. Even after ten years of experience, our cooks do not dare to say they understand Teochew dishes. So, learning to cook Teochew dishes is a very long process."

Even drinking tea in Teochew proves much more particular than in other areas. One day ago, I listened to Mr. Huang Wuying, from Hanshi, explain the meaning of Teochew Gongfu Tea, which required unusual care, as even a few grams of tea leaves should be weighed in advance. During the talk, Mr. Zhang's assistant kept a careful eye on whose cup was becoming empty, and he would quickly refill the cup. The teacup was the size of a walnut, and one could drink it up in a single sip.

Mr. Zhang was very frank. When asked why he was in the business, his answer was to increase his income. He further said that nothing could be accomplished without a solid economic foundation. I had heard the stereotyped opinion that the pursuits of Teochew people were unrealistic, but it turned out that they were pragmatic and down-to-earth.

## Nov. 7th, House of Cypress Shade

At night, we had an exchange with a few local Teochew students from Hanshi. Honestly, I didn't expect much, thinking it may be just a quick chat. It was only when we sat around together in the open-air garden where one by one, the Teochew students shared the profound influence of Teochew's tea culture, food, and Teochew opera on themselves, from childhood to adulthood, that I realized the true meaning of our research. Those young ladies, born and raised in Teochew, talked to us about their experiences growing up under this strong and deep-rooted culture. One said she grew up listening to Teochew opera with her grandparents, and when she was a child, she had to squeeze into the crowd to see countryside performances; one said she grew up drinking and making tea, and wherever she went, she would bring her tea set with her, which led to her dormitory communally drinking tea; another said she helped her mother make traditional Teochew red peach cake at festival time every year.

All night long, listening to their heartfelt sharing, I felt that I experienced a deeply immersive cultural experience. The moonlight cast on our faces and bodies, lulling me into a trance, as if I had been transported into a Teochew family, as if I had been born in Teochew, as if I had been nourished by Teochew culture in this way. As we gained an understanding of what made the culture of Teochew so unique and strong and enduring, I began to see the significance of the research. As Prof. Dai said at the end of our trip, when others talk about Teochew in negative light, we are likely to want to defend the culture; after so many days of in-depth research conducted along various lines, it seems that we belong here too.

## Nov. 8th, Phoenix Mountain

We arrived early in the morning at the tea factory in Phoenix Mountain, which is located in Teochew, and on the way up, because the main path was blocked, we turned onto a path that proved to be steep and narrow, with the soil loose and slippery, and fraught with coiling tree roots that left us half rolling, half crawling down the mountain. Still, I found it very touching that all of the teammates in the team proved very sweet and caring.

When we arrived at Phoenix Mountain, it was hard to quell our group's deep love and attachment to the floating dried tofu without trying the authentic *Fenghuang* Fried Tofu, as the day before, our guide Mr. Ke Min from Hanshi told us that they were different. Today, when we tasted it, we found it unusual, with a crispy and hot outer skin, wrapped in juicy tofu with a fresh and fragrant soybean flavor and undertones of *Caozi* (a local species of mint that grows in Phoenix Mountain) and fresh mint, evoking the clear mountain spring water of Phoenix Mountain. If the *Fenghuang* Fried Tofu, eaten for the first time in Paifang Street, was an experience in the bud, then the one tasted in Phoenix Mountain amounted to the same experience in full bloom. Even Lin Han, who had eaten the snack for countless times, was convinced that the Phoenix variety was unique. Only when I arrived at the place did I know that the *Fenghuang* Fried Tofu was made from grass, lightly tinged with mint, a traditional ingredient native to Phoenix Mountain. As it turns out, a variety of plants retain their authentic flavors when they grow in their local areas, hence delicacies made with plants in the two places could be very different.

## Nov. 9th and 10th, Teochew Cuisine Base in Hanshi

On this day we went to the Chinese Teochew Cuisine Research, Development and Training Base at Hanshi. I couldn't wait to put on the provided chef's uniform, tie the black apron around my waist, and don the striped chef's hat with a brim.

Upon entering the base, I saw rows of neat and shiny cooking tables, and all the student trainees were in chef's uniforms. I felt a bit apprehensive. We would learn how to make a classic dish called "shrimp ball" in Teochew feasts and home cooking, due to its spherical shape, which invested it with the symbolic meaning of *Tuanyuan* (meaning reunion). When I learned that I would have to deal with seafood with a shell, I immediately had a headache. Prof. Chen Jing, the Dean of the School of Geography and Tourism · School of Teochew Cuisine, taught us to peel the frozen shrimp, and cut twice down the back to remove the shrimp intestines. Prof. Dai Fan, who was a member in our group, observed that other groups had already outdone us and they obviously had learned faster. We did the hard work of removing the shrimp shells before pounding the shrimp meat. Wang Xi, though not having had much training in cooking, quickly mastered the various tricks. The next step was low-temperature frying and frying twice or three times before the shrimp ball turned golden brown.

This was a standard banquet fare, but the process was complex. As Wang Xi said, having come to know the great effort put into the making of a dish, we would no longer rush chefs in the making of food in a restaurant.

The next day, Dean Chen Jing invited two Chinese culinary masters, Wu Qianqiang and Su Peimin, to demonstrate their high-end Teochew cooking skills. Before the chefs positioned themselves in front of the wok, our group got ready to take notes. After so many days, we had begun to treat every meal as "work time", something we looked forward to and were also apprehensive about; we looked forward to taste the food and were apprehensive about becoming so engrossed that we missed cooking details. Master Wu and Master Su, as conservators of the intangible cultural heritage of Teochew cuisine, showed us some of the techniques of ancient Cantonese cuisine, including the cooking of high-end dishes such as Snow Mountain Golden Swallow, Double Plum Buckle Pork Knuckle, and Honey Pumpkin Taro Puree.

I was impressed by the pumpkin taro puree, which the chefs introduced as one of the most classic desserts. The pumpkin is marinated in sugar for two days until the water is completely removed by evaporation. In the evaporated original mix, heat with a gentle fire without adding a drop of water until the pumpkin is extra sweet and soft. There are also double plum pork knuckles, cooked until gelatinous, and a little red date are added to soften the sourness and saltiness of the plums, which can help to invigorate the blood in the medicinal sense. This reflected the Teochew cuisine's concern for health and nutrition.

As Prof. Dai mentioned in the evening wrap-up meeting, many of us were not likely to have noticed that these dishes were so full of art, but now we would look at them with awe and respect. We now understood the hard work and thought behind them, and we would no longer treat any dish prepared by the chefs casually. Every industry has its art, and the greatest significance of our trip is to discover and help preserve it.

## Nov. 10th, Hostel

Because we left Teochew the next day, Prof. Dai held a little wrap-up meeting in the evening. I can't remember the details, but one sentence resonated strongly in me. That is, after nearly seven days of in-depth research, we seemed to have gained a certain authority concerning Teochew culture. When someone repeats rumors or stereotypes about Teochew culture, we are likely to act like the locals and tell them, "No" or "It is not so". I came to realize that I had already integrated into this culture and would not be able to resist looking for its traces when I got back to my routine.

Prof. Dai also shared that, because she often needed to do hands-on projects, she had a heightened appreciation of the importance of images and words. The next time we come to Teochew, it would be difficult to have similar in-depth experience of the Teochew culture like we did this time, much less with the same group of people. It is an experience that would only happen once in a lifetime, and it would be a pity if it were not recorded in detail, as the memory would disappear with time. I now understood why every time when there was even a small activity, Prof. Wei's team would organize a group photo. Every photo or video is taken in a different time and place, with people's moods changing like the seasons. As a research group, we left early and came back late every day, and wrote stories and papers after we returned. It was impossible to do so simply for the sake of credits and grades; rather, it was for this once-in-a-lifetime experience, for commemorating the encounter in Teochew, and for keeping a record of all the people and memories.

## Nov. 11th and 12th, Under the Dormitory Building

This was the last day of our trip. We said good-bye to Prof. Dai at the Chaoshan Station. After dropping us off at the station, she would stay in Teochew for another day for another obligation. We took turns to hug her. As some moods will surely stay in Teochew, I hugged her extra tight, being afraid that if we saw each other again in Zhuhai, these lovely teachers and students would be different from the relaxed ones I knew in Teochew. Parting words followed, not only to the people but also to a period of time.

Finally, at Guangzhou Station, Senyan parted with us, just as she had met us. It was almost midnight when Lin Han, Lu Hui and I arrived at the dormitory building. When Lin Han was about to say goodbye to us, Lu Hui suddenly said, "Wait a minute!"

It then dawned on me that Lu Hui's birthday happened to be on Nov. 11th, and Lin Han's birthday was exactly on Nov. 12th. Lu Hui was a graduate student, Lin Han was an undergraduate, but their birthdays were just one day apart. Given such a coincidence, we somewhat believed that our meeting was also an arrangement of fate.

Lu Hui said, with emotion in her voice, "This year, I spent my birthday rushing to finish tasks. I hope you can have a good birthday."

"Indeed!" I agreed, and we sang the Happy Birthday song to Lin Han under the dormitory building.

At 00:00, November 12, 2021, Lu Hui and I, in Zhuhai, with a temperature of 17 degrees, sang the birthday song. Attended by Lin Han's slightly embarrassed and shy smile, our group's research drew a successful conclusion.

In retrospect, at the beginning, we had communicated with our teachers and group members under a spell of strangeness. Afterwards, we found fun throughout the field trip—which was brought out by the culture of Teochew. We came to know and understand our classmates and teachers better than ever while immersing ourselves in this six-day in-depth experience, and of course, we found out about Teochew culture by tasting its food, visiting Teochew embroidery, and appreciating Teochew opera.

Teochew culture proved to be a great invader of all our senses: taste, hearing, and touch. After we went back to the university, we couldn't help but missing our favorite "gold and silver bricks" and *Fenghuang* Fried Tofu. Senyan said she started to make tea every day as a result of the "invasion of Teochew DNA"; Lin Han was hankering for the reopening of the authentic Teochew restaurant at the north gate of the school. I feel that this memory and cultural invasion are properly placed in a corner of my heart; when there is a corresponding evocation, it can trigger a tidal wave of memories, because, from now on, we all have a place in our heart belonging to Teochew.

# Trip Journals

## TAN Xueming

## Prologue

Teochew is a city that dates back to the Spring and Autumn Period (770 B. C. —221 B. C.). During its long history, the city has developed a unique regional culture, featuring Teochew embroidery, Teochew opera, Teochew merchants, and Teochew Gongfu Tea. Accordingly, it is lauded as one of the most significant cultural centers in China.

Nevertheless, I could hardly comprehend such uniqueness, since I was born in Guangzhou and have never been to Teochew for even a glimpse of its brilliant culture. In my last year at university, I joined the Creative Writing and Translation course offered and instructed by Prof. Dai Fan. This year, Prof. Dai Fan cooperated with Hanshan Normal University (hereafter "Hanshi"), and organized a field trip to Teochew to learn about its culture. Fortunately, I became a participant in the course, and on November 6th, 2021, we embarked on a six-day journey.

Prof. Dai Fan divided the class into three groups, each bearing different survey topics: Teochew food, Teochew tea, Teochew embroidery and Teochew opera. Each group would be responsible for an investigation of the given field, and group members were required to write reports and stories based on their experiences in Teochew. I was in the group of Teochew embroidery and Teochew opera, the group members being Zhang Xiaoyan, Mo Yanchi and Ma Changjun.

Over the next five days, we interviewed several masters in Teochew embroidery and Teochew opera. We were impressed by their talent but also moved by their passion and devotion to Teochew culture. About the problem of cultural development, some of the masters were distraught while others were extremely frank. Different opinions in the interviews resulted in the birth of new ideas. Through this journey, I have come to deeply appreciate the importance of preserving traditional and local culture.

To express my gratitude to the masters, and also to record their passion, I am composing an account of our encounter, so that the effort for saving Teochew embroidery and Teochew opera will not be in vain.

## Journals about Teochew Embroidery Teacher

In Chinese, skilled people may be called "teacher". For Li Xiaodan, the term "teacher" is more than what she deserves.

Li welcomed us for an interview outside her workshop. She wore a white cheongsam and long hair, which gave her an elegant and graceful look. She showed us around the workshop, where numerous Teochew embroidery works were hung on the walls, including pictures of *long* (dragon) and *feng* (phoenix), flying birds and so on. These works were mostly stitched by her mother, an outstanding embroiderer. After visiting the workshop, Li led us to a desk and took out a piece of work. She slowly unveiled the piece, which turned out to be a golden arowana.

"The skill of padding the embroidery is special in Teochew embroidery, which makes Teochew embroidery distinct from other embroideries in China. In contrast to other embroidery works, Teochew embroidery is three-dimensional." She explained the skill patiently, her fingers pointing to the specific part of the golden arowana where the skill had been applied.

"Please pay attention to the belly of the fish. It was filled with lumps of cotton, so that the belly could be full instead of being sags and crests. The most difficult part is forming cotton lumps into the proper size for padding." She pressed on the belly to show how full it was.

"As for the scales of the fish, it was made by another skill in Teochew embroidery, *dianbian*. It requires the embroiderers to fold Chinese art paper up and embroider it to the canvas with golden strings. The skill of *dianbian* is capable of creating distinct lines in the embroidery picture." She then showed us some Chinese art paper that was folded up.

After the introduction to embroidery skills, we started our interview. We soon learned that we were not the only group of "students" for Teacher Li, as she was also a teacher at Hanshi, and students majoring in Art could take her course on Teochew embroidery. To show us the students' work, Teacher Li took out another bag, which was full of Chinese fans.

"These are the tasks I assigned this semester. After the students have all learned some skills in Teochew embroidery, I asked them to embroider one picture on the Chinese fan. Since I believe that embroidery works should have a topic, I decided to have them embroider pictures relating to the 100th anniversary of the Communist Party of China (CPC)."

Li then opened one fan fashioned by her student. There was a train on the left and a CPC flag on the right, with the embroidered Chinese character for "stay true to one's original aspiration" at the bottom.

"If you look carefully at this work, you will find him (the student) quite innovative. The train consists of two parts, the latter being an old-fashioned green train, symbolizing the past of China, and the former being a modern high-speed train, symbolizing the modern and prosperous era now."

When speaking of her students, Li could not contain her delight. She opened another fan, with a lion of Chinese traditional style on both sides. "She is a talented girl and could understand my instruction quickly, so I taught her more skills in Teochew embroidery, to make sure that she could embroider more complex pictures on the fan." In high spirits, Li showed us additional fans.

While listening to her description, I found it quite fitting to call her by the Chinese term for teacher in accordance with her excellence as a teacher, and I hoped that many students would be able to inherit such a special art.

## Craftswoman

"I can recognize whether the work is a genuine Teochew embroidery by a simple glance." As an embroider with a national certification, Kang Huifang was confident and even egotistical to a degree. When Prof. Dai mentioned that one of her friends in Teochew was trying to organize classes to teach Teochew embroidery, Kang expressed her doubt. Prof. Dai then showed her the works of her friend via smart phone, Kang squinted at the photo and smiled without any comment.

Concerning the problem of inheritance of Teochew embroidery, Kang had her own ideas:

"If about thirty young girls could learn under my instruction on Teochew embroidery for a month, I could easily identify the talented ones among them. Only with my further guidance would these talented girls become qualified successors. If it is done like courses in schools, with only several lessons a week, our goal of preservering Teochew embroidery would never be achieved."

She then showed us her workroom, where four women worked. Three of them have learned from Kang from an early age and now they were doing embroidery in the workroom with their children. There was, however, one girl in her twenties. Kang's voice showed excitement as she mentioned her, "She is quite a rare talent in embroidery. Since she is willing to learn from me, I spare nothing in my guidance." When we went near the girl, Kang said, "This is the very apprentice I just mentioned." She went to closely observe the embroidery of the apprentice and muttered, "Sometimes I am too strict with you. This is because I value your talent, and I hope that you put up with my temper."

For me, Kang constituted a bygone craftswoman in the modern era. However, in the following interview, I discovered how difficult it is for a craftsman to find a successor in this epoch. When we asked Kang about a successor in Teochew embroidery, Kang did not answer but asked a question as a response, "Have you met anyone in Teochew doing embroidery?" We shook our heads. Kang said, "This is the situation for Teochew embroidery."

The lack of a successor was Kang's major problem. Prof. Dai asked her how she made her living while paying rents and salaries, given that she had to keep such a large workshop and the apprentices going. Kang answered, "My wedding dress business is in demand. So are my other embroidery products. The only problem is that I am too short-staffed to fulfil the demand."

At the end of our interview, Prof. Dai sighed and said, "We are so sorry as well as worried to see the problem of the preservation of Teochew embroidery unsolved." Kang said nothing but forced a smile. As she looked up and out the window, dusk had already fallen.

# Artist

Cai Minqiang and Cai Zhonghan were a father-son team in Teochew embroidery. Cai Minqiang, the father, was the former Director of the Teochew Embroidery Factory, while Cai Zhonghan, the son, was an overseas student who returned from the U. S. Their special personal experiences resulted in particular concerns on the preservation of Teochew embroidery.

After the reform and opening-up policy was adopted in China, the Teochew Embroidery Factory, formerly a state-owned enterprise, became Famory Gallery. We were welcomed by Cai Zhonghan into the Famory Gallery. During our visit, Cai Zhonghan expressed his view on traditional culture preservation:

"I always tell others that intangible cultural heritage will inevitably suffer. Such cultural forms are the symbols of backwardness in productivity, which is no longer suitable for our industrialized times. Therefore, I believe that these cultural assets should and could only be preserved as exhibits in museums."

I was shocked by his words. He added, "Beauty, however, is a concept with staying power. We can hardly find successors of Teochew embroidery, but we may see the beauty of the masterpieces of Teochew embroidery in the museum indefinitely. This is why we set up this gallery."

After this little speech, Cai Zhonghan brought us to see the works of Teochew embroidery. I was convinced that Cai was not boasting when he referred to "masterpiece". The skill of splitting strings in Teochew embroidery made pieces extremely vivid. From whatever angle you viewed the portrait of Qi Baishi, a well-known artist, you would always find his eyes looking at you, which made the embroidery work even more lifelike than photos. This portrait of Qi Baishi in China is as skilled as that of Mona Lisa in the world.

During our visit, Cai Minqiang, also joined us. He told us that these works were done under his supervision, based on his understanding of art theory. Cai Minqiang also told us that the gallery was very much appreciated by senior officials who would stay much longer than their scheduled time. The embroidery works would also be exhibited abroad under the recommendation of the Ministry of Culture.

When I left, I was still at awe with all of these incredible artworks of embroidery. Moreover, I appreciated the opportunity to visit such a brilliant gallery in the field trip.

# Journals about Teochew Opera Idealists

The interview for the master in Teochew opera took place in the conference room in Chengnan Chinese-English school. We invited several people for our interview: Li Yingqun, a former playwright of Teochew opera, Chen Hanxing, a critic of Teochew opera, Chen Yuejuan from Teochew Culture Research Center, Li Danli, Chair of Puning Playwright Association, and Liu Yingni, an actress in the Baihua Teochew Opera Troupe.

Li Yingqun was in his eighties. He remained energetic and talkative when discussing Teochew opera. He said, "Teochew opera bears a close relation to other Teochew folk cultures. Experts in Teochew opera are also likely experts in Teochew folk cultures." He added that even he had not understood Teochew opera thoroughly. However, as he began to discuss the circumstances of Teochew opera in the rural areas of Teochew, I knew his "not understanding Teochew opera" were only words of modesty.

Li placed great emphasis on the adaptation of scripts from traditional opera. He took *Meeting in a Wood House* as a case in point: "This script was from other places. When my predecessors rewrote it for Teochew opera, its elements were representative of Teochew life that viewers commented that the main characters were just like their neighbors. The audience, consequently, laughed for the whole performance and had a very good time. Therefore, I hold the strong belief that a script is good enough if it can be amusing to ordinary people."

While Li Yingqun recounted amusing anecdotes about Teochew opera, Chen Hanxing sounded worried and even resentful concerning the problem of heritage in Teochew opera. He said, "I can hardly see the significance of developing traditional culture. Many Teochew opera troupes invite directors from outside to direct new plays. However, these directors know little about Teochew opera, and their so-called innovation would only make Teochew opera lose its distinctiveness."

He complained about the new scripts of Teochew opera, saying, "The stories of Teochew opera mostly come from daily life. The plots of wars and other grand historical events are seldom in Teochew opera." When speaking of practical solutions, Han suggested that Teochew opera should not focus on new plays for the next ten years. Instead, all troupes should return to the old scripts.

Liu Yingni sat silently on one side of the conference room. About our age, this young lady wore make-up and manicured after the fashion like many of her peers. However, when she was invited to perform a portion of Teochew opera, everything changed. She went to the front of the room and started Teochew opera music on her smartphone. Then, she slightly raised her head as if looking at the audience from afar and bent her right arm as if she were wearing a long sleeve in a Teochew opera costume. When she started the performance, she instantly became the main character she was playing in the opera, singing with intense emotions. Meanwhile, she danced gracefully and moved her right arm as if moving a long sleeve in a real performance. Everyone in the conference room was moved by her performance. When she finished, the conference room was filled with applause.

After the performance, Mo Yanchi, one of my group members, asked Liu, "What is the biggest difficulty in learning Teochew opera?"

Liu answered, "It is hard work to practice, but it doesn't matter, since I love it. However, there is one thing I can never accept. I cannot stand being asked why I am still learning Teochew opera when so few people are interested." The latter half of her answer became a sob.

As I rode in the bus back to the hotel, I reflected on the wonderful night. It was, after all, moving to see the effort of idealists.

## Realist

Outside the Teochew Opera Troupe building, Guo Mingcheng welcomed us, wearing glasses and a suit. Before the interview began, he showed us around the building. On the second floor, we saw four girls practising the movements of long sleeves under a teacher's guidance, while three boys learned the basic movements of Teochew opera. One other boy was practising Teochew opera in costume. Guo told us that these were all of the students learning Teochew opera.

After the visit, we sat down in the hall and started our interview. Guo, as the Head of Teochew Opera Troupe, gave us detailed information on the difficulty of finding a successor in Teochew opera: "It has to take at least three years to learn the basic skills of Teochew opera. Practising your voice would only extend the training. Therefore, children who do well in school would not want to learn Teochew opera."

He further pointed out, "The decline of the opera derives from the decline of dialects. We used to have Teochew dialects for classes, but now schools use Mandarin. How can we expect the young generation to become our audience if they can hardly understand what we sing on the stage?"

When we asked him about the future of Teochew opera, he said, "I think it will last, but the quality of its performance will inevitably decline. The reason is simple. We cannot find enough performers, not to mention talented ones. When I was young, many were eager to join the Troupe. Nowadays, there are so few applicants that we must admit all applicants willing to study."

During the short interview break, Guo asked the student apprentice to perform Teochew opera for us. The students came and went up to the stage one by one. The boy in costume proved the most skillful. His pace on stage and the waving of his long sleeve felt just like an experienced actor. However, Guo just watched the performance silently and did not applaud. When the students returned upstairs, he sighed, "The boy's voice is far from what is considered satisfactory. It is the same with his basic stage skills."

We were astonished by Guo's strictness. He continued, "When I was young, actors could never go up on stage until their voices were properly trained. For this young man, it was a difficult case since he had passed the voice changing period when he came to our Troupe. The basic skills are also challenging for him."

We followed up with more questions. Guo knew that the golden time for Teochew opera had clearly gone. During the interview, I watched Guo's expression, but I found him quite calm, with no upwelling of emotion.

I was confused. Even as an outsider, I could feel the desperation of the lack of successors. As a person witnessing the dilemma day in and day out, how could Guo remain so calm?

At that moment, Prof. Dai asked, "With what kind of emotions do you work every day?" This was also the very question I wanted to ask.

Guo did not answer directly, "I get on with my work no matter how I feel." He hesitated for a while before saying, "If I become depressed because of the problem of qualified successors or other dilemmasat work, how could I enjoy my life?"

I finally understood him. Guo was also frustrated by the reality, but he had already become accustomed to the frustration, so he was able to carry on his career despite the frustration. I thought of Hector. Everyone knows that Achilles was invulnerable. However, if Hector was easily frustrated by the invulnerability, who could protect Troy? If a realist is easily frustrated by reality, who could ensure the future of Teochew opera?

Respect filled my heart. I wished I had a glass of wine to toast to Guo: *To the Greatness of Realism.*

## Postscript

Having done all the research, I would like to draw a conclusion.

What does "cultural development" mean? I used to consider this question simple. According to what I learned at Senior High School, cultural development means giving up some parts of traditional cultures or making them adaptable to modern times. However, it is far more difficult in practice. After the field trip to Teochew, I found this question similar to the Ship of Theseus: If the traditional culture survived after transmogrification, could it still be recognized as the same cultural form? Thus, a dilemma arises. It seems a choice between the slow decline of traditional culture and the effacement of the core of traditional culture. I do not like either of these choices, so I don't know which to choose.

After understanding the dilemma, I have become increasingly pessimistic, since I am not able to find a solution.

However, it occurs to me that there is still something I may do. As the Chinese saying goes, "To write is to propose an idea." While not overly assured of my own prognosis on the dilemma of traditional culture, I can at least transmit my awareness of the dilemma to a greater number of people, thus fostering discussion. With the effort of many, I believe that some solution may arise.

Therefore, if you have finished reading this article, please pause for a moment to think about the dilemma. Teochew embroidery and Teochew opera need your wisdom, as do other endangered traditional cultures.

# Stories from Teochew

Drawn from interviews and field trips, this section includes three stories concerning related aspects of Teochew culture: tea, food, embroidery and opera.

# The Story of Tea, the Story of Us

## YU Zhigao

When I was young, I did not like drinking tea at all. I could not understand why adults liked to sip the "bitter dark water". It smelled nice, I had to admit, but that was all.

Tea did grow on me though, and the bitterness became an acquired taste, and its deep color even provided me with a sense of maturity—I am not a child anymore, and it suits me. Although I have developed a soft spot for tea, if you ask me, can you tell me something about it—its history, how it grows, how to brew it—I have to say, Sorry. Though I like tea, I knew quite little about it. Still, I am not quite empty-handed, for I can show you a picture of tea. This is on account of my participation in a six-day field trip to Teochew, a small city located in the east of Guangdong Province, southern China, where tea is rendered *Chami* (written as "茶米" in Chinese), or "tea rice", since food, tea and art in Teochew are well known, it is a perfect spot for us to explore its culture.

Would you like to join us? You won't regret it! Our leader is Prof. Dai Fan. She is leading the Creative Writing and Translation course to investigate the tea, food, embroidery and opera of Teochew.

OK, by now, you must have figured out that I am a student of the course and I am in the field trip, and that my job is to write a piece on the tea culture in Teochew. Sorry? Do you want to know about China's tea culture? Not a problem. If you have interest in the tea culture in Teochew, please follow me.

## Day 1

Hey! We finally made it here! Yes, this is my first time in Teochew, too! Oh, here is our bus! Do make yourself comfortable. As you know, we are due this evening at Hanshan Normal University (hereafter Hanshi) to listen to students there talking about what Teochew culture is like.

Now it is the tea group's turn! Let's see what they bring to us!

"Gongfu tea, which is symbolic of Teochew, requires TWENTY-ONE procedures, including presenting the articles of the tea set one by one and the washing of the brewer's hands."

"Why is it called Gongfu?"

"The term reveals Teochew's tea culture, *Cha Dao* (meaning the Way of *Cha* or tea). Gongfu tea shows the skills of performance, as a manifestation of Chinese Gongfu. It also reflects Teochew people's understanding of tea, that is, drinking tea can be more than simple drinking—we can make it serious if we choose."

That's interesting, isn't it? Sometimes we take something for granted, using words like "awesome" and "fantastic" as they are the best compliment we could give. But nothing extraordinary could be simply done. If something is important for us, we can't help taking it seriously. So it is with tea in Teochew.

Have a good night! Tomorrow is another busy day!

## Day 2

Did you enjoy Teochew's embroidery, opera and china over the day? Yeah, I know, the tour was a little intense and exhausting. You know, I always wonder how our leader Prof. Dai can be so energetic. Yes, she has planned everything, from the cozy hotel where we are staying to the feast we enjoy for almost every meal, but we, the young people, are already out of energy. Anyway, guess what? Tonight she has invited Teochew students from the School of Foreign Languages at Hanshi to share their understanding of Teochew tea culture.

...

Isn't this cool? This is a tea house. We are going to talk about tea as we drink tea! I can't think of a better way to learn tea culture! Oh, let's keep quiet! The girls are beginning to share their stories. Let me interpret it for you.

"My families drink tea every day, from seven in the morning till bedtime. We like to have tea together, and it seems like something is missing when any of us drinks alone. Usually, we have tea after the three daily meals. My father will sit in front of the tea set and brew it for us, each time, every day. For ages, I did not realize that it is a tradition for a father, the head of the family, to make tea."

Oh, that is not uncommon in China. Almost every family has a tea set for personal or guest use. Tea drinking is part of our life, you know. Sorry! Another narrator has just begun her sharing:

"At the very beginning, every family had three, only three teacups, which were put into the shape of a Chinese character *Pin* (written as "品" in Chinese). For example, *Pinde* (written as "品德" in Chinese) refers to morality in English. If the number of family members is more than three, the young must let the older use the cups first; when there are visitors, the host should let them go first to show respect."

Well, nowadays people seldom keep only three cups for a tea group of more than three people—you have found that out on our trip, haven't you? But the spirit of "guests-first" is still carried on not only by the Teochew people but across the rest of the country. Yeah, you can always see China through some fragments. As a nation with a history of five thousand years, an ancient morality has long been engraved into every Chinese person's mind, past and present, here and there.

Oh, the host is making tea for us! Drinking tea is a very good way to keep the conversation going! When you have nothing to say, you can stand up and pour tea for guests; if you are the guest, you can ask for more to break the ice. We are doing it now, aren't we? When I explain this to you, the conversation is already set! That is also the reason why in daily interaction or business negotiation, drinking tea is a necessity in Teochew, and to a lesser extent in China as a whole. No matter how little we know about each other, when we drink the tea poured out of the same pot, we are closer, bonded and activated by tea: When someone is offering you tea, you are likely to treat the host as your friend, which is also the way he or she sees you. So, my friend, are you excited about the new adventure tomorrow? We are heading to Fenghuang Mountain in Teochew. At Fenghuang, we will see where the tea trees are grown, what they look like, etc. Have a good night!

# Day 3

Are you okay? I know, the rugged and zigzagging mountain road makes me feel ill, too. But we made it! See that mountain with wreaths of mist swirling upon its top? We are in wonderland now! Breathe in that fresh air, and let's start our trip! We can have a brief tea talk in a tea farmer's house before we head up to the tea garden!

This is the farmer who drinks tea grown by himself. No worries—your interpreter is here:

"I guess you have tried *Yashixiang* (*Yashi* means duck shit in Chinese) in Teochew?"

"Yes. But why is it called that? I don't think it smells like the shit of duck."

"Well, the tale goes that *Yashixiang* type of tea leaves smells so wonderful that the tea farmers called it that to prevent others from stealing."

Let me put it this way. In China, tales often function as ways of explaining things that started a long, long while back. Some are verifiable, and others are not. But that does not matter. What matters is how the listeners feel. The story only matters if the listeners take it seriously.

Now it's time to climb some mountains and see the tea trees! Let's go!

Be careful of these stairs. They were made specifically for mountain climbing. But you see, it is still steep. Can you see where the tea plants are? They are not far away!

They are just beside you! Yes! These are tea trees! When hearing "tea plant" for the first time, I would imagine a picture of trees several meters tall with their leaves covered all over their branches. That could be true if we let them keep growing, especially in tropical areas, where tea trees can be as high as 30 meters. But to better manage them, their heights are kept to around one meter, you know, convenient for picking tea leaves and pest control. Aren't they pretty? They grow in rows on terraces, but from afar it looks just like a wooded mountain! Look closer! See? These oval-like green leaves are the origin of what we drink these days: those dark green wrinkled things we drop into the teapot were once bright, fresh and succulent! Smell it! The scent in the mountain tea garden may even be subtler than the dry tea leaves we have encountered in recent days, but the subtle fragrance is another new experience!

## Day 6

Did you enjoy Teochew's food, embroidery and opera culture in the last couple of days? Yes, tea can be an inseparable part of local people's daily lives, but so can embroidery, opera and food, which are also passed down from generation to generation. Yes, I had a great time, too.

What impressed me most? I think it is the stories behind Teochew culture, especially those relating to tea.

I was born in Fujian Province, to the east of Guangdong Province, and we drink tea too. Before I came to Teochew, I thought I had this covered. My job in the team is being the English writer, and the topic was tea. I know tea! Not too hard. It could be a little bit boring, though, you know, experiencing something I already knew. But the truth is, we can always learn something, can't we? Even from what we encounter every day. At first, I thought all I would learn would be how to brew Gongfu tea, the history of tea in Teochew, different sizes and shapes of teapots used on various occasions, etc., but I was wrong, totally wrong. I remember our second day especially well, as I was touched by people's stories here. It was a relaxing night. We had gathered together, sitting in some low bamboo chairs, with annoying mosquitos biting me now and then. Our teacher invited some students from Hanshi to share their experiences with tea. I got distracted easily, but I did pay attention that night. One student said she used to brew a strong tea for herself when she was little; another told us that she could tell if the tea leaves were high quality or not, as she lived in the town where people make a living by growing tea. Their experiences resonated. They reminded me of my past, as I had similar experiences too. That is when I realized that tea is not what matters most, but the stories behind it, which was buried deep in one's heart.

But don't I worry about the disappearance of these symbols? Young people nowadays do prefer drinking milk tea. Some of them even don't know how to make tea.

But I think, symbols may go; stories, never.

I used to see tea as tea. When I was little, even before I went on the field trip in Teochew, tea was only a "dark drink" for me, whose flavor did change with time, but not much else. But now, I realize that tea is more than tea, it carries our memories, and our life attitudes, accompanying us from childhood to adulthood, and turning us into who we are today.

All in all, the story of tea is the story of us.

# The Making of Teochew

## HUANG Senyan

I'm in a stalemate with my breakfast.

It's a rice roll, but not the Cantonese one that I know, with its thin, crystal sheets of rice flour and tapioca, with fillings like pork, beef, shrimp or egg, served with mystically seasoned soy sauce. No, the dish in front of me does not deserve to be called a rice roll. It's a pile of rags, soaked in a fishy, glutinous, and brown sauce. Withered coriander straggles over the pile, adding absurdity to the dish.

I take a picture of my breakfast and send it to my Teochew roommate Zheng with the message: *I should've realized that I have to try all your food on this field trip.* There are two other groups, their research topics being Teochew embroidery, Teochew opera, and tea culture, respectively. And I was appointed to be a researcher in the food culture group. I told my family that a course called "Creative Writing and Translation" dispatched me somewhere 400 km from Guangzhou on a freezing day, just to taste a weird plate of food. Now I'm a joke in my family WeChat group.

*What?* she replied, together with two furious emojis.

*I've told you a million times, and I'll never stop telling you, Teochew food is DELICIOUS! Take my word for it. What's more, the Teochew region consists of three cities, Teochew, Shantou and Jieyang. You can't just directly compare our food to Cantonese cuisine.*

*Come on, I've tried your rice roll. It made me vomit like a dysfunctional auto-teller.*

My criticism isn't groundless. For one thing, I'm a fussy eater. In my mind, a rice roll is a fixed, divine symbol. If it is titled with the sacred name *rice roll*, it has to be a Cantonese one, with neat wrappers, plentiful fillings, and a salty taste. Whenever I encounter someone who dips rice rolls in peanut sauce or even chili jam, I would shoot him an irritated glare. This is as offensive as putting pineapple on pizza in front of an Italian! I also curse restaurants that put mango or chocolate in a rice roll and soak it in coconut milk in the name of innovation. If such a heterodox business doesn't go bankrupt, justice does not exist.

For another thing, a Teochew rice roll did give me a nightmare nine months ago. After a whole day's full schedule, I went back to my dormitory in Zhuhai, a city near Guangzhou, and ordered a Teochew rice roll from a local vendor as late dinner. It looked totally different from the rice roll I knew, strange, yet tempting. That Teochew rice roll was floating in brownish soup, placed on top of a bunch of bean sprouts and rice noodles. Light, salty, and slightly sour. Tormented by hunger, I wolfed down the rice roll and even drained the soup. Thirty minutes later, the growl in my stomach kicked off the drama. I started to feel a sense of fullness, slow but irresistible, spilling across my guts and creeping to the ends of my limbs. The mixture of undigested food and gastric juices rose to my throat. I was stiff, suffocated, muted. Frozen on my chair, I sat like a volcano about to erupt. With one more gasp, I would burst from the inside like a balloon.

Mouth shut, I gestured to my roommate for a digestion tablet. But the moment I opened my mouth, yellow vomitus fountained from my throat. After throwing up seven times in the bathroom I still felt the burn in my stomach. Even when I was asleep, it didn't stop—I was nearly drowned in my chyme. The following days remained torture. No vomiting, to my relief, but that was because I hardly ate anything. Gloom haunted me for over a week. Even the smell of food made me sick, which had never happened to someone like me, who always stuffed herself. From then on, I avoided everything with the prefix Teochew and would hasten my pace whenever I came across a Teochew restaurant.

"Hurry up with your breakfast," Prof. Dai, the teacher of the course, called out while I was still rummaging through my rice roll, "We're leaving in ten minutes." I couldn't start my day with an empty stomach, so I picked up the chopsticks and pricked the stack. Well, no bean sprouts, no rice noodles—at least this one seemed less suspicious. I picked up one layer of rice roll and carefully dunked it into the sauce, then, put it in my mouth and chewed.

Well, there was neither a golden light effect nor Hallelujah background music, no, do not expect that. But to my surprise, this Teochew rice roll tasted pretty normal. The thick sauce matched well with the bland rice flavor, and slices of mushroom add to its texture. Although it's not as juicy and springy as the Cantonese one, it's good enough to be breakfast.

I texted Zheng, *Fine, sorry for being mean to your food. I mean, honestly, it's better than I expected. HOWEVER, it's just ordinary. Cantonese rice roll is the best.*

She replied to me with a smirking emoji, *Get ready, Teochew food will blow your mind.*

That's the way Zheng talks. She is a typical Teochew person. I'm not stereotyping the people, but every Teochew person of my acquaintance follows the same pattern: excessively proud of Teochew cuisine, in possession of a mother who allegedly cooks better than any chef (hence, the derision for all restaurants). Meanwhile, at least one of their relatives runs a restaurant. Teochew people are tightly connected by a strong bond, be it lineage, language, or I'd rather believe, the same odd penchant for their cuisine. You can tell them by their aura. But, as a Cantonese, I seldom pay attention to them. I stay in the comfort zone of my own culture. No matter how vigorously Teochew people advertise their food, I'll take that as pride, or to be precise, tribal self-identity.

So, the whole night, as we strolled through a local food street, I kept my arms crossed. Other members of the food culture research group considered this place a perfect spot for fieldwork. With contented smiles, they drifted from one side of the street to another, shopping like they'd missed the dinner, seaweed jelly in one hand, tea in another, bags of takeaway dangling from their arms. Lin, a local, stuck his head over the partition of a food stand.

"Ay! Come and look at this," Lin beckoned to me. "You must try this snack." He was holding a plastic tray, each of its three compartments filled with irrelevant stuff: yellow fried tofu puffs heaped up in one, fiery-red chili garlic vinegar ripples in another, dewy mint leaves joggling at the brim. The combination of yellow, red and green made the whole dish a wild, surreal palette. "It's called *Fenghuang* Fried Tofu (written as "凤凰浮豆干" in Chinese). I recommend that you eat all three in one bite."

"Huh?" I raised my eyebrow behind the cluster of mint, "Nobody's gonna eat grass. It's weird."

"Well, just think of the peppermint in Mojito."

"Who would eat the leaves in it???" His analogy was so hilarious that I uttered my question in a wry tone.

"Just give it a try. You can put just a small sprout at the top. It won't bite," Lin tilted his head, the look behind his glasses turning playful. "You will probably take your words back."

Brimming with confidence, Lin talked like he knew everything, his instruction taking on a hint of sarcasm. In a fit of pique, I pulled out a stick and skewered a piece of tofu together with a mint leaf and then rolled them in the spicy vinegar. Moist leaf was garnished by crushed chili, and sauce kept dripping from its tip. Before I stuck it into my mouth, I closed my eyes and prepared myself for the aggressive piquancy of mint.

Our first meeting was fragrant. The freshness of vinegar softened the sharpness of the chili, while the combination in turn balanced the punch of garlic. Under the cover of sauce, the tofu puff manoeuvred between my teeth and tongue. Dried on the husk, its inside remained spongy and bouncy, from which outflew streams of flavor. My face must have shown visible relief, yet I was still wondering where the mint went.

Chew.

Once. Twice.

Herbal aroma ascended. It spiralled, with every grinding of the teeth and stirring of the tongue. The mint scent was both impressive and humble. Without sacrificing the base, it arose, distinguishing itself from the spiciness, garlickiness and sweetness, the mint added another layer of flavor.

Thrilled, I let out a cry, "Whose idea was that? Peppermint leaves are fantastic!" My voice disturbed the tranquil night air. Soon I began to notice that my friends, chewing tofu, were restraining their gloating laughter. "Whoa," I exclaimed, "forgive me, alright? I used to have misconceptions about Teochew food, but now I love it!"

Soon, I found out Teochew food had more to unveil than snacks. The next day, Zhang Sheng, President of Teochew Catering Association, invited us to have lunch in his seafood restaurant.

"I used to be a regular of Fengchun Seafood Restaurant (written as "枫春海鲜大排档" in Chinese). To me, every meal here sparked new inspiration. When the business, unfortunately, failed in 1999, I took over the place." Mr. Zhang took a sip of tea. It sounded like he was beginning to spill the tale. I opened my notebook and uncapped my pen. But the nostalgic look on his face faded when he lifted his chin and signaled to the waitress, who was setting the table behind us. Now, ambition sparkled in his eyes.

Mr. Zhang continued, "I've always wished to present the essence of Teochew cuisine through a single meal, as an expression of my gratitude and love for this city. In 2019, I got the chance. In memory of Han Yu, a master of classical prose in the Tang Dynasty (AD 618—907), also the best-known official in Teochew, my partner Mr. Zeng, a bunch of chefs and I developed a menu containing 14 dishes, all their ingredients inspired by Han's poems."

"What kinds of ingredients?" Jing asked as she turned her head back to the dishes. Her pose looked funny: she twisted and craned her head backwards, but her right hand stretched forward, holding a recorder. "A wide range of seafood. Let's continue our talk at the dining table. Shall we?" Mr. Zhang clapped. While other group members exclaimed, I cast an eye upon the table—like magic, a rich feast had popped up.

One dish arrested my attention. A mythical creature, carved out of carrot, arose from a collection of crispy fish, marinated goose and mussels. The sculpture bore the head of a Chinese dragon; each hair flew as if a storm were brewing under the dragon's feet. But underneath was the body of a stallion, raising its forelegs, ready to jump off the table at any time. "You won't see anything as stylish and vivid as this one elsewhere," Mr. Zhang said with a proud smile on his face. "We Teochew chefs seek perfection in all aspects of a dish. It should engage both the stomach and the eyes."

Looking around, I could hardly tell the ingredients of other dishes, because instead of being prominent, the meat or vegetable became part of the design. Octopus slices were used to imitate the ripples behind a cute tomato swan, while a crystal-like geoduck hid among scrambled eggs. Thanks to the effort of Mr. Zhang's team, I got to catch a glimpse of the Teochew lifestyle a thousand and two hundred years old, for each bite could be traced back to Han Yu's original verses. Perhaps that's the reason for the strong bond between the Teochew people. Their food, their ingredients, their recipes, and even their unique matching of sauces, as they are passed on to a new generation, bear the weight of a thousand years. Local specialties, similar lifestyles, experiences and memories of the city mingle and are digested in the huge stomach of society, to become the flesh and blood of the Teochew people.

Back home, I immediately ordered a Cantonese rice roll. We are the same as Teochew people, with our identities and emotions interwoven with our food. This introduction to Teochew food deeply impressed me, but it also made me more Cantonese. However, henceforth I shall keep one thing in mind, that the fillings of the rice roll are diverse.

# A Glimpse of Teochew Embroidery and Opera

## MA Changjun

As I sat by the window on the bus, rays of sunset came into sight, dyeing the world a jubilant gold orange. Once the sun rays touched the surface of the Han River, they broke into sparking fish scales. I looked out of the window as things flew past me in shades of orange.

Suddenly I found myself in a forest, with trees so thick that only a few rays of sun pierced the dark-green leaves. All was magical, yet so real. A few steps from me was a serene river. The lighting and shadow changed as I was drawn closer and closer, and the tree trunks were covered by green mosses. I couldn't help reaching out to touch the sun. For a moment, I was convinced that light has texture—soft and thin like silk, as is everything else in this forest! A golden dragon and phoenix flew close to me and passed on.

I opened my eyes, and found myself on the bus that was driving us back from Teochew, and the sunset and my schoolmates came back into view. Oh, it was a dream; I had entered a piece of Teochew embroidery that we had encountered in recent days. I smiled, feeling relieved. My teammates and I had been worried about this aspect of traditional culture at first; but once we realized the charm of embroidery, we began to be inspired.

From November 6th to 11th, 2021, led by Prof. Dai Fan, a group of students from the Creative Writing and Translation course travelled to Teochew, a city in Guangdong in Southern China, to explore its unique tradition and cultural heritage. The 12 students of the course were further divided into three small groups, focusing on three themes respectively—tea culture, Teochew food, Teochew embroidery and Teochew opera. Our Teochew embroidery and opera group had 4 students, Xiaoyan and Xueming, who were junior undergraduates, and Momo and me, first-year graduate students. We visited several shops and museums related to Teochew embroidery and conducted some interviews about its current situation and future.

Our first stop was Teochew Baishiyuan, a gallery showcasing Teochew art crafts. We were amazed by the exquisite works of embroidery incorporating a range of techniques. Curiosity drove us to a lady whose hands were moving rapidly up and down. In front of her was a desk on which many small baskets were placed. Inside those small baskets were tiny beads of varying colors. Take green as an example, we saw light green, grass green, moss green, emerald green, olive green, etc. The *xiuniang* (female embroiders, written as "绣娘" in Chinese), as she's called, invited us to try threading the beads with a needle. When the *xiuniang* was embroidering, she never looked up to see the beads; she only gazed at the embroidery work. Our group member, Xueming, had a go at it. Taking a needle in hand, he stared at the beads and gave it a shot—zero beads onto the needle. He gave it another try, none again. Changing his gesture and squatting down a little bit, he tried again, and finally, there were two beads on the needle. We cheered. We were very happy to get to experience one actual process of the Teochew embroidery.

Li Xiaodan, a Teochew embroidery conservator, took a different route in developing Teochew embroidery. Her studio was crowded with works of embroidery. Her mother, Zhuo Guifen, had been a *xiuniang*, too. Li showed us several of her works, which were quite different from the traditional embroidery. Many themes were related to the battle against Covid-19 and the history of the Chinese Communist Party. She had combined embroidery with paper-cutting, creating her style.

Li said, "We must go with the tide of the times and create new work. Only in this way will Teochew embroidery develop and advance." I added her WeChat before we left. Now, I often see her taking part in artistic competition activities and asking for votes for her new work. My teammate Momo said, "This is what we should do! Even though we face some difficulties, we always seek a new way out!"

On the next day, we visited Teochew Embroidery Museum. Having got up early in the morning, everyone was seizing a nap on the twenty-minute bus ride. When we arrived, Cai Zhonghan, the manager of the Mingrui Gallery, welcomed us. He gave us a tour of the works of embroidery and introduced us to the history of Teochew embroidery. "Teochew embroidery used to be commonly applied to Teochew wedding gowns, the building of halls, temples and the costumes in Teochew opera, as well as daily decorations." He went on to introduce us to the unique techniques applied in Teochew embroidery.

Through his explication, we learned that two unique symbols in Teochew embroidery were the golden dragons and phoenixes that bulged from the background, and we realized that by adjusting our angle, we could observe the effects of lighting and feeling. We also learned that by dividing a thin thread into four strings, a fuzzy lustre of animal fur can be created.

A man with glasses showed up. He was Cai Zhonghan's father, Cai Minqiang, who was the former manager of the state-owned Teochew Embroidery Factory. Behind that pair of black-frame glasses, his eyebrows frowned a little, seeming serious.

"I was the head of state-owned Teochew Embroidery Factory. To finish one piece of work required several days and several workers. However, with the development of our society, I can say, mass production and machine manufacturing are bound to take over the handicraft industry. To prepare for the arrival of that day, we have collected the best works, representing the highest standard of Teochew embroidery, and displaying them in our Gallery for people to appreciate. We have also recorded weaving techniques in a book. The craft may diminish, but at least these fine works never fade."

Mr. Cai continued, "I feel sorry too, that there are fewer craftsmen nowadays. In the past, thousands of people thronged into our factory. The only thing I can do now is to preserve these best works of Teochew embroidery. These works have been on exhibition in Paris, Moscow, to lots of other places, to high praise. We also integrated the characteristics and patterns of Teochew embroidery in the making of evening gowns and western-style wedding dresses."

"I am quite shocked by what Cai Zhonghan said today," Momo told me while we were heading out of the gallery. "I feel more relieved, and I am not so worried about the situation of Teochew embroidery anymore. This craftsmanship is preserved, and now Teochew embroidery has been integrated into modern dresses that sell at home and abroad. Maybe we don't need to worry too much about the inheritance of Teochew embroidery. I felt relieved, hearing all the masterworks and weaving techniques are now recorded."

Yet, Master Kang's worried face made me worry a bit. Kang Huifang is a national-level conservator of Teochew embroidery. She was in a dark green dress that day, sitting by the green window.

She was straightforward, with a tinge of impatience. Leaning on the back of the chair, she started asking, "So, tell me, what do you want to know? What questions do you have?"

Xueming raised a question, "We learned from a *xiuniang* previously that it takes a long time to finish one piece of work. Now in the age of industrialization, are there a lot of people in this industry?"

"It is indeed very hard to find or keep people in this field. Many prefer other jobs with a brighter future and more job security. It takes at least five years for a green-hand to learn, not to mention the precarious working situation and low salary."

We nodded as we took notes. "Why not hire some masters and trainees?"

"It's easier said than done! Let me ask you, where can you find qualified teachers? To be a teacher, one must not only be an expert in weaving but also be able to explain and teach the method and technique of Teochew embroidery. As you know, the reality is, many *xiuniang* didn't receive much education, and some of them can't even speak Mandarin!" Master Kang sat still. She was leaning a bit forward.

"What can we do to reverse this situation?" Momo asked, concerned.

Sitting upright, Master Kang replied, "A lot of people and students come to visit, and they conduct interviews. So what? When they finish their task, they put Teochew embroidery behind them. So many people come here only to have the EXPERIENCE. They couldn't care less about the survival and inheritance of our Teochew embroidery. I'm glad to see that you do care about it."

We followed Master Kang to the third floor. On entering the workshop, I saw a lady sitting nearest to the door. I felt very sorry for her because she was weaving with only one arm. How could a person be so wretched, having to weave embroidery, with only one thin arm? She was so thin that I could see the bone of her arm, her jaw crooked, reminding me of Yennefer from *The Witcher*[①]. I then looked up to see the whole room. There were five women and one girl, each placing one arm under the woven fabric. It was not until I saw the other *xiuniang*'s gestures that I realized that they all put one arm under the woven fabric to coordinate with the other

---

① *The Witcher* is an American fantasy drama TV series created by Lauren Schmidt Hissrich for Netflix. It is about a monster hunter, Geralt of Rivia, who struggles to find his place in a wicked world.

hand. The girl, who answered in a low, shy voice, said that she was 16 years old. "I like embroidery," She whispered to us. Master Kang went to her station and checked her weaving technique, giving extra instruction.

"She's a new and the youngest apprentice. She's very talented. I hope she'll become an inheritor of Teochew embroidery."

We then went downstairs to the first floor. Attracted by a work of embroidery, a vivid blue peacock, Prof. Dai bought this piece, as a way of supporting Teochew embroidery. There, I noticed a wall of news and pictures of Master Kang and President Xi Jinping shaking hands.

"The President came to visit our Teochew embroidery and praised us for what we did. President Xi said Teochew embroidery is our traditional culture, and we must protect it and carry it forward," Master Kang told us proudly. "I have made a promise to our president; as an inheritor of Teochew embroidery, I will do everything I can to carry it forward, no matter how hard it might be. It's my mission."

The interviews with Li Xiaodan and Kang Huifang got me worried about the future of this ancient cultural heritage. What if not all people were as dedicated as Master Kang? What if few people realized the situation Teochew embroidery is facing? Master Kang said Teochew embroidery might face extinction, but now, seeing what Mingrui Gallery had done, I thought Kang Huifang would be relieved.

"I agree. I think, regarding how to protect traditional Teochew embroidery, they all have found their answers," I told Momo. "They are preserving and carrying it forward in their own way." These people have already taken up the responsibility.

## Teochew Opera

Teochew embroidery is widely used for the traditional costumes of Teochew opera, where the padding patterns, symbolic dragons and phoenixes, and grand and bright colors are often featured.

With its own long and storied history, Teochew opera faces similar challenges. Kexin, one classmate in the course who was born and raised in Teochew, told me that as much as her grandmother loved it, she was not into it—it was too long and slow-paced.

A well-known scriptwriter, Li Yingqun, kindly agreed to accept our interview. He is now in his mid-80s.

Xueming asked, "Teacher Li, could you tell us the characteristics of Teochew opera?"

"Ah, there are several characteristics. Firstly, it is very distinctive in its local feature. We call it Teochew opera, it is sung in Teochew dialect. Secondly, it is vivid and humorous. If a play does not make people laugh, then it's a failure. Thirdly, it tells people's stories and expresses their feelings. All the stories, no matter whether they are adapted from old stories, or written recently, concern daily topics, such as marriage, family ethics, etc. It uses the grassroots language so that all can relate to it."

As the outsiders who have never heard or watched a single Teochew opera, we expressed our concern, "Teacher Li, do you think Teochew opera might extinct one day because the audience is diminishing?"

"Well, I am confident it will never disappear. Teochew opera has a solid foundation among the people. As I said, the culture of Teochew opera is the culture of life in Teochew. It is in our blood and bones."

We invited Liu Yingni, a Teochew opera actress, to sing a small part for us. Most of us do not speak nor understand the Teochew dialect, but when she finished singing, our teachers' eyes had reddened, along with some of the students, I guess, that is the charm of Teochew opera, connecting and touching all human feelings, although we understood nothing about the language.

We also visited a local professional school that trained actors and actresses. Instead of calling it a "school", the word "building" might be more suitable. All facilities of this school were included in this building. The first floor was the students' canteen, the second was for dancing and training, the third for performance, and the fourth was the students' dormitory. Each classroom contained three to five students, and the total number of students was about 20.

The principal told us about the enrollment situation, "There used to be many students, and we got to choose those with real talent. But now, few students come here, so we need to take all candidates. Otherwise, we don't have students!"

The principal sat down and crossed his leg, explaining, "Like any other vocational art school nowadays, only those who can't get enrolled in high school will be willing to come to this school."

Prof. Dai raised a question, "This sounds like a depressing situation. How do you feel about it?"

"Yes, the situation isn't promising, but I'm not depressed. We should all keep positive thoughts! We can't feel miserable or bad because of a situation or our work. We simply do the best we can."

"What do you think can be done to improve the current situation?" Momo asked.

"The government needs to step in! If this industry cannot provide students with a promising future, then no one will come and watch Teochew opera. Therefore, the only thing that may be done is to secure the government's attention and support."

Although I do not have a very deep understanding of Teochew opera, I have a sense of the deep feeling Teochew people hold for it. Maybe, when they are away from home if they watch Teochew opera, they will be brought back to their experiences and their hometown. I believe that, like me, all human beings wish to have a sense of belonging to their hometown community. Teochew opera is such a cultural identity that can create this sense of belonging, so as Teochew embroidery.

I recalled what Mrs. Xie, our teacher, born in Teochew, had told me. She said she had started making Teochew embroidery when she was five years old. "At that time, we all made embroidery. Every day, our mother gave us a piece of work, and we would work on it after school. For each piece, we would get paid. At a young age, we knew we should help our family, and we all paid our tuition fee with what we made from our own embroidery." When I asked her whether she missed Teochew, she said she did, but she couldn't go back anymore, as most of her relatives had left Teochew. She also said, "Sometimes I don't know who I am. I feel as if I am floating like a rootless lotus."

I am grateful for this trip because it allows me to gain an understanding of Teochew embroidery and Teochew opera, the problems they confront, and what people do to protect and inherit them. Without encountering these people, I would never have known all of these individuals doing what they can to preserve their cultural heritage.

Maybe we should not have worried that much about the conservation of

Teochew embroidery and Teochew opera. Certainly, traditional culture faces some challenges, yet whether we visited or not, quite a number of people are putting forth the effort to keep local culture alive and to keep it up with the times. As long as people live, as long as Teochew stands, the culture stays. I've heard a saying: *Teochew culture is like the salt in water—not visible, yet everywhere in Teochew.* Rooted in the folk, its vitality is undeniable. We should have faith in it.